Architecture Essays

Andrea Branzi

Weak and Diffuse Modernity
The World of Projects at the beginning of the 21st Century

Cover
Andrea Branzi, For a
Non-Figurative Architecture, *1968,
typewritten diagrams in preparation
for the project* No-Stop City
Centre Georges Pompidou Archive,
Paris

Editor
Luca Molinari

Design
Marcello Francone

Copyediting
Emily Ligniti

Layout
Paola Ranzini

Translation
Alta Price

First published in Italy in 2006 by
Skira editore S.p.A.
Palazzo Casati Stampa
Via Torino 61
20123 Milan
Italy
www.skira.net

© 2006 Skira editore, Milano
© Fondation Le Corbusier, by SIAE 2006
© The Estate of Francis Bacon, by SIAE 2006
© Richard Hamilton, Mark Rothko, Andy Warhol, Frank Lloyd Wright, by SIAE 2006

All rights reserved under international copyright conventions.
No part of this book may be reproduced or utilized in any form or by any means, electronic or mechanical, including photocopying, recording, or stored in any information and retrieval system, without permission in writing from the publisher.

Printed and bound in Italy.
First edition

ISBN-13: 978-88-7624-651-7
ISBN-10: 88-7624-651-7

Distributed in North America by Rizzoli International Publications, Inc., 300 Park Avenue South, New York, NY 10010
Distributed elsewhere in the world by Thames and Hudson Ltd.
181a High Holborn, London
WC1V7QX, United Kingdom

Photo Credits
Dario Bartolini, pp. 62, 78, 79
Hélène Binet, pp. 124, 125, 126, 127
Photo Francesco Milanesio, p. 26 (on the right)
Photo Giacomo Miola, p. 120
Photo Raghu Rai, p. 26
Photo Studio Ueda, Tokyo, pp. 174, 175, 176–177, 178, 179
Interfoto/Alinari, p. 69 (above)
National Geographic Society, p. 105 (above on the right)
Kaj Bell Reynal © Photographs of Artist. Collection I, Archives of American Art, Smithsonian Institution, Washington, D.C., p. 69 (below on the left)
Annalisa Sonzogni, pp. 166–171

Contents

9	Introduction For a Non-Figurative Architecture	98	*Master Plan Tokyo City X*
		104	*Domus Academy Master's – Incubators*
		106	The Sensorial Revolution
13	A Strong Century	110	*Tokyo Forum*
16	Architectural Link	114	Architecture and Agriculture
18	Fuzzy Thinking	122	*Focus Commercial Center, Munich*
20	Liquid Modernity	124	*Osaka Pavilion*
24	The Genetic Metropolis	132	Models of Weak Urbanization
28	The Man without Quantities	134	*Agronica – Weak Urbanization*
34	Elastic Classicism	147	*Domus Academy Master's – Flexyroad,*
36	Minimalist Politics		*Reversible Infrastructures*
38	The Economy of Innovation	148	*Monumental Cemetery of Carpi, Modena*
40	*Master Plan for Eindhoven*	152	*Parco di Fossoli of Carpi, Modena –*
50	New Forms of Enterprise		*Architecture/Agriculture*
54	From Brand to Buzz	154	*Competition for Fiabilandia*
56	Transitory Enterprise and the Social State		*Theme Park, Rimini*
60	Business Art	155	*Domus Academy Master's – Agropolis*
62	Urban Dismissal	156	*Cemetery of Sesto Fiorentino, Florence*
66	Cities without Architecture	160	*Porta Nuova Gardens – Virgilian Park,*
70	*No-Stop City*		*Milan*
82	*Residential and Commercial Center,* *San Donato Milanese*	166	*Glass Garden*
		172	City and Music
86	Time and Network	174	*Ghent – A Sonorous Sponge*
90	*New York Waterfront – Architecture* *as New Territories*		
		180	Bibliography
94	*"La Certosa" Real Estate Complex,* *Sesto Fiorentino*		

This is a book of theoretical physics
Andrea Branzi

Introduction
For a Non-Figurative Architecture

This book proposes two goals: to analyze the innovations that the twenty-first century is introducing to the world of design, to the passage from the strong and concentrated modernity of the twentieth century to the weak and diffuse current one, and to investigate whether there is, in this passage, the possibility of imagining a future for non-figurative architecture.

An architecture that becomes an urban semiosphere, surpassing its constructing limits and becoming a producer of immaterial qualities that change over time.

It is a question, therefore, of setting oneself outside of the architectural tradition seen as a formal metaphor of history, which limits to solely figurative and symbolic codes its function with respect to the major questions of the contemporary urban condition.

This urban condition is made up of services, information technologies networks, product systems, environmental componential practice, microclimates, commercial information, and above all perceptive structures that produce systems of sensorial and intelligent tunnels that are contained within architecture, but cannot be represented by architecture's figurative codes.

Contemporary architecture still suffers from a delay in respect to the previous century's culture, which derives from the fact that this culture attributes its fundamental urban and civil role to a figurative function.

This culture is unable to imagine itself as an abstract, immaterial reality, which does not have a direct relation to the form of structures, but to the contemporary metropolitan condition, which cannot be related to formal questions, but instead to physiological, internal questions of the urban organism.

Contemporary architecture still attributes its own foundation to the acts of building, constructing visible spaces; metaphors limited to a single building and single typologies, and does not take the opportunity to represent a dispersed, inverted, and immaterial urban condition.

Today, it is a question of imagining an architecture focused not on creating definitive projects typical of classic modernity, but focused rather on creating imperfect and incomplete subsystems typical of the new modernity of the twenty-first century, following the logic of relational economy, diffuse work, and mass entrepreneurship.

The constructed world today seems to derive evident advantages from the ever-weaker connections that unify the city, architecture, and the world of objects. The strong programs that used to unify all dimensions of modern design have melted, allowing each of these three spheres to acquire autonomy and efficiency. The functioning of the contemporary city is deeply influenced by the world of objects and electronic instruments: the processes of urban "refunctionalization" caused by lay-offs and new forms of entrepreneurship are spontaneously actuated through the sole interior transformations of the buildings. The urban landscape's whole image no longer corresponds to the activities carried out within it.

The close relationship between form and function has dissolved: the computer has no function, but has functions as numerous as the operator's needs. We have gone from the age of functionalism to the age of functionoids, instruments that do not possess a single function, but as many functions as the operator's needs.

This search is therefore aimed at:

- designing models of weak urbanization, in other words, reversible, evolving, provisory models that correspond directly to the changing necessities of a reformist society that is continually elaborating its own social and territorial organization, dismissing and re-functionalizing the city;
- an architecture that is less composite and more enzymatic, meaning an architecture capable of inserting itself in the processes of the territory's transformation without using external figurative codes, but internal environmental qualities, dispersed throughout the land, not closed within the building's perimeter;
- an architecture aimed at surpassing the limits of building as a structural and typological concentration, to activate methods and services diffuse throughout the environment, beyond the traditional confines of the single construction, becoming an open system of environmental componential work;
- a traversable architecture that guarantees the penetration of territory and space, no longer marked by closed confines, but by open filters like a three-dimensional agriculture;
- an evolving architecture where the variable of time is a structural, dynamic element, integrated in and symbiotic with nature;
- an architecture that corresponds to a fluid society and an elastic democracy free of ideologies that produces programs as a result of a diffuse genetic energy utterly without metaphysics.

It's not the first time that architecture attempts to go *beyond architecture*, but in the twenty-first century this utopia seems to be for the most part realized within the contemporary city, where the environmental evolutionary processes and immaterial reality of computer networks have already created a de facto, dynamic,

Agronica, 1995

invisible, and abstract metropolis that is progressively substituting (or moving to the background) the physical and figurative metropolis.

It is a matter, therefore, of moving on to an adaptation (non-violent) also in designers' way of thinking; too often they deny or refuse this extraordinary opportunity to try out new logics and new operative dimensions, taking refuge in the myth of architecture as a producer of only certainties.

But today uncertainty has become a rock-solid reality; un-reinforced (weakened) concrete can be the best-adapted laboratory for experimenting with a vaster architecture—a swarm of sensorial input, services, and products.

A Strong Century

Europe came out of the twentieth century proving the deterioration of its principal cultural and political theorems. On the one hand is the failure of right- and left-wing political programs born of its generous revolutionary hopes and exported with negative effects to many countries of the world. Fascism, Communism, and Nazism—in various forms and with various rewards—lie buried among the ruins of the brief century that has just ended. The ethical supremacy of the Old World, cradle of Christianity and moral philosophy, has been discredited by the atrocities of the second-half of the century. Add to this ethical-political debacle the crisis of European rationalist modernism, whose hopes have failed under the uncontrollable complexity of its own creation: a progress made up of an industrial and social growth completely different from (if not opposite) the universe of order and logic upon which this modernity had founded its purist prophecy.

The code of classic modernity presents itself today as a rigid concept, overwhelmed by the fluidity of commerce, the invasion of innovations, the ungovernable nature of the world economy, and a climate facing a constant pollution crisis. Neo-capitalism, which has trumped throughout the world since 1989, seems to survive itself solely on the condition that it knows how to reform, modify, and in practice deny its own doings on a daily basis.

Seen from the viewpoint of an ever-growing distance, the period of time from the French Revolution to the end of the twentieth century was, in the West, a long season of grand ideologies that were incessantly fed by the energies of extreme and irreversible transformations. These transformations were the fruit of archetypal thoughts and expressions of a society that tried to combine secularism and theology, leaving the search for designs and definitive solutions to politics and culture—as though these were the instruments of a human science, aimed at solving once and for all the unresolved problems of the selfsame human sciences. In this sense, the key physical and metaphysical technology of the last two centuries has certainly been mechanics; this strong technology, based on the transmission of movement through the friction of bodies and the stress of gears, has been interiorized by modern man and his machines, which were seen as instruments of work and as perfect motors for the transformation of history and of the world. The end of this epoch of forced modernization, marked by strong logic and the search for irreversible and definitive solutions, therefore coincides, as François Fouret claims, with the end of the historic epoch begun by the French Revolution and ended in 1989 with the fall of the Berlin Wall. Revolutions and the vanguards of future (artistic) revolutions have been the studios where creative minorities worked, driven to a quest for the new. This was always understood as a discovery of the *true*, of the *authentic* hidden under the overstructures and hypocrisy of history. This was a search, therefore, aimed at broadening the available repertory of certainties, always looking for a truth that already existed, but was previously unseen. Very few among the heroes of that distant season, particularly among the architects, had the doubt that their work was not aimed at seeking the deep foundations of a new secular, rational civilization capable of confronting the long time periods of an eternal modernity—finally and definitively eternal because they were founded on inviolable principles.

That long period of violent and genial structural transformations is followed today by a different, more experimental epoch. This is an epoch more attuned to the values of normalcy, even if composed entirely of ex-

Jacques-Louis David, Oath of the Jeu de Paume, *1790–1791, Louvre, Paris*

Metro construction site at Place Saint-Michel, Paris, 1907

Etienne Louis Boullée, Cenotaph, *18th century*

ceptions, in a context where spread out laboratories of permanent vanguards work, intent on producing daily their due measure of innovation and research, without making reference to global models, and above all without having any sort of stable certainty at their disposal. The current epoch is open to obstructing the weak and diffuse energies of new politics, like the weak and diffuse energies of nature and of informational networks. This is an epoch in search of energetic systems capable of producing, without trauma and earthquakes, vast social and physical upheaval.

No more, then, will there be the strong, concentrated cathedrals of the old modernity; in their place will come articulated cognitive processes, reversible climactic transformations, invisible and penetrating network systems. This will be a modernity capable of using weak and diffuse energies that do not produce the din of mechanics, but create forces similar to those created by stars, the moon, and the planets, capable of moving each night and all the oceans of the world without producing a single sound. The twenty-first century has begun without the stimulus of mega-designs for the future; the new times are signaled by an ability to work in a world constructed according to a logic that we will call weak and diffuse, and that we will try to illustrate as the theme of many designs and research programs.

The concept of weakness that we speak of does not imply, however, any negative value of inefficiency or inability; this indicates rather a particular process of modification and cognition that follows natural logic, not geometric logic—diffuse, diluted processes, reversible and self-stabilizing strategies. Gianni Vattimo was the first to talk about a weak thought, that is, a type of hermeneutics that develops without looking to the great syntheses of the twentieth century, or to the unifying systems of politics and projects that were typical of classic

The twentieth century is characterized by strong and concentrated processes of transformation, both in the environment and in society, through political and structural revolutions that are the heirs of the spirit of the French Revolution and the reign of secular reason.
Illuminist architects proposed the birth of a new monumental classicism—one that is solid and eternal, of which modern architecture was the spiritual heir.

François Kollar, Saint-Etienne, *photomontage, 1930 ca.*

modernism. Instead, this hermeneutics proceeds following more incomplete, imperfect, disarticulated types of cognizance and transformation, which are more ductile and therefore able to absorb the new and confront the surprises and complexities that this produces.

The same weak word is now used in relation to new information technologies, fed by the low energies (i.e. ten volt, etc.) of electronics; from this derives its performative ability that follows logical and productive processes very close to those of physiology and the human brain. Electronic technology is, therefore, less traumatic than the old mechanics in its relationships to man, and is certainly able to deeply modify the logic of work, the economy, culture, and the relationships among people.

Such a silent mutation has not yet truly entered the world of design, doing so thus far only in the most superficial manner, often associated with the possibility of simulation offered by graphic computers.

The investigation of the vast and deep consequences produced by information technologies and the weak logics they create—in the contemporary world, and above all in modern architecture and the city—is the theme of this book.

Various research experiences are collected here, beginning with the birth of the radical movement at the end of the sixties to the moment in 1995 when for the first time the theme of a weak modernity emerges, like a new statute under which architecture sees itself as a threshold presence among major metropolitan mutations (and endings) and the universe of informational networks. This is a non-compositional, anti-typological architecture, like an enzyme capable of transforming vast terrain according to criteria of reversibility and navigability, completely new with respect to the typological, physical, and reinforced limits of classic modernity.

Architectural Link

We see today that contemporary architecture, after a long period of silence, is opening new studios of design research in order to finally develop a positive reflection on its own crisis. This reflection is capable of developing an investigation of design that is not exclusively bound to building opportunities, but parallel and autonomous from these; not bent, therefore, on resolving short-term problems, but rather focused on opening new ones for the future to better understand the often obscure and misunderstood present. Just as theoretical physics precedes and feeds applied physics, providing the latter with the necessary information and base theorems, design research must be an open studio for reflection as a manifestation of a designing thought that does not lose itself in the pure practice of building.

In an epoch like the present one, continually traversed by the new, incurable conflicts, a permanent reformism, and by an absence of general models, design has chosen the route of incessant research, following the fluctuating dynamic of the market and history.

In other words, the whole culture of design has entered a state of permanent crisis, which is in a condition of permanent difficulty, corresponding to the slow pace of a stably experimental epoch. This is an epoch in which conditions of social, cultural, and economic crisis, as Kevin Kelly asserts, are the premise for any sort of social, cultural, and economic growth. The crisis, therefore, functions as a positive developmental concept, as a premise for the elaboration of a dynamic adjustment to the new.

The crisis of contemporary architecture is one that feeds on a double difficulty. The first difficulty consists of the end of design's unity: city, architecture, and products are no longer synergetic universes, but conflicting and alternating systems that follow diverging logics.

The city no longer foresees architecture; architecture presents itself as an alternative to the city. The world of industrial objects affirms its centrality with respect to the city and architecture. Design itself often comes forward as pure creative energy—one that cannot be reduced to the act of construction, but rather to the definitions of autonomous metropolitan theorems and behaviors, already complete in themselves, which therefore do not refer to successive processes of realization.

This state of things no longer has to be lived as a negative condition, as the disappearance of the epistemological foundations of architecture, inasmuch as a discipline bringing order and unity. On the contrary, the schizophrenic state of the designed world opens the possibility of finally deepening the by-laws of architecture so that it is no longer seen merely as an art of construction, but as a complex and mutable cognitive thought process that no longer refers to the (impossible) unity of technologies and idioms, but to the weak and diffuse energies of transformation of terrain and space. This is architecture, therefore, that is no longer architecture, for a city that is no longer a city.

To this completely new, historically unprecedented operative condition is added a more specific difficulty, born of the confrontation between the virtual world and the solid side—the constructed side of reality. This solid side is one component of the (positive) crisis in the transformation of urban space into a virtual system of information, services, telecommunication products, and relational networks independent from architecture as a constructed presence.

It seems almost as though the reign of

James D. Watson and Francis Crick, discoverers of the helical form of DNA, 1953

The contemporary city is made up of a sort of plankton of information, services, products, and relations in continuous evolution. Ungovernable currents traverse the structures, creating a mobile backdrop, often immaterial, that no longer coincides with the rigid passage of architecture and with its formal codes.

Architectural Link, *exhibition organized by the Domus Academy, Milan, 2003*

that which we call architecture has now been transformed into a thin, traversable diaphragm, in a sort of transparent screen placed between two continents—that of the networks and virtual urban services, and that of internal spaces, of operative systems, of ambient component ware, flexible and ductile, capable of following the continuous mutation of productive and social functions.

The term "architectural link" indicates precisely this perimeter-oriented nature of architecture in the contemporary city, of its being an interface between two formative processes of urban dynamics, a filter that must be thought of as a fluid, traversable, reversible reality. No longer a carrier of metaphors and definitive solutions, architecture is an active presence in a context that foresees the theoretical and practical nuance of future layouts.

Hence it's a question of a mental and technical search that aims to go beyond the impassable disciplinary limits that have held twentieth century architecture back from a courageous and radical confrontation with the crisis of its historical foundations. Because of these disciplinary limits contemporary architecture significantly lags behind other modern cultures such as painting, music, writing, and logic.

Fuzzy Thinking

Contemporary scientific thought tends to surpass the rigidity of mathematical and geometric logic, stabilizing new relationships with the complexity and indeterminacy of nature; this follows a more fluid logic that in turn traces more indeterminate and exploratory paths and modalities that brings science closer to new forms of creative knowledge.

Mechanical representation of the human brain (from Culture Technique, *no. 14, June 1985)*

Albert Einstein, 1945 ca.

This term was first used in the sixties by logician Lofti Zadeh, and more recently by Bart Kosko; it belongs to a specific tradition in modern science that propelled the field towards a previously unexplored boundary, going beyond the rigid dual logic upon which science itself is based.

Bart Kosko affirms: "One day I realized that science isn't true," in the sense that is not part of the real world, but is a parallel abstract thought, and as such is not capable of giving certain answers. As Albert Einstein said in *Geometry and Existence*: "When the laws of mathematics refer to reality, they are not certain. And when they are certain, they do not refer to reality." The inquiry regarding the limits of science belongs to the thinking of many twentieth-century scientists and philosophers, from Mach to Heisenberg, Thomas Kuhn to Paul Feyerabend, all the way to Karl Popper.

They took scientific thought to its most extreme consequences to reveal its contradictions and limits as well as to enlarge its cognitive capacity.

Paul Feyerabend, in his 1975 piece *Against Method*, declares: "Science is an essentially anarchistic enterprise: theoretical anarchism is more humanitarian and more likely to encourage progress than its law-and-order alternatives."

This sort of skepticism regarding the scientific method has now become the only scientific position possible, because it is the only one that permits the development of an integration of science and nature—two realities that as of yesterday were irreconcilable. On the one hand are science's great mathematical geometries, its universal laws, and its perfect speculations, which are accepted only when reproducible in the laboratory. On the other hand are nature's great complexity, chance, and accident, produced by phenomena everlastingly different from one another, builders of reality that are utterly irreproducible in a laboratory setting. A universe where time changes reality, pro-

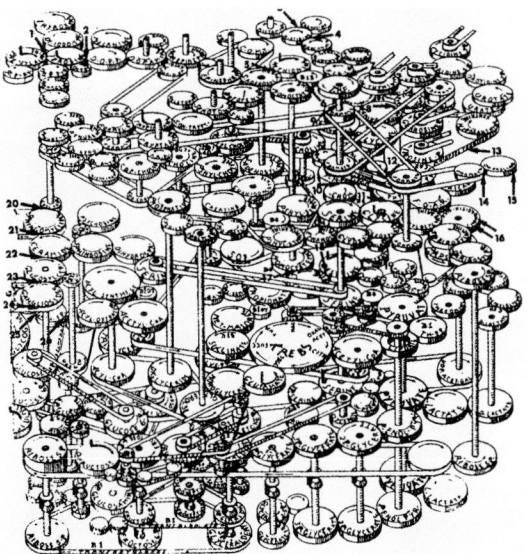

Electronic instruments, with new calculating possibilities, have permitted for the first time the laboratory reproduction of the structural and spatial complexities of natural phenomena (fractals), opening a new age of knowledge for science, logic, and culture, including design culture.

Fractal detail by Mandelbrot

ducing fluid systems of experience in continually evolving contexts.

The possibilities of electronic calculation of large numbers, and the ability to enter a very high number of variables into these calculations, now permits us to recognize and reproduce in fractals the logical vortices of nature's elementary phenomena. We could say that if Galileo Galilei had removed air's friction for the sake of demonstration of the law of gravity, today we are looking to give back to science the real world's high level of friction and viscosity. The refusal of the scientific method, which Bart Kosko claims to promote, is therefore the sign of a structural passage of science, which now—pushed by the influence of Eastern cultures, by Shintoism and the vision of great Asian nuances, but also by the new instrumental possibilities and new logical methodologies—disputes its old, rigid statutes.

This evolves as so-called fuzzy thinking, which no longer represents the purity of geometry and the precision of mathematical paths, and instead represents very well the fuzzy reality of the universe, of its evolutionary stage—a nebulous, milky intermediate between mass and energy. This way of thinking is the figurative metaphor of a new, expansive period of science, as a positive end to its methodological crisis, leading towards a new naturalism.

This scientific and technological naturalism, which no longer considers nature a primitive phase in need of change, but rather an evolved model to imitate in the process of building the new, belongs wholly to this regime of a different modernity, intent on elaborating richer, less rigid design instruments in order to realize diffuse transformations that take advantage of previously unknown ambient and social energies.

Liquid Modernity

In 2000, the sociologist Zygmunt Bauman published with Polity Press "Liquid Modernity," an essay in which he outlines a long analysis of the transformational processes of the concept of modernism at the beginning of the twenty-first century.

For Bauman, the term "liquid" positively indicates the idea of a state of material that does not possess its own form (rather, that of its container) and tends to follow a temporal flow of transformations. These conditions converge to describe "the nature of the current, and in many respects new, phase of the history of modernism."

The concept of liquefaction belongs to the primitive processes of modernity, as a movement of liberation from the structural nodes of history, the melting of the academic disciplinary blockades, dispersion of the aggressive structures of repression (William Reich). The same authors of the *Communist Manifesto* proposed to "merge the solid bodies" as a preliminary act in a process of political and creative liberation. One must remember, though, that the "liquefaction of solid bodies" that the first modernity proposed did not in the least presuppose the formation of a permanent liquid state. On the contrary, it represented a transitory phase, a necessary premise for the construction of new, more resistant solid bodies. This search for new, more solid foundations in the twentieth century happened without success for culture and politics, but for Bauman it was at the formative base of modern capitalism's entrepreneurial spirit and its capabilities to construct large, stable economic empires.

Let's not forget that the great political dictatorships of the twentieth century were born also as an attempt to confront the devastating reality of the economic and methodological apparatus of national and international capital, based on the naked laws of profit. To confront this major historical collision twentieth-century politics looked to construct new (and disastrous) societies—Fascist, Communist, Nazi. This happened even contradicting, at times, those libertarian premises from which the dictatorships originated.

In 1922, Lenin said: "More socialism and less State," but Stalin, in reality, effected "more State and less Socialism." Mussolini, influenced by Bergson's philosophy, wanted to create a political movement "contradictory as life," and ended up founding a dictatorship. The freed individual was therefore promptly thrust back into new niches that were more solid than the previous containers.

These containers, these solid bodies, have become—in the current, high-complexity societies of extremely rigid organisms, and because of the extreme normative force that they must exert in order to organize reality's multiplicity—obsolete, fragile structures, utterly unusable and distant from any efficient praxis. The resulting operative void is, for Bauman, now filled by the spontaneity of individual behaviors, local initiatives, constant reform, and the destruction of all chains, up to the point where the system's flexibility "is the product and the sediment of freedom expressed by human agents."

Deregulation, the freeing of enterprise, flexibility, the fluidity of unions, and free access to financial markets all together represent the inverse process of all that solid modernity had created as a container of the liquid state of all that was modern. In this sense, the end of the epoch of Revolutions, as producers of normative mega-containers, derives from the definitive (and apparent) identification between entrepreneurship and society, economy and its over overlying structures, spontaneity and politics—between the fluidity of institutions and that of the market.

The fusion of solid bodies carried out by current modernity has been directed towards the liquefaction of political processes, understood as instruments for transmitting aggregating designs and the radical transformation of the existent; already in the seventies individual freedom tended to identify itself with consumption, seen as an indispensable act of constructing one's own identity. The political clout of society, after the failed revolution of 1968, has been greatly lightened, and no longer tends to elaborate designs and global statutes for substituting the system.

Modernity becomes the sole judge of modernity itself; it folds over on itself and proceeds on to its own modernization. The powers of coercion have gone from the system to life, descending from a macro to a micro scale.

Bauman concludes that "ours is a type of individualized, privatized modernity, in which the onus of connecting the dots and the responsibility of failure fall mainly on the shoulders of the individual."

Individual freedom therefore presents itself now in apparent coincidence with the freedom of the system's liquefaction from the moment when, in the era of mass entrepreneurship, there is no longer any apparent distance between the whole and a small part of it, between private interests and collective interests. The free creativity of the market drags along the free creativity of enterprise.

Archizoom Associates, No-Stop City, *1969–1972*

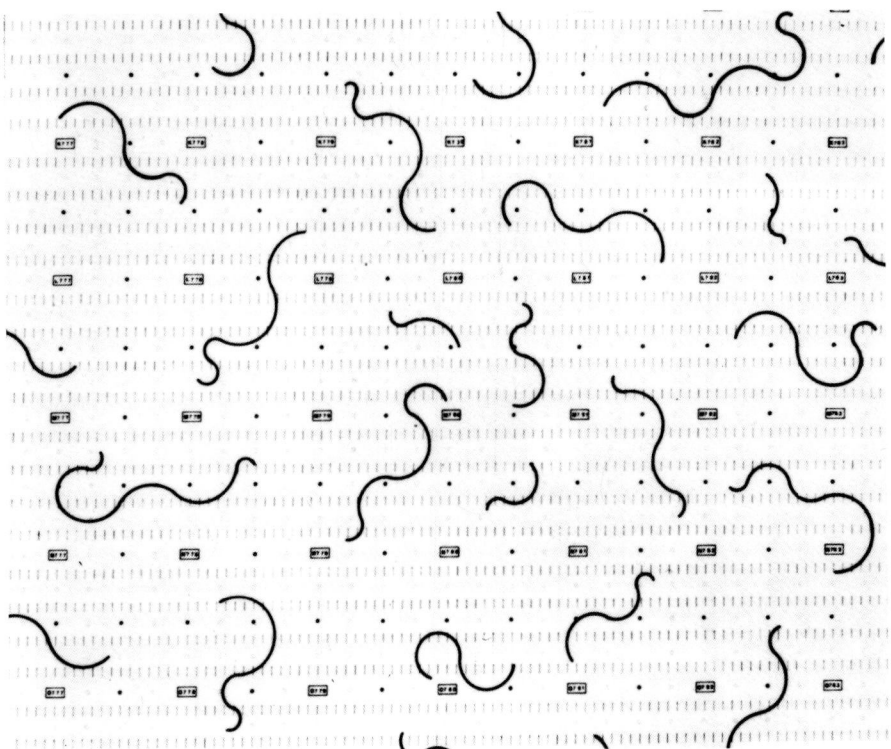

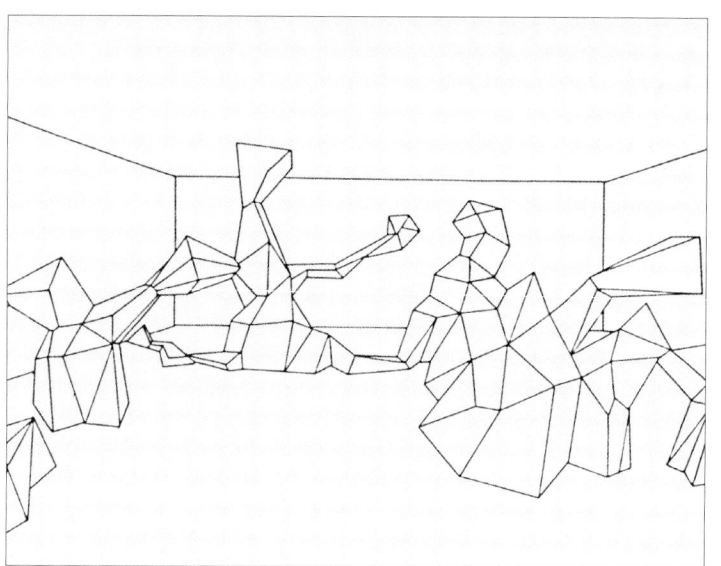
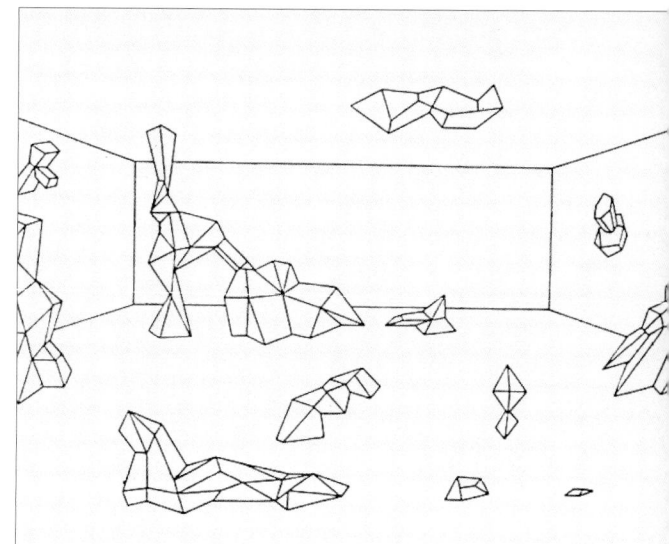

The processes of dematerialization of solid bodies and their transformation into dynamic fluids which Bauman spoke of also correspond to the search for new devices of representation of urban territory as a highly complex and changeable reality that no longer corresponds to the figurative and rigid systems of architecture.

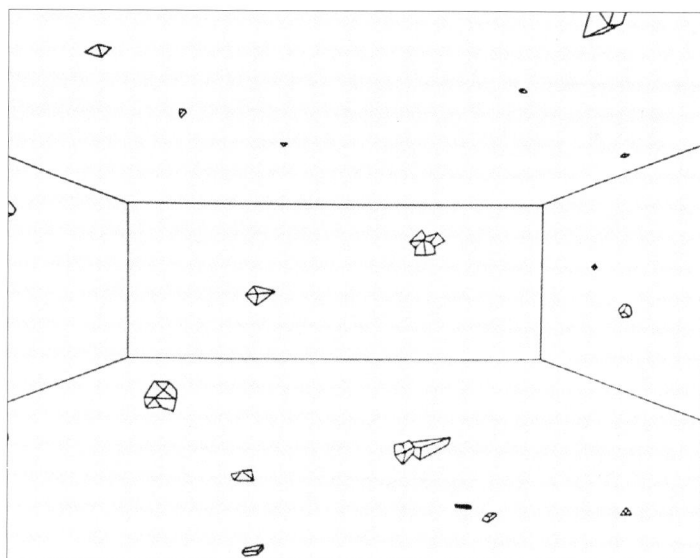
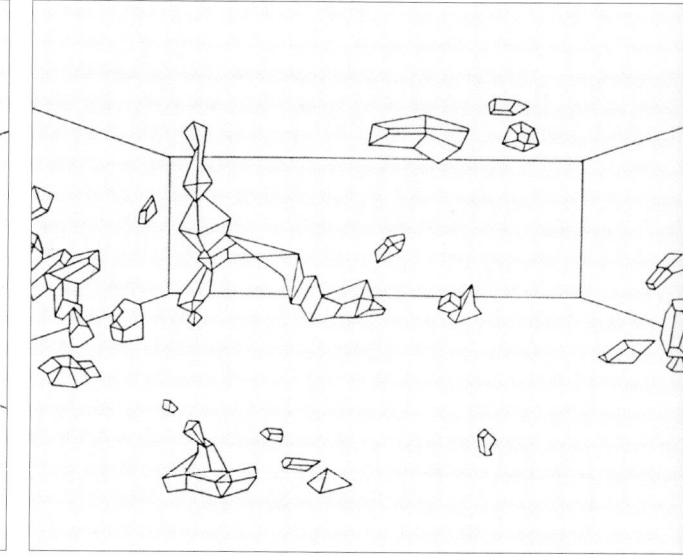

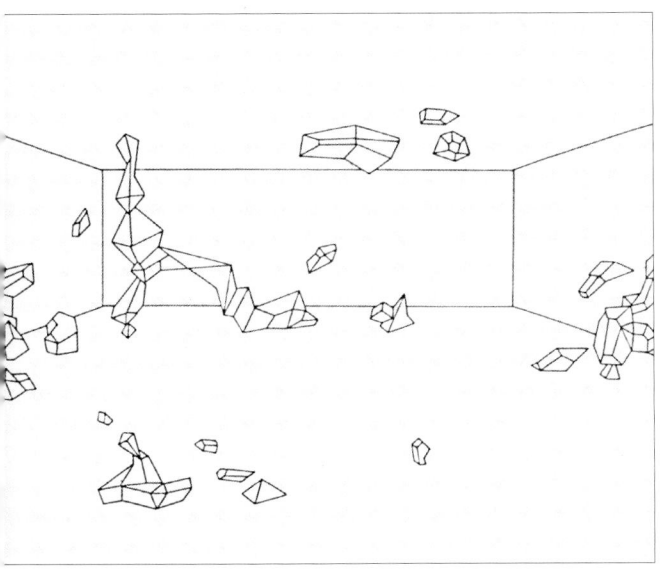
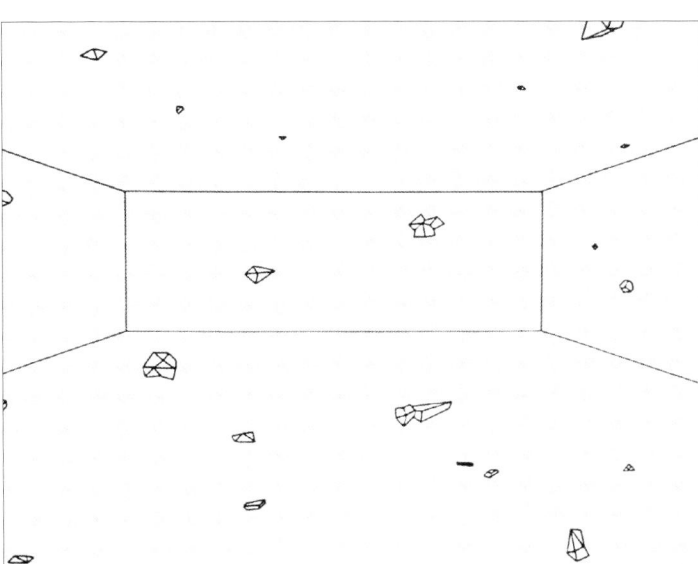

Andrea Branzi, Strutture in liquefazione, *1969, FRAC Collection, Orléans*

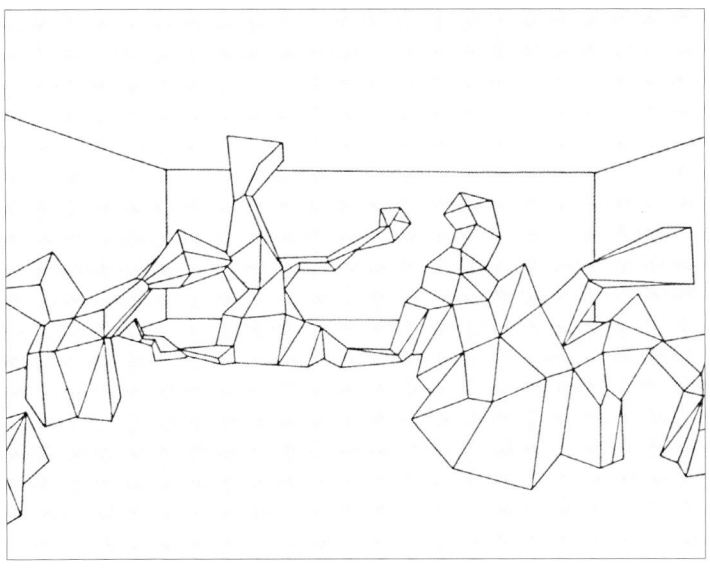

The Genetic Metropolis

This vision of a conclusive coincidence between subject and system, individual and entrepreneurial market, introduces a new definition of the metropolis as a great genetic bed—a layer in the ancient sense that we can imagine in Imperial Rome, in current Mumbai, or in the great African capitals like Lagos: an urban reality where architecture is nothing but a weak system connecting a heap of human presences, relations, interests, and exchanges that completely fill the space.

Kevin Kelly, in *Out of Control*, writes: "There's only one epoch in the history of the planet, when each single individual and each single thing become connected, and we are alive in that exact moment. This enormous interconnection, permitting us to exchange ideas, information, intermediations, and money everywhere, anytime, and with whomever, is our promised land."

The metropolis of the information age is not, then, the capital of technology; it is rather the land of the humane, in all its ability to connect its own DNA with that of business, disseminating its own genes in a tight network of parental and entrepreneurial relations. The genetic metropolis is one where the biological energies of society free themselves and reach their maximal level of liquefaction, fully invading every infrastructure and overflowing every possible designed form of containment.

This promised land that Kelly speaks of consists in a vast bio-technological system, moved by weak and diffuse energies aimed at the expansion and defense of the system's genes and the search for better conditions to protect and reinforce them in order to improve living conditions.

It is therefore a large vital system where the interests of a single being intertwine with the analogous, primordial interest of others and outside distinctions of class, religion, and culture; in other words, a class, religion, and culture that have not disappeared, but which change the statutes governing solid bodies in order to become instrumental values and a means by which to legitimately defend the amniotic liquid in which the metropolitan gene moves.

In this evolving logic, any paradigm or organized model is always to be considered transitory, traversable ground in the search for better environmental and social systems for the defense and consolidation of its own lineage.

This defense no longer occurs in its aggressive form, which sought the elimination of the weak or the different, but rather anticipates a reinforcement of the defenses of its own DNA through the mingling with that which is different, creating preventive systems that protect the weak component of society. The ethic of information networks has taught us of the existence of great advantages that social interconnection offers. Or—as Hinduism, a religion that greatly influenced twenty-first-century electronic thought, teaches us—these advantages exist in an interconnectedness of all that is vital, in a unique system that extends itself from the human world to the plant world. It's strange that precisely the two great twenty-first-century technologies—information technology and genetics—have not yet adequately been joined in order to be understood as weak and diffuse technologies that work within all the processes of liquefaction now underway. The genetic metropolis is, in fact, the vision of a territory within which architecture no longer defines a permanent segmentation of space, but becomes the theater of a vast elastic (in other words, reversible) modification of infrastructures, services, and metropolitan underpinnings from the bottom up.

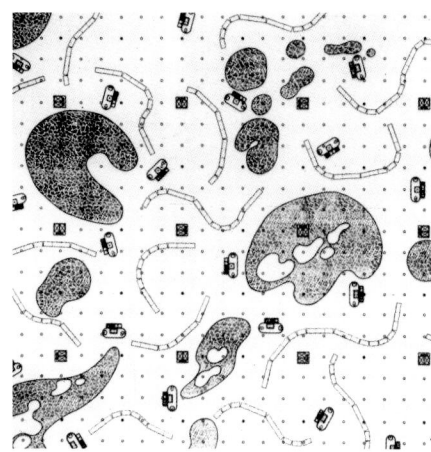

Archizoom Associates, Bosco residenziale, No-Stop City, *1969–1972*

The contemporary metropolis as a genetic bed (that is, an intense space of genomic exchange and economic relations) makes up a sort of aquarium full of amniotic fluid from which aggregative forms of a society based on exchange and information take shape and are in turn dissolved.

Andrea Branzi, model for the Die Zeremonien des wetliches Europas seminar, Hochschule der Kunste, Berlin, 1988

There is a great fear of speaking about genetic energy as a positive factor because the affirmation of race, genetic manipulations, and the uncontrollable egoism that this concept brings to mind suggest an extreme prudence. Nevertheless, there is a need to create a less limited, less fearful vision of this great vital patrimony, this anthropological layer that moves history; the great creativity expressed by genetic systems, in their unstoppable tendency to free themselves from the limits and chains that genes manifest in their growth, cannot be the object of misunderstandings.

In a great book entitled *In Praise of Imperfection*, Rita Levi Montalcini described man's ability to design as a positive result of his biological imperfection, of his never being completely and definitively homogenous with the physical and historical environment. This imperfection, with respect to the surroundings and history, pushes the human genetic system to design, experiment, and search for the best survival conditions for itself and its lineage. The absence of a final model and pre-established path within this search represents in the most complete manner the condition of contemporary man: freed of many impediments and false models, he seeks out his path starting from within his own nature.

The genetic metropolis represents this level of evolved aggregation as the best market of opportunities and parental mingling. Its constructed form is not significant because current society can no longer be represented by a succession of forms and places. Current society more and more resembles the great textile-based civilizations of the past (or present) like that of the In-

dians—societies which represent themselves in a continuous network, a flexible and transparent fabric able to resist the knocks and tears of the internal transitions and collision with the new.

Indian civilization is based on textiles, and is therefore an anti-architectural, anti-mechanical, anti-logical, and anti-constructive one capable of understanding interweaving processes as a cosmic philosophy wherein each person's life continues beyond death, within the warp and weft of other lives. Mahatma Gandhi began his revolution by returning to the primordial act of spinning cotton as the base of a radical re-foundation of society. Thus, by skipping all the processes of modernization connected to the strong energies of mechanics, India landed autonomously in the world of the web via a religious path, becoming in a very short time the world's third largest producer of software, behind only the United States and Japan.

The backdrop of Indian society, with its codes of metropolitan identity still linked with the presence of textile colors and patterns, coincides, much more than does architecture, with the mobile system of bodies in a bio-technological environment.

Speaking, then, of a genetic metropolis, we mean a theoretical model of a land where the vital and entrepreneurial energies coincide with the form of the city itself, through a constructive, reversible, and traversable apparatus. A model that corresponds to an asset that is not necessarily chaotic, but rather to an elastic system that changes with time and the needs of rela-

The Temple of Khajuraho, New Delhi, detail (from Louis Frederic's Khajuraho)

Indian women

Indian civilization developed the idea of architecture as an aggregation of human bodies and erotic relations (the Hindu temples of Khajuraho) that correspond to the non-building logic of their culture, which instead finds in weaving processes its own deep adhesion to universal laws, where life and death, good and bad, technology and sacred animals all intertwine without contradiction and without end.
The traditional urban landscape is made up not of architectures, but rather of people's bodies, colorful textiles, and the decorations of their dress, which create a lively, fluctuating backdrop that is seemingly fragile, but in reality very resistant to the impact of the cultural and technological changes of society.
India's spiritual identifications in the sacred rites of weaving foresaw the electronic thought of a web civilization where everything is associated and interconnected, and corresponds to the symbolic gesture of Gandhi, who began the revolution for independence by weaving a new fabric on the loom.

tions. This type of bio-technological environment is closer to the management of agricultural systems, linked to seasonal cycles, weather, and the reversibility of crops more than to the paradigms of the urban government, which act through traditional architecture.

The genetic metropolis therefore resembles a high-tech *favela* more than the great American cities. It is more similar to ancient Dharavi in the center (not the periphery) of Mumbai—where for three centuries 500,000 people have lived in a unified, fluid system of thatched huts—than to the historical European city centers, which are rigid, fragile, and untouchable. The architectural links we have spoken of correspond to the idea of a constructive, reversible, and traversable system, perennially incomplete and imperfect, but adapted to contain a space made up of networks, services, and relations, thus always open to transformation over time.

The Man without Quantities

The Man without Quantities is a man who lacks information on the quantitative dimension of certain phenomena occurring around him; in lieu of having such information, he continues to refer to superseded criteria of evaluation that lead him to make often grave errors. He still believes that looking at the world is enough to understand it; instead, there are many invisible new levels of reality, on which one must be prepared with organized packets of information. The twenty-first century is characterized by progressive, deep, often barely evident changes that grow within an outline until they suddenly determine general, very visible transformation that only a few observers had suspected.

The Man without Quantities is therefore a characteristic figure of our time because he hasn't any consciousness of the existence of phenomena in slow and progressive growth that are silently changing our overall picture. After the end of the great ideologies the state of intellectual awareness fell; we lack the condition of social pre-alarm, people are more distracted, and therefore there is a greatly diffuse absence of sensitive point of observation that is able to keep these slow mutations—typical of an era of tremors (not of earthquakes) in an age of weak and diffuse modernity—under control.

Among the many underestimated novelties of the twenty-first century we can list: all the processes of "refunctionalization" of the contemporary city carried out directly through the universe of objects; the advent of mass entrepreneurship and the *relational* economy derived from it (based on virtual, as opposed to real, exchanges); and many other things that are silently and irreversibly changing our way of designing (both interior and exterior) architecture.

But there exists a natural, purely human phenomenon that our designer colleagues seem not yet to have understood in all of its innovative dimensions.

The phenomenon consists in the fact that, for the first time in the history of the human consortium, the number of the living has reached the record point of 6.5 billion people. Fifty years ago there were just over half that number, and fifty years from now we'll number far above 10 billion.

This is a rapturous number of people who move freely through the constructed world and determine an absolutely new landscape phenomenon.

Beyond the political, social, and economic questions this phenomenon brings with it, 6.5 billion people (a temporary and growing number) represent a physical and corporeal reality expressive of completely unusual dimensions; it is this very original aspect that now calls for reflection.

In our cities, a sort of active filter has formed, a dynamic curtain composed of the bodies of hundreds of thousands of people, which form a bona fide mobile landscape made up of expressive presences that invade every space and every place, substituting the traditional architectural backdrop and inducing new qualities and new devices for the elaboration of the real quality of the environment.

Fashion must now be seen as a new type of urban quality; the fabrics and colors are part of the environmental structures, and tailoring belongs amid the other metropolitan technologies.

That which differentiates one city, street, and territory from the next is no longer architecture and its formal, rigid, immobile, and distant symbols—rather, it is the invasive, lively, varied human presences; unique cells that bring true diversities, exceptions,

Tokyo

and deep cultural information; terminals of living memories of various stories. It is the quality of the people, their gestures, their dress, their (inevitably no-global) physiognomy that marks the evident differences between Delhi and Milan, Paris and Naples, and there are increasingly fewer local architectural repertoires that create the recognizable elements of a metropolitan environment.

Human presences interrupt the perspective and create unrepeatable flows of not only anthropological, but also corporeal, scenes.

Six-and-a-half billion people make up a sort of horizontal, enveloping plankton that invades space and creates, by extension and density, a specific visual experience. The city's space, once empty, where architecture was the sole protagonist, is now made up of a whole full of objects, products, messages, and, above all, people. Thus the true result of the electronic revolution consists not in the presence of information technologies within the environment, but rather the human presence, which invades the scene and imposes, with its uncontainable formal anarchy, a serious revision of all the traditional strategies that govern the quality of the environment.

Factories have emptied and millions of workers, who were once gray, monotonous laborers within the industrial cycle, have been liberated within the environment, and build it like a colored and changing surface within which human physiognomies, qualities of dress, relational gestures, and urban ceremonies and rites act together.

For those who design the environment and for those who are bent on governing it, all this is paramount to a verification that the unique and concentrated act of designing is now substituted by a sort of diffuse crowd of design vibrations that each subject present in space produces in order to signal itself, its creative presence, its economic search, and its genetic energy.

Thus design and architecture begin the twenty-first century comparing themselves with this unexpected invasion on the part of all that is human, and what all that is human brings with it.

The direct relationships between people, the ability to manage interpersonal contacts with the necessary social gallantry, the good manners of the accounts and salespeople, and the efficacy of operative rituals and ceremonies have become a fundamental element in the qualities of places within the contemporary city.

The human metropolis is therefore a reality that cannot be taken on in unified operative terms; and perhaps, as an overall result, it also cannot be designed.

But if the environmental effects of the presence of 6.5 billion people can be difficult to imagine, there exist other urban phenomena whose dimension hasn't been intercepted by the *man without quantities*.

For example, in all the large industrial cities of the world, the phenomenon of factories falling into disuse is noted and very evident: our suburbs are spangled with former industrial areas that are no longer in use, which present themselves as a grouping of decaying structures, obsolete machines, and rusted looms. (An entire region like Germany's Rhurgebiet, which in the eighties was converted completely into cultural and leisure-time activity spaces.)

But there also exist less evident dismissals, which have reached large proportions: the abandonment of tertiary spaces is rapidly growing. Globalization, the surpassing of old office typologies, and the reduction of spaces (and workers) has created a large void within buildings and skyscrapers that seem to be in full use, but have actually become dead structures where the lights are no longer turned on each evening.

From a recent study conducted by the Engineering University of Tokyo in the Japanese capital alone there are 2,270,00 square meters of abandoned office space. This means that within one of the most congested metropolises of the entire world there exists an entire region that has succumbed to desertification, technologically equipped and perfectly maintained, but without function.

What is even more revealing is that, if one considers that ever since the fifties the largest Japanese metropolises have suffered from an unbalanced setting created by the occupation of city centers on the part of industry services, offices, banks, and shopping malls, residential areas are relegated to a peripheral ring of exile made up of very small, uncomfortable home typologies. The effects of this imbalance also produce serious social problems; because of this lack of residential market, an intrinsic fragility has been produced in the Japanese economy because it cannot guarantee an individual wealth based solely on mobile goods (stocks, consumer goods, automobiles), nor can it be based on immobile goods (houses) as in the West—real estate that is the traditional shock-absorber in the cases of recurring national economic crises.

Thus, in a very rich nation like Japan, individual wellbeing is not sufficiently guaranteed. If this great real estate patrimony of now unused tertiary spaces could be within a short time transformed into a newly conceived residential park, finally placed in the city center, it would be possible to make a turn for the positive in these structural insufficiencies from which the national economy suffers.

Milan, as an innovative district in the nineties, found in its unused industrial spaces areas available for the development of new professions and the services indispensable for its growth; activities which would never, in the traditional city setting, have been found—cities that had not foreseen and never could have supported this type of development.

There exist, then, realities submerged within dimensions that make up an important resource for national and local economies.

The national and local economies need, in order to consolidate and expand, adequate spaces and resources. The adequate resources now consist not only of the availability of technicians and entrepreneurs, but also of an elevated number of creative people—not necessarily designers and artists, but subjects able to operate like a (weak and diffuse) innovative energy; in other words, elements able to activate dynamic strategies for setting offers in motion, renew the domestic market, and confront international competition.

In this picture, the demand for professional education corresponds to the exponential growth of universities and design schools that aim to educate not only traditional designers, but also experts in innovative strategy.

In the last ten years, a worldwide phenomenon has occurred that has completely eluded the *man without quantities* (and many designers as well).

This phenomenon consists of the major growth in the number of universities and design schools, and is connected to the new role of design in national economies.

We can provide some data about this growth.

Numbered series of 20,000 small vases, each with a different face, Genetic Tales collection, Alessi, 2000

In Italy, at the beginning of the eighties, not a single course of design existed at the university level, while in 2003 there were eighteen degree-track courses of study at eleven different universities, with a total of nearly 8,000 students.

The number of continuing education and post-graduate schools in Italy has grown from one to seventeen over a period of twenty years, and in Milan alone there are eleven post-graduate and ninety-six continuing education design courses of study, of which twenty-three are funded by the European Union (FSE).

In Europe, between secondary schools and universities, seventy-one design courses of study are active, and from which approximately 50,000 students graduate each year.

In Japan, where in the seventies the design profession was limited to very few designers who worked within large industry, there now exist thirty-seven design departments with a total of approximately 70,000 students.

In North America, there are now 224 active design schools (144 fashion schools), while in India there are 311 design universities.

The large trade fairs for modern furniture and interior design have also developed greatly.

In Milan, the Salone del Mobile (Furniture Salon) has grown to the point of becoming a large world-wide design festival where each year not only the most important producers in the field converge, but also young designers who present their proposals (in 2005 there were 367 auxiliary shows during the fair). Each year eleven fairs take place here, one after the other, dedicated to trade sectors specialized in furnishings (from design objects to kitchens, lighting, and upholstery). Each year twelve cities throughout Italy host approximately twenty international fairs dedicated to home furnishing components.

In Paris alone, each year nine international salons dedicated to design are held, and important fairs take place in Frankfurt, Hanover, Cologne, Valencia, Birmingham, Dublin, Stockholm, Tornoto, Düsseldorf, Porto, Chicago, Shanghai, Hong Kong, Madrid, New York, Copenhagen, Montreal, Tokyo, Lisbon, Brussels, London, Moscow, and Istanbul.

This growth of the educational opportunities and commercial promotion accompanied neither by unemployment of design graduates nor by a crisis in the public flow toward the numerous design weeks presented around the globe.

This is, therefore, not a superficial phenomenon, but a stabilized trend that has roots in the typical processes of our time, such as globalization, mass entrepreneurship, the relational economy, and demand for innovation within various industrial systems.

All of these phenomena began in the final years of the last century and have rapidly grown (silently and in the penumbra) to the point of producing completely new general situations that signal the true beginning of the twenty-first century.

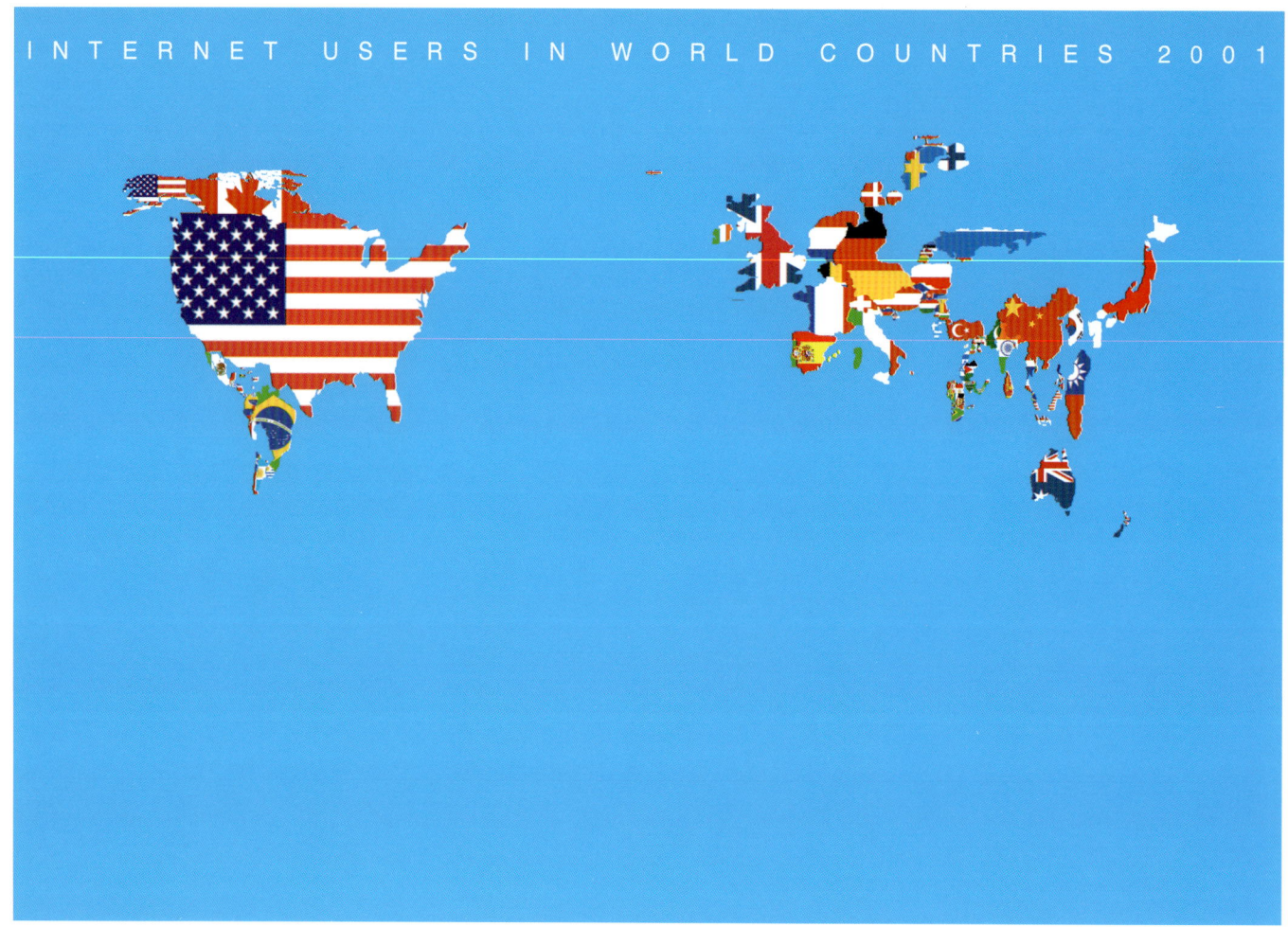

Antonio Scarponi (Master's in
City-Planning, IUAV, Venice),
Human World, Internet Users
in World Countries, 2002–2006
(from Nua, 2001)

Antonio Scarponi (Master's in City-Planning, IUAV, Venice), Human World, Population in World Countries, *2002–2006 (from United Nations, 2000)*

Elastic Classicism

In our critical tradition, classical architecture is represented as the greatest producer of movements, triumphal arches, amphitheaters, and imperial palaces. But the cities of ancient Rome and the Latin world had nothing of the formal unity of the Greek *polis*, above all that of the Athenian model, unified around the hill of the Acropolis, upon which the Parthenon rested. Rome was a polycentric urban system distributed over seven hills, capital of an endless empire that extended from Latium to Africa and the distant East.

That territory urbanized through a very simple architectural system, based solely on post and lintel construction where stylistic elements totally coincided with the static elements. With that system it was possible to build an imperial palace or a shepherd's hut, supports for a vineyard or a temple of Minerva; it was sufficient just to change the construction material, be it wood, stone, or marble, to change the sense of architecture.

The city, its forum, and its agricultural land were constructed from a vast system of columns, pillars, and posts, all placed in an orderly fashion at a distance that corresponded to the length of the lintels. Atop this regular fabric the wall segments were connected, until they composed the city's warp and weft, and around this were the fields where crops were equally ordered according to the same rule. The classical nature of agriculture (and the agricultural nature of architecture) originates from this process of the land's transformation, where single constructions are joined as a visible intensification of a theoretical mesh.

This type of traversable, indifferent, extensive continuation, which contained cities, buildings, cultivated fields, and streets, corresponded to the Latin concept of a civilization founded not on single cities, but, as Cicero explains, on the principles of the Right and on civil institutions, summarized by the abstract formula *Senatus Populusque Romanus*.

The classical city therefore had its foundation in an immaterial judicial system that the troops defended and expanded, and that architecture rendered visible. Thus the Roman Empire presented itself as a great symbolic system where style and politics coincided—an expandable framework within which it was possible to hold all the most contradictory cultures, crops, logics, and religions.

The Italian Renaissance of the fifteenth century returned to this elastic nature of classical architecture when the end of the medieval unity opened an incurable crisis in the rapport between faith, science, and politics. The Renaissance's aesthetic apotheosis originated from the role assigned to (classical) art as a symbolic paradigm, able to hold together a polycentric system of weak and irreconcilable truths. Each was imper-

Fresco sinopia of landscape with construction site, Villa San Marco, Stabia

Le Corbusier, Profile of the Parthenon *(from Le Corbusier, La maison des hommes, 1942)*

Brunelleschi, Old Sacristy of San Lorenzo, Florence, 15th century

fect, incomplete, but with a totalizing vocation: a Christianity that lives together with pagan culture, science that signs along with Galileo its own abjuration, politics that refound themselves with Machiavelli on the ashes of their own failure.

Since its birth the classical code of the Renaissance was made up of an elastic material, able to make those opposites live together: from the oval in Brunelleschi's cupola up to the eighteenth-century revivals, that code demonstrates its ability to stitch together incompatible spaces and philosophies. Modernity inherited that same role as a great cosmic system, of a stylistic, civil nature capable of continually changing in order to remain always itself. It kept together the most incurable contradictions: opulence and minimalism, liberalism and planning, local realities and globalization, mechanics and electronics, monuments and virtual webs, technology and spontaneity, innovation and tradition. For the next two or three centuries modernity will construct the (evolving yet stable) landscape of Western culture, providing the highest levels of freedom within those stylistic and intellectual confines determined at the beginning of the twentieth century and continually revisited with new sensitivity and methods.

When speaking of a liquid modernity as an evolutionary phase of post-modernity, one nevertheless speaks of modernity. When speaking of an uncertain civilization one nevertheless speaks of an advanced phase of society's secularization introduced by modern reason. The weak and diffuse modernity that marks the beginning of the twenty-first century is the result of a diffuse and extensive refinement of a culture that now spreads beyond design disciplines to collide with the enzymatic transformation of land and environment. This is an expansive phase in the porosities of a world, still in large part divided into heterogeneous jurisdictions and velocities.

Elastic classicism is the model to which our elastic modernity refers as a deformable system, within which social, technological, and productive transformations of society find space, thus avoiding trauma and fracture and continuing to finely construct the best conditions for freedom and knowledge.

Minimalist Politics

One of the most original contributions of fuzzy logic is the proposal to accept certain families of home appliances (such as small, self-regulating air conditioners) as new moral models: as sweet elaborators of a microclimate's spontaneous self-regulation, no longer looked at in relation to hot and cold, but to the intermediate conditions of the environmental context.

In other words, electronic technology becomes the producer of a new ethical model, based on the ability to establish an ever-relative equilibrium through its intelligent interface. No longer, then, the Hot or Cold, Good or Bad, Everything or Nothing mode of dualistic logic, but the tepid, humid, intermediate that constantly changes in relation to the contextual conditions, reforming itself along with their changes.

This metaphor of a ductile, weak, and self-regulating morality corresponds well with the ethic-political condition that emerged at the close of the great revolutionary era. The twentieth century, for a very particular series of historical events, has produced, as Mario Tronti said, a singular synthesis between social politics and theology: poor against rich, right against wrong, black against white, worker against employer. This type of strong and mechanical politics ended up producing great simplifications, and reduced politics to a schematic process of often banal formulas that no longer correspond to the absolute contents for which they had been designed. Let's say that last century's politics, after the failure of the global alternatives, seems to have taken the two-fold road of a return to the rites of parliamentarianism together with the nostalgic search for a heroic season, which began with the Oath of the Jeu de Paume and had its mythic moments in the Spanish War and the Resistance.

This nostalgia has fed terrorism and its refusal of the return of politics in its traditional source, of weak praxis, which no longer compares itself to grand ideologies, but rather works on systems of local succession, on a very diligent reformism that aims to continually modify and reform the system's developmental model in order to avoid its rupture.

This is a politics, therefore, characteristic of a highly complex, conflicted, and uncertain monological system—a system lacking in global alternatives, but also lacking a sure democratic model. This is a globalized system that produces a virtual democracy lacking both *demos* and *cratos* (people and power), and that holds its oldest institutional rites along with brief, violent, anarchical revolts.

Revolts and seditions are born from time to time from the desire to purge, even temporarily, the possibility to recommence the games, to question the system; they are looking to follow the Palazzo and Piazza in which history continues to visibly, simply, and directly happen.

Hence this political praxis happens in minimalist and irreversible terms, in the sense that long periods of virtual participation alternate with brief moments of violent collision between two minorities, that of the Powerful and that of the Antagonists, who confront one another reciprocally disputing the mandate to represent all the others, the absent, the indifferent people—those who make up the scattered majority.

That dispersed majority is, however, an evolved majority, totally secular, but not indifferent; it follows a fuzzy ethics and diffuse reformism, and has a sporty, televised, minimized impression of politics, far from the return to the twentieth century's teleo-

Francis Bacon, Untitled, *1954*

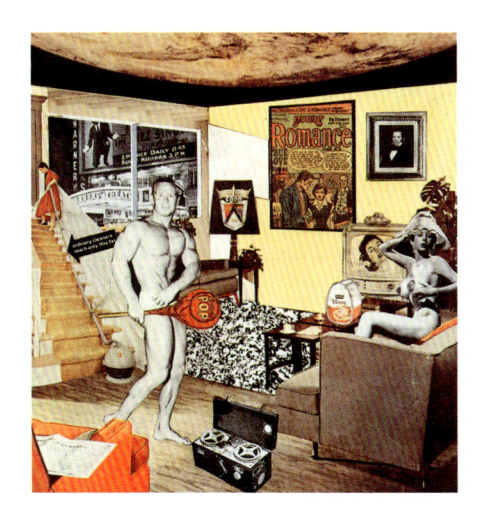

Richard Hamilton, Just What Is it that Makes Today's Homes so Different, so Appealing?*, 1956*

Ruins of the Twin Towers in New York after the 9/11 attack

logical confrontations. This dispersed majority is the champion of an elastic distance, of a weak, indirect democracy, but precisely for this it is difficult to beat. Precisely because it is a democracy as diffuse as a protective film around a discomposed planet—a planet that could from one minute to the next begin its decomposition, opening an irreversible crisis, if robbed of this anesthetic level of democracy.

Any absolute theorem, any definite solution, becomes dangerous in this context because it can be perforated, producing unmanageable rigidities and therefore fragility. Ours is an epoch in which one must know how to produce flexible models of development and government able to adapt to the changing conditions of society and the market. This is an epoch marked by minimalist, reversible, televised, and at times violent politics produced by a diffuse society of indifferent people, but also of unpredictable new believers. This is an epoch of sporty democracy, in the sense of a democracy where only formal rules and insurmountable prohibitions count; where the referee is no longer parliament, but the magistracy or the stock market, who contest violations and decide expulsions. President Nixon and his later successor Clinton, Microsoft, and Enron are all familiar with this.

From all this a deeply minimized vision of the world emerges, a product of analgesic contact with history and the absolute refusal of lacerating comparisons with the crushed systems of metaphysics.

In fact, with the disappearance of the great metaphysical systems, or the reduction of ethics and politics to a merely social question (just as happened in the second-half of the twentieth century), one could truly say that the real modern tragedy is the disappearance of tragedy itself, which marked the complete fracturing of the eternal hierarchies of metaphysics.

After the terrible proofs of the slaughter Europe was capable of, in confrontation with the death—which happened in the media-saturated society—of human identity's ancient roots, Europe ran the risk of paralysis before the nightmares of a forever-lost innocence. Ancient tragic masks, their forms lacerated by anguish, could have been the catharsis to which hopeless contemplation could be entrusted, before which even art retreats and refuses to go any farther. But it is precisely from art that we received the sign that these extreme historical conditions could be gotten over and positively resolved. Not through the removal or forgetting of the past, but with the innocent acceptance of the present, with a curious and unconscious smile of one who asks *why not?* Why not accept the world as it is? Perhaps there are still extreme margins of survival, spaces for play!

In the London of the 1950s, there were two artists who better than all others represented this extreme dilemma: it is a question of stopping oneself, horrified, before the present, as painter Francis Bacon said, marking the limit beyond which there are only tragic masks. Or try timidly to look innocently at this world made of figurines, and try a cut-and-paste approach, rearranging it in demented scenes, where nevertheless self-irony is possible, as Richard Hamilton did in those same years. Perhaps it is from that moment, fruit of the poet's unconscious, that the present world slowly found that weak energy that permits it to follow new, light logic, and thereby save itself, move ahead, observe and accept the world as it is. Smile at the world as a premise for (perhaps) changing it—certainly not to die artlessly, crushed by tragedy.

The Economy of Innovation

The new economy (or net economy) originated in the eighties, following the vastest project of industrial renovation of contemporary times. It was a process of productive and managerial reorganization made up of the introduction of robots and electronics in the chain of production, and of computers in the management of warehouses and tertiary activities.

This industrial renovation, which was the first response to the segmentation of markets and society, was the first step towards globalization with the consequential outsourcing of production to more convenient countries, and therefore one of the first developments of e-commerce. All these processes made a massive layoff of workers possible, a drastic reduction of commercial and factory personnel, and in fact favored, beginning in the nineties, the formation of two parallel economies.

On the one hand is the classic industrial economy, still bound to the salary of factory and office; an economy that is ever more divided into autonomous sectors managed by enterprises that are willing to invest in new technologies, under the condition that they permit the reduction of the number of workers. On the other hand is a social economy that is always more extensive, made up of a great number of laid-off workers, that is, workers not boxed as usual into the frames of wage compensation, and therefore dedicated to reinventing day by day new forms of enterprise and work.

This scenario has turned the classic schemes of twentieth-century political economics upside-down. These schemes assumed a leading role for industrial economics over social economics, in the sense that as the former grew, jobs grew, and therefore the social economy was also buoyed. In this new order, the two economies act autonomously, with indirect, even paradoxical relationships: in fact, the better business goes for industry, the more it invests in substitutive technologies, the more it expels workers and the more unemployment grows. The unemployed flow into and augment the reservoir of a social economy based on entrepreneurship in the sectors of service, small business, and aesthetic markets (fashion and design), where the initial costs of investment are very low.

The creator of growth of this new, post-industrial economy is therefore made up of a permanent state of crisis in which, however, the lay-offs do not necessarily coincide with recession, but rather with the increase of a social economy that produces research and innovation.

This laid-off society, excluded from industrial cycles and a guaranteed salary, has begun to invent work and enterprise, and often has successfully entered the market of technological, aesthetic, and commercial innovation using information technologies as a new condition of working independence.

This is a revolution that Jeremy Rifkin calls an economy of access, which is marked by the arrival of a new mass society no longer made up of anonymous consumers, but of small financial operators, from independent small business owners, inventors of aesthetic enterprises, new metropolitan services, and virtual relations in the world of e-commerce.

This vast productive renovation also invests technological research, now spread out over many specialized sectors where young, autonomous researchers are capable of offering an imposing mass of micro-inventions for the world market of innovation, which regards above all the electronics industry and its derivative products.

Following the functional model of artistic research produced by independent workers, musicians, designers, or stylists who, moving in various districts of urban innovation such as Milan, Tokyo, London, and New York, create collaborations with the sector's large industries, even the large electronics enterprises like Apple, Microsoft, and Sony have begun to create relations with the various Silicon Valleys throughout the world, where a free population produces spontaneous technological research and innovation. This is a microscopic research and innovation, which does not produce masterpieces or Nobel prizewinning inventions, but creates a continual push for the updating of the aesthetic and electronic market through innovative new products, styles, links, software, portals, services, and enterprise. It is a question of a weak and diffuse energy, able to constantly move the sector's global market, producing a new social economy as well.

All the industries that act on our mature, high-saturation markets constantly need technological, commercial, aesthetic, and goods-oriented innovation; innovation is, in fact, the only energy that permits industry to deal with competition and punctually renew its catalogues and offerings. Today this type of innovation is not solely a product of the great centers of scientific research like NASA, MIT, university campuses, large design studios, or the bastions of taste, but is also and chiefly produced by the juvenile districts, by the dispersed population of independent researchers, by those who spontaneously take on a determined technological or design problem as if it regarded not an industrial problem, but rather the realization of their own personality.

These often follow unorthodox work methodologies, based on a very up-to-date knowledge of the sector; a knowledge that is freely reworked according to creative intuition. Musicians like Peter Gabriel and children's game inventors provided the first uses of CD-ROM technology, which had long been unused by Philips because of its challenging, ramified logic, demonstrating how the improper thinking of artists and children are often among the most adequate ones for interpreting the potentialities of new technologies.

Like artists who live in their studios, producing research and innovation without base investments, creating added value solely through their creative work, today's freelance researchers move in complete independence from any and all programs, often using "inappropriate" places, in an urban context saturated with relations and stimuli, using the most sophisticated electronic installations now available at low cost on the second-hand market. Artistic behavior, then, once considered characteristic of small, excluded, marginalized, and unpredictable social groups once viewed as foreign to the business world, has now gained a new centrality in the social economy. It has become the example of a spontaneous, creative entrepreneurship that works according to the logic of self-branding, requiring close to nothing in initial investments.

Master Plan for Eindhoven

Client
Philips Design
(director Stefano Marzano)
Municipality of Eindhoven

Year
2000

Design
Andrea Branzi
with
Ernesto Bartolini, Lapo Lani

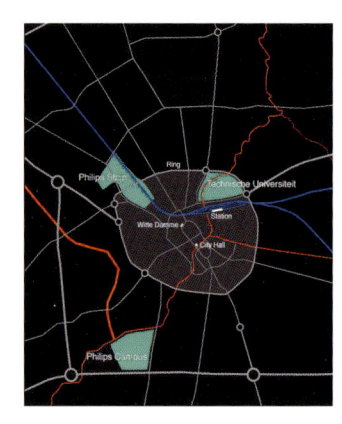

Street plan of Eindhoven

The city of Eindhoven has been, since the beginning of the last century, the historic seat of the Philips industries; it was here that the first electric lamp, the first CD-ROM, and the first walkman were born. Up until the early seventies almost 90% of the population worked for Philips. Then, progressively, a process of transfer within the productive centers began, and Eindhoven, like all the other mono-cultural cities, began a long process of rethinking itself.
The industrial dismissal of the Philips *Strijp* (982,000 p.) is occurring in a progressive and controlled manner, along with the construction of a new Philips Campus south of the Eindhoven ring, which has the characteristics of a scientific research center.
In June of 1999, the design seminar on the Philips *Strijp* took place, followed by one on the city's historic center by Atelier Mendini, and a studio presentation on the new train station with Peter Eisenman.
Our design studio—with Ralf Brodruk, Lauren Kolks, Jan Kinings, and Sonia de Jong from the city government of Eindhoven—was largely programmatic in nature, as a moment for preliminary discussion of the city's marketing and the programmatic characteristics of the project. Additional elements for a master plan were later worked out with Ernesto Bartolini and Lapo Lani. The idea elaborated during our June seminar was to preserve the Philips *Strijp*'s characteristic of an autonomous territory with respect to the urban context, like an open

agricultural park that allows for the reactivation of connections between the city's separate parts. The problem of the zoning of the various internal urban destinations was overcome by our request, initially posed to the Eindhoven city administration, to consider this area an experimental territory from both typological and normative points of view. An area, in other words, where different volumetric activities can take place over time, with end uses not defined and which can be effectuated as in agriculture, following criteria that change over time and with the seasons, and according to supply and demand. The area's layout was not, then, traced out with a system of roads, but with a pattern of pedestrian, cyclist, and tram routes—a sort of large tartan cloth of weak, crossing penetrations traced on the park's grass, constituting a homogenous fabric of light distribution that reconstructs a diffuse ability to traverse the whole area.
Upon this great urban tartan a series of autonomous layers of services, constructions, gardens, illuminations, specialized transport, and commerce are laid out—layers designed separately and superimposed on one another. A fairly limited number of industrial buildings were identified (together with the current aerial circuit of energy distribution) for preservation.
Within the European marketing plan for this vast area there was a proposal to make it a protected area for the new enterprise of the post-industrial economy, for those entrepreneurial initiatives that develop in a sprinkled fashion,

across the territory and various sectors, connected to technological, artistic, and mass design creativity. These could all find in Eindhoven their own European Silicon Valley, a district of great industrial tradition, already served by research laboratories, international connections, and university campuses within a historic city.
This type of young, diffuse entrepreneurship calls for the creation of intense relational spaces, an urban mix where residences, scientific research, laboratories, commerce, free time, and agricultural production are all indifferently layered one atop the other. In contrast with the old industrial zoning, the new economy, as a mass entrepreneurial inclination, happens not on separate campuses, but within the contexts of cultural and critical information that only the urban market can offer.

Unused areas of the Philips industrial campus with a plan of internal circulation routes

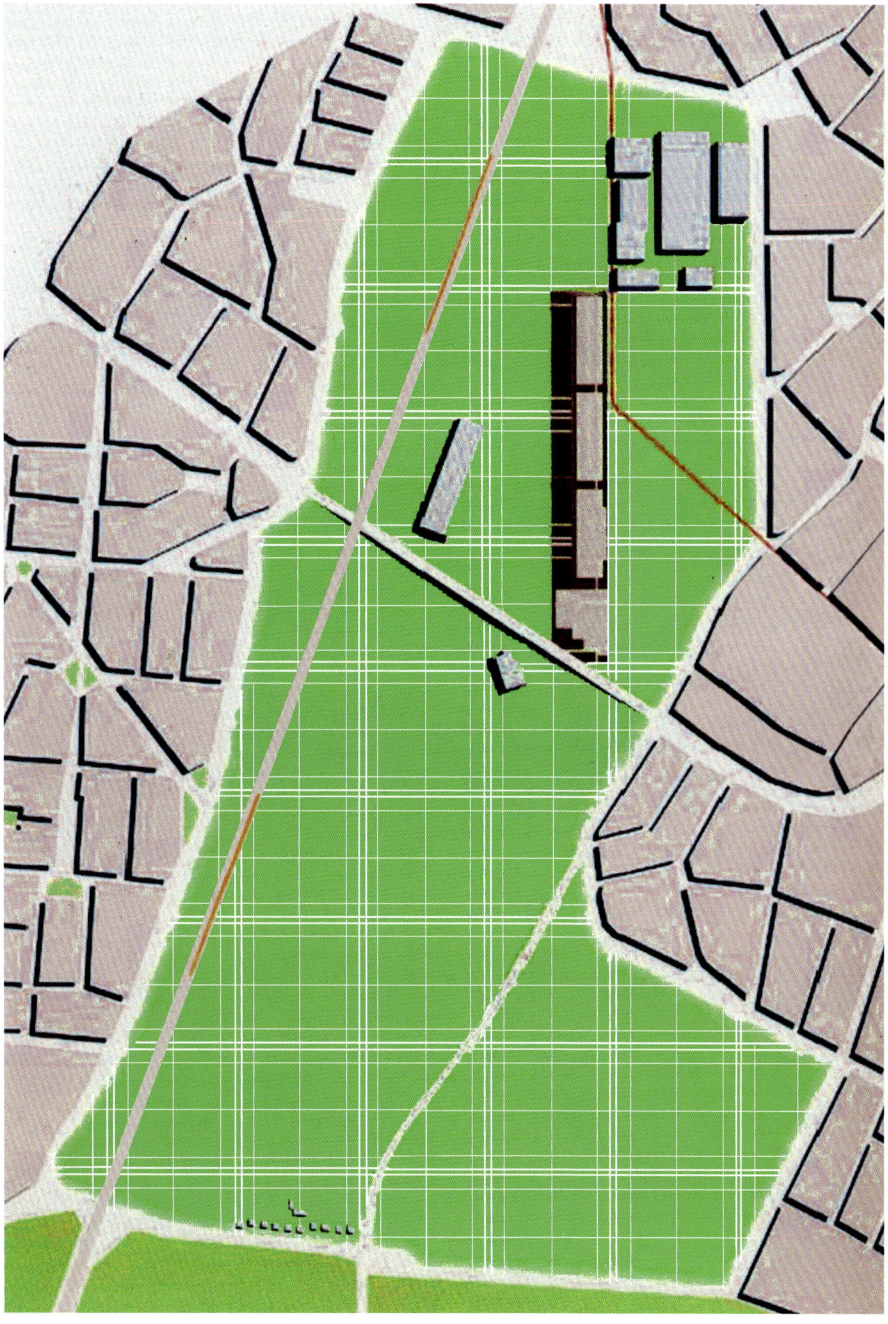

In the age of globalization, the laws of international competition force the industrial system to enter into the market solely on the condition that it is able to propose products or services different or alternative to those already in existence. Every industry active on the market needs to assure itself of its capacity to incessantly construct catalogues and new products that follow the continuous changes of taste and the economy.

Innovation, therefore, becomes the energy indispensable for the survival of enterprises in the highly competitive markets. Today, the production of this energy is no longer limited to the large technological research centers (NASA, Aerospace Enterprises, MIT), but this is also a result of a new creative social economy, made up of small business owners and independent workers who carry out aesthetic and technological research in territories (districts) with a high density of cultural information and human exchange.

Andrea Branzi, Ernesto Bartolini, Lapo Lani, Eindhoven, Model of Weak Urbanization, 2002–2004, *diagrams*

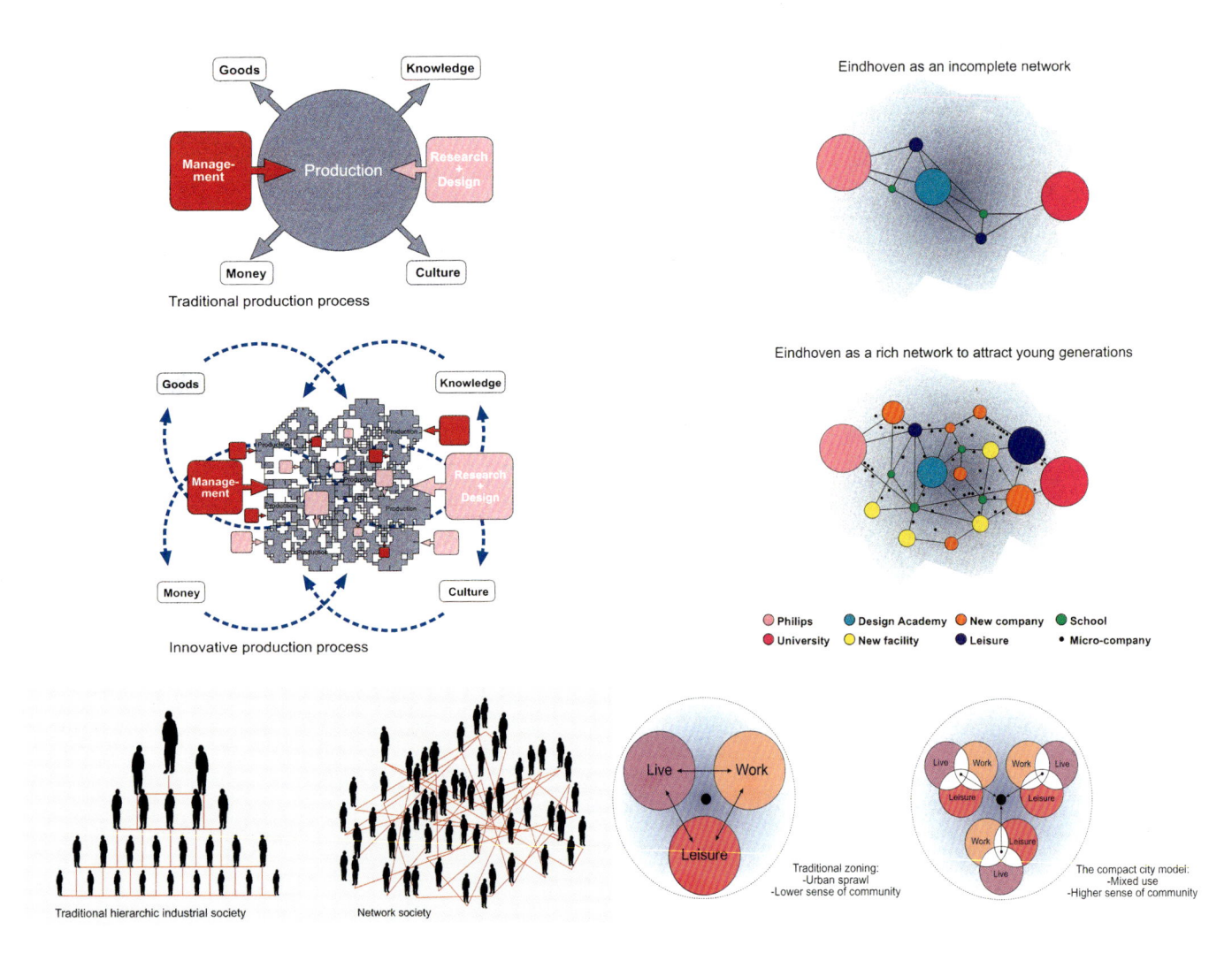

42

Mass entrepreneurship is one of the most interesting phenomena of the late twentieth century. This is the result of industrial processes of transformation begun in the seventies with the introduction of electronic technologies (robots) into production lines and the consequent progressive lay-off of workers. The phenomenon, accompanied by the move of many production activities to distant, more economically convenient and less unionized countries, favored the formation of a new social economy in the West, no longer directly associated with industry, but made up of a diffuse system of independent subjects who invent innovation, new products, and new enterprise, feeding into an often virtual economy characterized by a turbulent and unstable course that is nevertheless capable of creating social wealth.

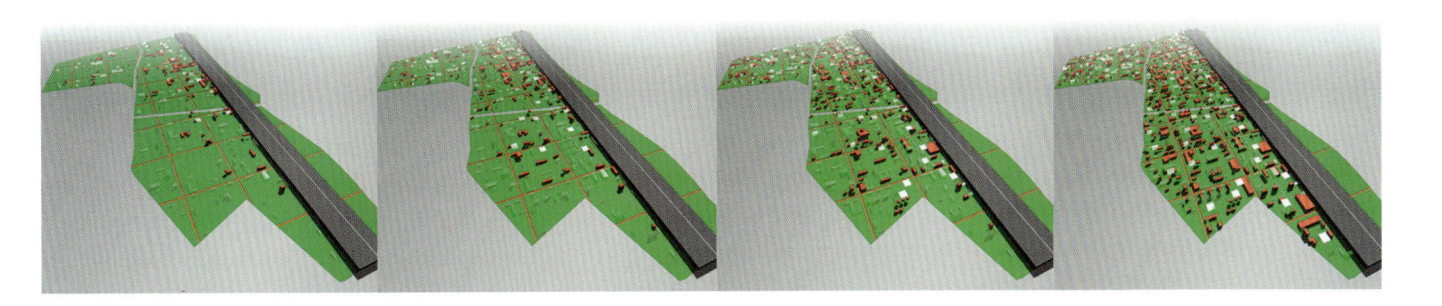

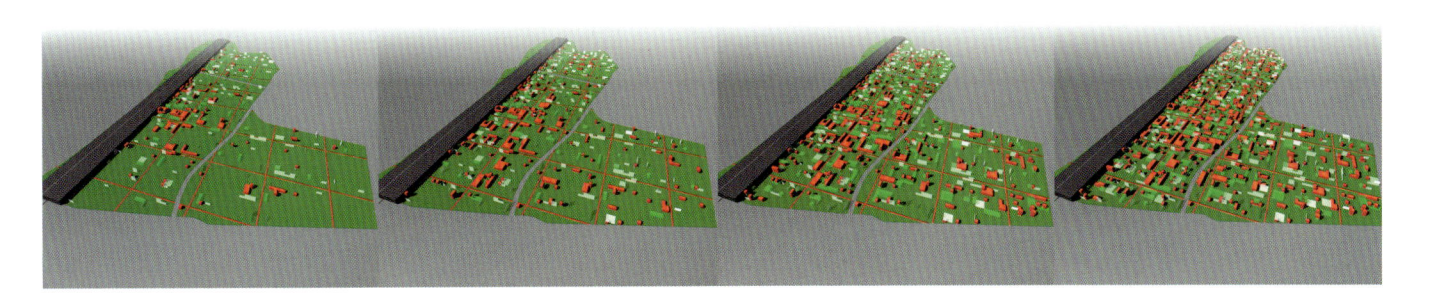

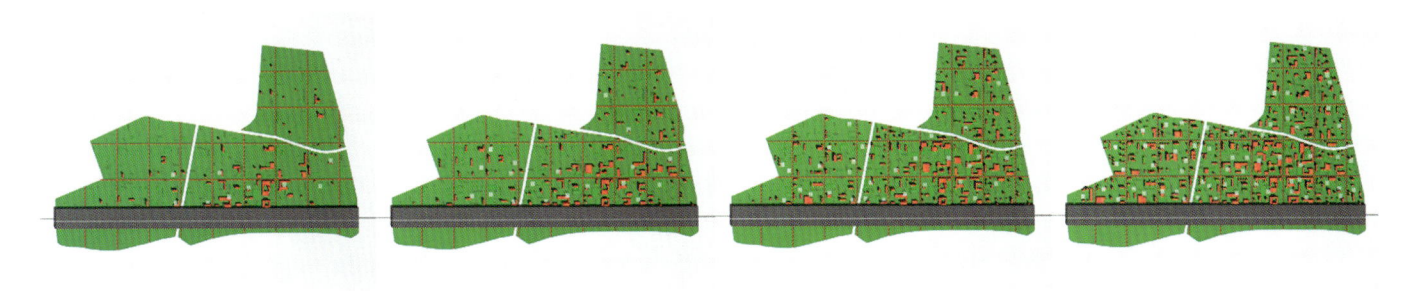

43

The meta-project for the future areas of Philips that are no longer in use in the city of Eindhoven foresees a weak model of urbanization, made up of a productive and traversable agricultural territory (where research laboratories, residences, and leisure-time structures are connected and intertwined, able to follow seasonal turnover in function) and of new dimensions. This sort of high-tech *favela* represents the hypothesis for a European district of research and innovation, an enzymatic territory with no stable image—rather one that seasonally changes its order like the agriculture with which it is unified.

Internal views of the innovative district of Eindhoven

Following pages:
Model of the innovative district within the agricultural park

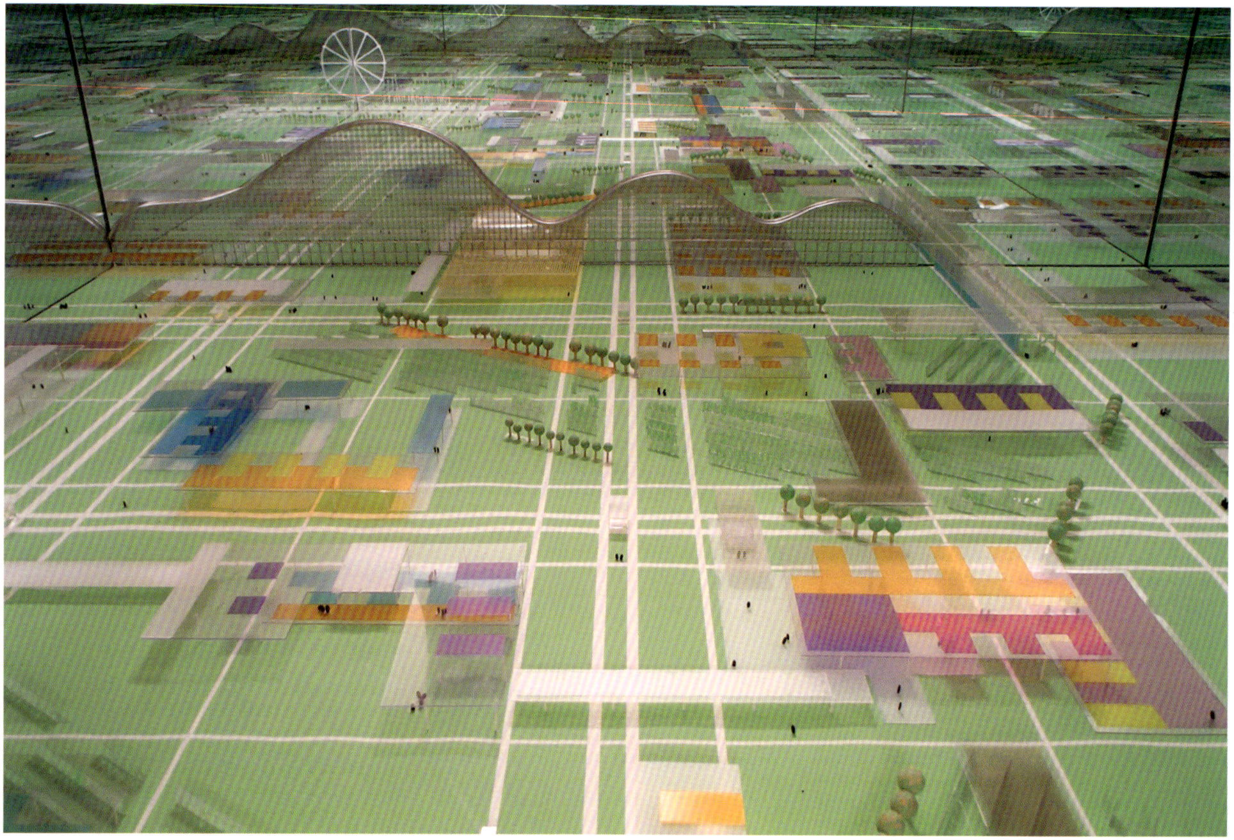

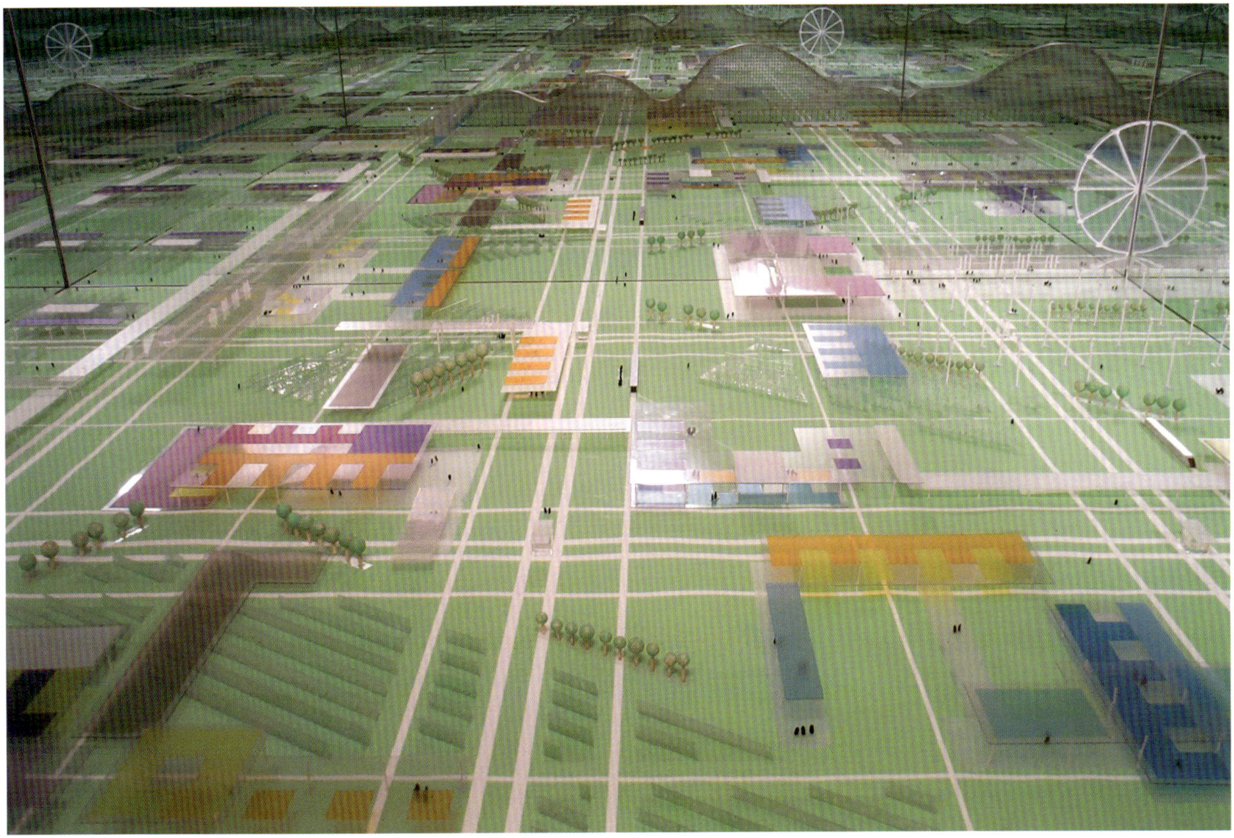

48

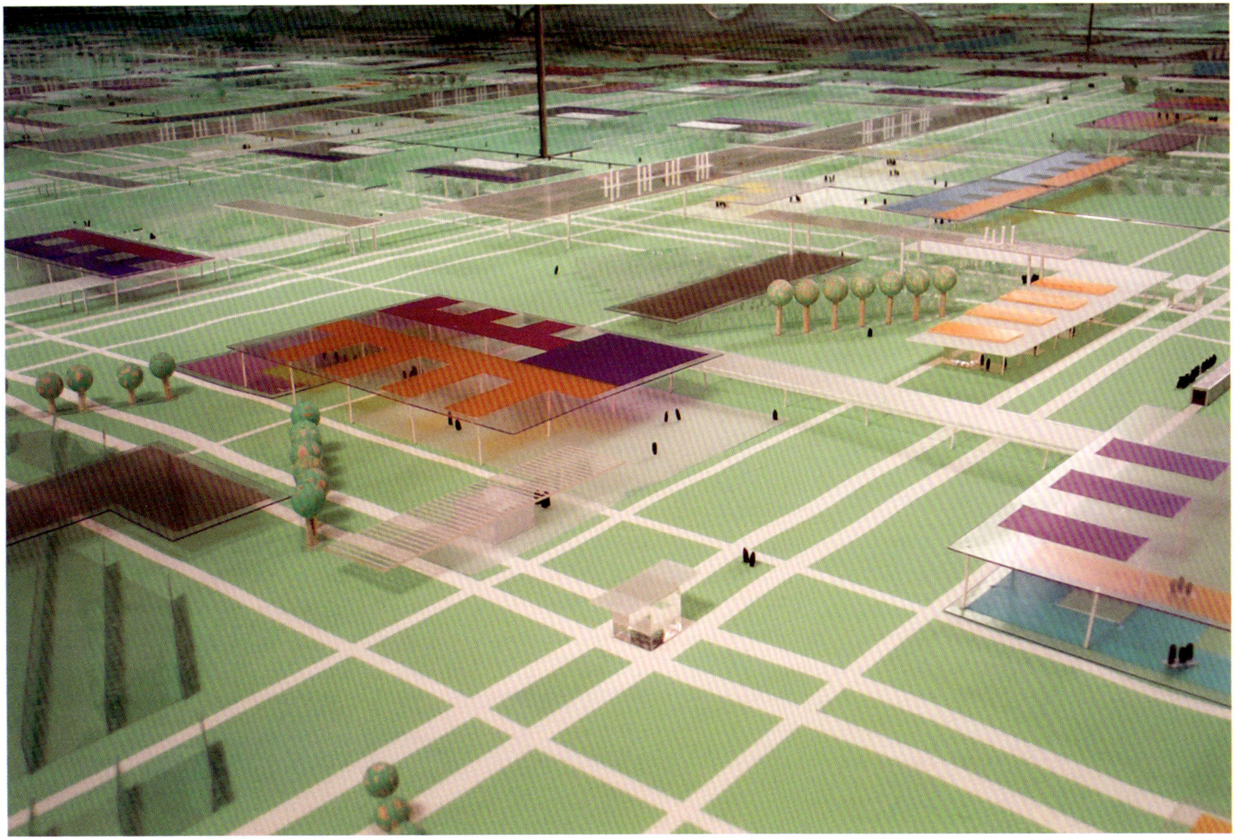

New Forms of Enterprise

Zygmunt Bauman's liquid modernity describes an age in which the political forms of both right and left are liquefying and often fluctuate among themselves. In the absence of the great consolidated values systems, the forms of politics once again become an object of creative research, like the invention of new logics, no longer based on great schemes of mechanical contraposition between workers and managers, or rich and poor, but between much more nuanced social subjects that contain less evident conditions of diversity—ignorant and informed, nomads and fixed populations, monotheists and polytheists.

The same form of enterprise (productive or commercial) is the object of new critical reflection. It is no longer considered a given form, a monad from whose aggregations the general economic system is composed. It seems more a form projected over time, a completely artificial structure, which has always corresponded to a theoretic/formal model of human and productive relations.

Imagining new models of productive organization is an integral part of any design culture: a new modernity is born only from a new model of enterprise. The form of manufactured objects cannot be separated from the form of the industrial nuclei that produce them, just as it cannot be separated from the consequential environmental structures.

In liberalism, just as in socialism, enterprise has always been the result of a theoretical model of the world, the formalization of productive energy and of the present exchanges in society. Enterprise is the result of a philosophy of human relations and the production of value. Therefore any design that does not presuppose a reflection on the organisms of production is always an inadequate design.

The concept of modernity in the twentieth century belongs to the ideology of the transformation of technologies, idioms, and behaviors used by industry; the "form of enterprise" has been one of the most adequate instruments for creating this transformation. The mechanical age produced a model of enterprise like a motor, a (strong and concentrated) machine of an economy made up of correlated but different, separate, antagonistic parts.

The classic enterprise is organized according to specialized, sector-based knowledge, capable of creating "definitive products and above all permanent wealth" that are situated in history as pillars of a new time-honored societal foundation—new permanent values, and new definitive riches.

With the net-economy and e-commerce, mass entrepreneurship, and the inclination towards diffuse innovation, the mechanical-military model has fallen into crisis: it no longer corresponds to the society of access and above all no longer corresponds to the ebb and flow of a global economy developed with no model of reference, without stable orders and fixed rules, with transitory virtual wealth and circumstantial economies. This is, then, a "buzz economy" that follows discontinuous flows of an energy that is more relational than productive.

This is an economy constantly in expansion because it is constantly in crisis, and vice versa; it is inadequate for governing its lively impulses, always on the brink of failure, as an indispensable premise for its leaps ahead.

From this tumultuous phase of maturation it becomes clear that the classic industrial economy, where wealth was produced by enterprise (a rigid form within a fluid society), is a rapidly setting sun. Enterprise and society coincide; the entrepre-

Little Wood Football Pools Offices, USA

Frank Lloyd Wright, S.C. Johnson and Son offices, Racine, Wisconsin, 1936–1939

neurial disposition coincides with the same vital energy of society and individuals.

In this sense, the social economy, like an evolving energy, coincides with the natural form of genetic systems—with the genetic metropolis. They are a conglomeration of weak and diffuse energies that traverse history and produce its unstable state. They are the symptom of a continuous evolution, produced by the individual's necessity to increase the conditions of environmental and social safety of its own genes.

It is a question, therefore, of rethinking the forms of economy and enterprise as specific parts of a new vision of history (and politics), one that makes reference to a fluid universe, a dynamic system in continuous evolution and renewal. The concept of new modernity must make reference to these new genetic, dynamic concepts, rethinking the present enterprise like an inadequate, rigid, fragile organism. This means moving from a closed, stable, specialized form to an open, provisory, liquid form.

It is therefore necessary to introduce new key words: traversable enterprise, reversible enterprise, that assume in their own organized form a state of permanent crisis, the instability of the market, the uncertainty of values, producing organization charts capable of liberating expansive energies beginning with its own dissolution. This means moving from enterprise to agency, from the armadas of Julius Caesar to the disposable army of Genghis Khan.

The design energy of the modern enterprise, its coincidence with the capacity to produce innovation, aims to surpass brand understood as a tribe of belonging, as a micro-society motivated by competition, to become instead a molecular system that traverses fluid plankton, continually liberating its form, and creating ever-new aggregations and new working alliances. No more, then, permanent forms, but fluid energies that coagulate and move only following terminal strategies and with working methods that are irreproducible in any classic form. In the essay "Treatise on Efficiency" by French sinologist François Joulien, there is

Andrea Branzi, Interior Garden, theoretic model, *Venice Architecture Biennale, 2004*

The new forms of enterprise, in the age of diffuse work and mass entrepreneurship, call for a very flexible type of logistic organization that is able to adapt to changing productive organizations and their objectives. The distributive systems of tertiary activities' interior spaces no longer correspond to rigid, specialized functional programs, but rather to elastic software that are able to provide different fabrics of service in real time.

mention of a surpassing of the Western concept of efficiency, based on Clausewitz's military model, in favor of ju-jitsu techniques, the Chinese martial art that uses adverse force to reach one's goal. The growth of enterprise is no longer, then, a dimensional growth, but coincides rather with its dynamic capacity, the continuous reduction of apparatuses, the dismissal of workers, and thereby the continuous betterment of its working capacities.

Today, the great operations can happen through the organization of provisory apparatuses, programmatically destined for dismissal; temporary apparatuses of a gene that grows only as a specialization, intelligence, experience, and not as a complex structure.

This complexity, as a qualitative category for organisms bent on surpassing environmental difficulties through the multiplication of their own components, leaves room for inverse processes of simplification of working modules, for the liberation of enterprise's energetic nuclei, freeing them from all formal over-structures.

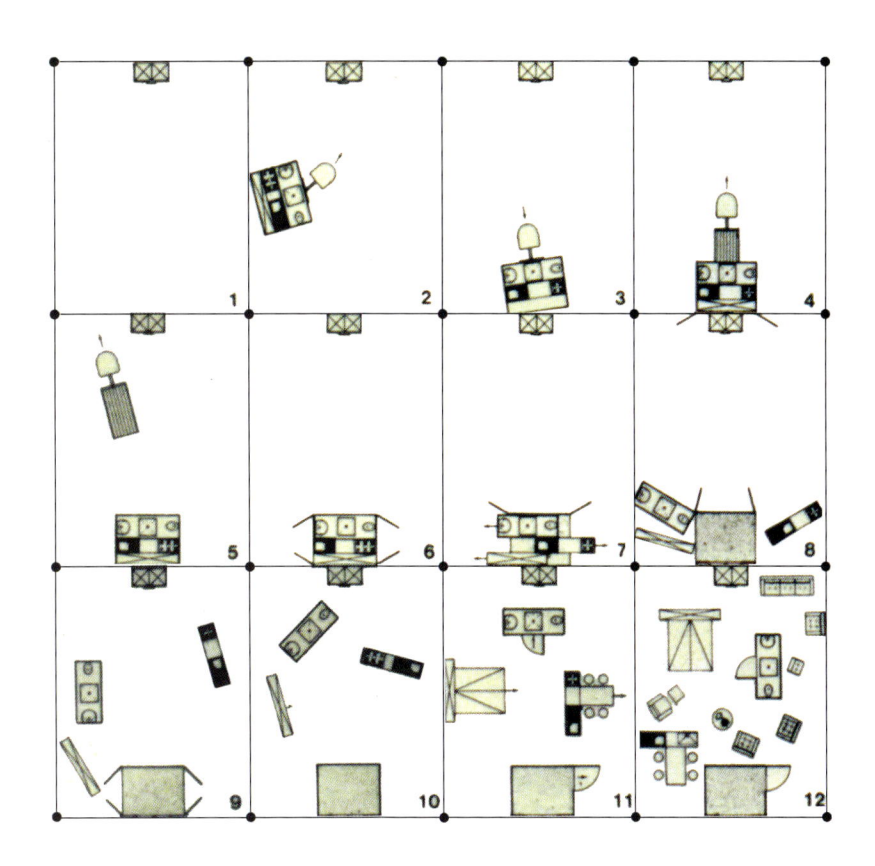

Archizoom Associates, No-Stop City, *1969–1972*

From Brand to Buzz

This consideration is important also from a communications point of view: the possibility of an enterprise's liquidation is no longer a surprise or danger, but is rather the condition by which to free its vital energies into a new form of dynamic flow, producing profit as a result of the capacity for expanding its relations, intermediations, and communications. All this follows the evolution of its vital nucleus and moves it definitively beyond the limits of the myth of identity. These are the politics of brand definition and defense as a recognizable element in the market. A nucleus of identity inalienable by enterprise must be redefined as the communication of a buzz, as a dynamic swarm, a nucleus of communication that is not exactly definable. This moves from the politics of geometric crystals to that of fuzzy, traversable embryos.

A brand does not stably occupy a space, nor does it have an identifiable form; rather it is set in a continuously expanding galaxy whose form is always temporary precisely because it is alive. This defines not an organization, but a genetic system. This system cannot be attacked for its weak and diffuse nature, and because of this it is also not easily destroyed. The elements of crisis, of inexpressiveness, or of communicative imprecision are characteristic of all the genetic elements capable of surviving in environments of tumultuous transformation, precisely because nebulae, swarms, and fluctuations impede its fracturing, elastically absorbing the traumatic processes, favoring the metabolic activities of strategic progression.

Authenticity, precision, and incisiveness in communicating one's own identity combine to create an intrinsic fragility; the classical

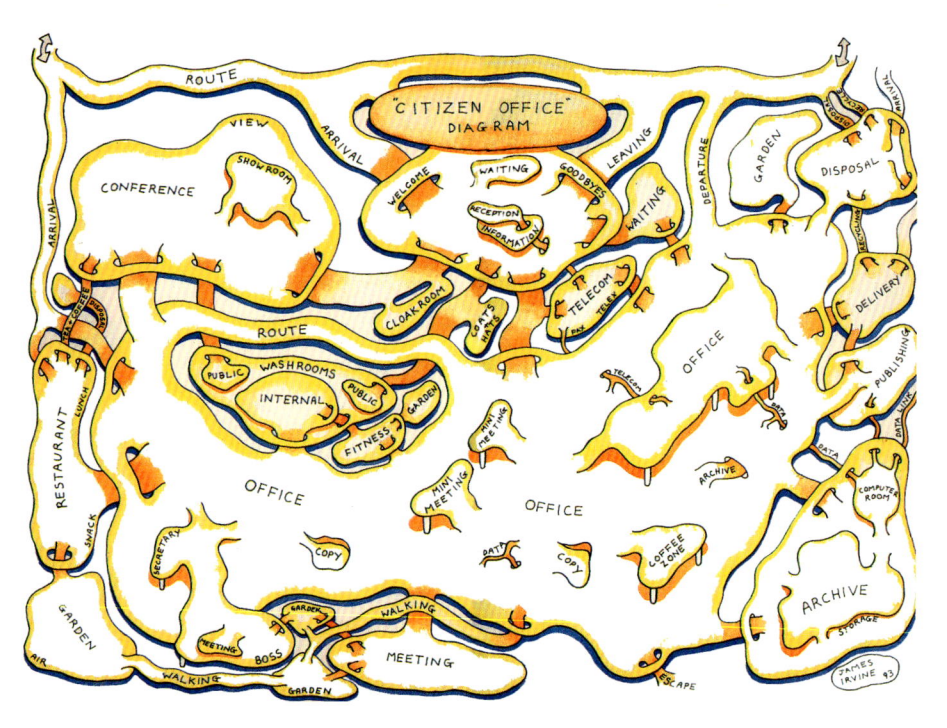

James Irvine, diagram for the exhibition Citizen Office, *Vitra Design Museum, Weil am Rheim, 1994*

concept of efficiency must be substituted.

At the end of the twentieth century a passage occurred from Fordist-model large enterprises of a single trademark to holdings. A fragmentation into specialized segments of the initial enterprise encouraged their penetration into post-industrial markets; each of these fragments, however, preserves like a hologram the precision of its mother image. In other words, they preserve all the informational elements of the original brand, augmenting where possible the precision of each sub-trademark in its own specialized sector. Operating like this a multiple system is produced where, however, each component element reproduces the fragility of the original nucleus, without at all improving its ductility, bettering only the offensive disarticulation, and not the defensive disarticulation.

Also in the model of business organization a progressive passage occurred from pyramidal organizational charts of military origin to matrix charts, where each function has its own specific autonomy (even competitive) with other joint compartments. This type of organization, where each operator is both client and business director, reproduces *in vitro* the processes spontaneously present in a territorial district where the forms of competition and collaboration between small businesses continuously intermingle following the conditions of the market.

A system of "ecology of an artificial environment" that guarantees the coexistence in the operative system of materials and objects that pertain to different logic, thereby creating complex and balanced systems: technical instruments and symbolic objects, artificial and natural materials, lasting and ephemeral products, mass-production systems and handmade goods. The internal space is therefore seen as an artificial landscape, a place of narrations that go beyond the functional specialization so as to become the bearers of corporate values and messages.

Andrea Branzi, corporate identity models for the exhibition Citizen Office, *Vitra Design Museum, Weil am Rheim, 1994*

Transitory Enterprise and the Social State

The industrial district represents a model of system-enterprise; this is the system that comes closest to the genetic concept in question, except for the fact that this, like all other earlier models, calls for the construction of permanent states of wealth, of definitive capital accumulation upon which to build other types of definitive wealth.

Temporariness as a new form-enterprise manifests itself, as we have seen, both in the processes of communication and in the methods of belonging. In the traditional enterprise, the employees live a contractual condition that binds them to the company as if to a closed system, destined to last through time and to which their energies must be exclusively dedicated.

The fact that enterprise is a finite process, or a transitory event, is not a foreseen fact (except in specific cases); the interruption of the relationship is one of many possible individual choices. The death of the enterprise is a negative, traumatic event that should always be avoided, inasmuch as it is absolutely unforeseen in the social and entrepreneurial setting.

The failure or liquidation of an enterprise always constitutes a pathological emergency, reparable through instruments of social rescue. The whole industrial system behaves as if only the conditions of the market exceptionally determine the death of productive organizations; when this happens it can be said that the whole social and productive system suffers.

Going into a historic phase of perma-

Archizoom Associates, model for the exhibition Superficie Neutra, *Abet Laminati, 1972*

In the city of mass entrepreneurship and diffuse work, the places of production become realities with a nuanced perimeter, without specialization, and with a low level of identity; bona fide functionoids able to adapt themselves (like personal computers) to the different necessities of the workers. The reuse of defunct structures, together with the inappropriate/unintended use of those already extant, determines a sort of continual dynamic refunctionalization of the city and redefinition of all its internal services and capabilities.

Andrea Branzi, Showroom abitabile, *installation for the exhibition* Italia e Giappone, design come stile di vita, *Yokohama and Kobe, 2001*

nent instability of markets and the constant state of world economic crisis it is necessary to elaborate a model of enterprise that is able to transform these negative conditions into positive elements—in other words foreseen, governed, accepted, and therefore socially innocuous elements. Confronting the concept of the temporariness of wealth and resources, the instability of the stock market and the exchange, as a vital condition in a state of definitive (not transitory) turbulence.

Enterprise in this context of liquid modernity, which does not anticipate the creation of definitive phenomena and stable empires, confronts the condition of uncertainty as the only possible certainty; it must assume the form of a dynamic accelerator—in other words, of an organism that is (secularly) temporary, open, and traversable; a sort of mobile reducer that accelerates the flow rather than obstructing it.

Enterprise as a mobile reducer makes the field's present energies converge, but does not trap them in an enclosure called brand, which reduces the dynamism of the system. In other words, the form-enterprise assumes the aspect of an organism not formally defined, but only as a segment traversed by relational forces, whose existence is defined in absolutely temporary terms. This collocation is not exactly retraceable. This process of liquefaction is rapidly happening throughout the West, and rightly finds great resistance on the part of political and union organizations that are worried about the impact this radical process of liberalization could have on society, thereby disintegrating the social shock absorbers. In other words, there is the danger that this deregulation is not accompanied by an adequate form of social protection, extended not only to dependant employees, but to all citizens, as a natural right that goes along with their belonging in society.

Traditional welfare that is reserved for the weakest minorities must be extended to all and act as a sort of general protection, like a well cared-for genetic campus for all those who belong to the social metropolis.

The state must directly guarantee the creation of this type of general protection of its members in order to guarantee the processes of liberalization of enterprise.

Up until now the reduction of the state's presence in society meant a guaranteed maximum freedom of enterprise (and its right to fire). Today we must begin to think that the maximum presence of the state is the only guarantee in order to have the maximum freedom of enterprise. In a civilization where all the citizens are entrepreneurs, this means guaranteeing the communal good. These considerations are not extraneous to the questions of design because they introduce a general concept that the processes of liquefaction that Bauman spoke of must now occur in a protected form, in a way that they are facilitated, not blocked.

Bauman's observation on the devastating effect of free enterprise based solely on profit in the age of proto-capitalism is important; the fact that it facilitated the re-composition of defensive solid bodies, which over time have produced political disasters and the preconceived refusal of many legitimate forms of spontaneity and liberalism is undeniable.

Currently the battle waged by union organizations in defense of welfare runs the risk of becoming a battle of the stragglers ("retrogard") because it must confront the conservative "retrogard" attack of those entrepreneurs who presume they have obtained the right to fire, and presume to obtain this result by demolishing the extant forms of social protection. The solution of this conflict, then, is not in the prevalence of one of the two sides in the conflict, but, on the contrary, in the formulation of a different, more extended welfare (public or private) that covers all citizens with new forms of social guarantees. We will see that this concept of a new rapport between the processes of liberalization and normative conditions will reemerge when we speak of models of weak urbanization, where the aim is to analyze urban regimes that call for volumetric fluidity, the absence of functional typologies, the surpassing of territorial standards, but also the introduction of new energetic formats that guarantee the governing of the land in non-traditional forms.

The current norms that regulate the formation of urban constructions and the programmatic use of buildings largely condition the order of current architecture because they anticipate in any case that the functions, typologies, and volumes be precisely predefined and observed. This type of regulation originated in the aim to prevent cities from becoming theaters of uncontrolled building speculation, which put infrastructures and sanitary conditions in crisis. But this type of normative apparatus, which in the twentieth century guaranteed to limit the damage produced by the large processes of urbanization, is now often a grave impediment to the functioning of the city in the age of diffuse work, industrial lay-offs, and e-commerce—all realities that require a high level of metropolitan liberalization, not for speculative reasons, but as an effect of the information technology revolution and mass entrepreneurship.

The comparison of the processes of liquefaction and formation of solid bodies of containment reemerges in the contemporary urban setting and collides head-on with the questions of design, which for a long time have been settled solely on linguistic comparisons, as if the political problem of architecture were already exhausted, resolved, or in any case foreign to the sign of modernity.

The traditional urban typologies defined by the Charter of Athens edited in 1933 by ICMA (International Congresses on Modern Architecture) and published in Paris in 1941, based on the distinction between residential zones, industrial zones, historical city center, and leisure time spaces, has been surpassed because of the diffusion of electronic instruments (computers) that favor diffuse work and the temporary forms of a relational economy whose working confines no longer correspond to recognizable and differentiated realities within the form of an object-oriented city, but rather to "informationalized" territories. The city has become a computer every 20 square meters.

The role of the *glance* as an instrument for gaining knowledge of reality is beginning to lose importance. The illuminist tradition to which Le Corbusier referred ("We must always say what we see and, above all, we must always—and this is more difficult—see what we are fording.") proves impractical when faced with the reality whose forms and functions no longer correspond to an inseparable unity.

Andrea Branzi, Vertical Home, *installation for Abitare il Tempo. Giornate Internazionali dell'Arredo, Verona, 1997*

Andrea Branzi, Showroom abitabile, *installation for the exhibition* Essere-benessere, *Triennale di Milano, 2000*

Business Art

Andrea Branzi, exhibition for the Bicentennial of the French Revolution, 1989

This new type of economy, diffused in an intensely relational way in society through information networks, constitutes a historical phenomenon that is completely new in its dimension and originality, and calls for a vast reflection on the form of the modern city, which is still largely organized according to classic industrial logic. This is a logic that, as we know, is based on zoning separated by function and closed enclaves, which have nothing in common with the fluidity of current productive activities and the intensity of exchanges, of work, and of the market.

The tendency to use land in less codified, more ductile forms corresponds to the different needs that individuals or groups carry out over time, often in the course of the same day, which require a great managerial autonomy and an availability of space and structures that are completely different from those foreseen by the factory's specialized mechanisms and the society bound to them.

During the past century architecture and design considered the reaching of a high level of rationalization of the constructed environment and human behaviors fundamental: industrial society could be defined as a society that used industrial products and therefore everything had to merge in favor of this type of market. The form of the city, but also art and politics, seconded this logic and this new anthropology linked to the series.

Today we have gone from an industrial society to a veritable industrial civilization, where everyone is in some way a part of the typical entrepreneurial values and logic. Everyone is becoming an industrialist, an entrepreneur, or their own manager (self branding) and considering the realization of their own personality in relation to directly industrial parameters like the execution of exchanges, the realization of profit, or the production of technological innovation, which is now experienced as though it were an artistic (autonomous and spontaneous) search.

To invent products means to create enterprise; to imagine the new means to expand the offer. To criticize the system means to optimize it, correct it, reform it. Global alternatives no longer exist.

We could therefore say today's age is that of Business Art, where these two once contradictory words collaborate to create wellbeing, information, development, and where creativity produces both aesthetics and enterprise. The current age is one that remembers the great commercial civilizations and marine republics where cultural exchanges produced wealth, where art served to create profit: art as business, then, but also business as art.

The passage from an industrial society, characterized by serial products and social specializations, to an industrial civilization where everyone is industrial brings with it the fact that everyone, in different forms, takes part in the values and problems born of industry and diffuse throughout the society. Just as in ancient Rome, where all the empire's inhabitants were Romans independent of where they lived or what they did, industry is now an internalized reality, a subjective and collective condition from which there is no escape. This context tends to reduce the distance between who designs and who produces because envisioning new products means designing new enterprise, and new enterprise always presupposes new products. The difference between who consumes and who designs is also disappearing; choosing, buying, and selecting are creative activities that produce fads and new trends. There exists a sort of buzz design that moves the market and indicates new spaces of the imagination, individuated from the crowd of micro-choices made by the consumer.

The post-industrial economy is largely based on the creative energy of society and its capacity to imagine "the new" in the form of products, enterprises, and new markets. In this context, even art becomes a leftover/advanced productive model, because it is based on a subject's ability to create value from a beginning investment of zero.
The artist and the entrepreneur are no longer opposed figures because both testify to the individual's inclination (through different means) towards innovation and change. The masterpieces of modern art thus become the new monuments of the contemporary city, children of a French Revolution that saw Reason not as a carrier of order, but as an instrument for eradicating the pre-established order of things and for renewing the world.

Andrea Branzi, exhibition for the Bicentennial of the French Revolution, 1989

The interface between who designs and who buys has therefore become interactive because both operate within the amniotic liquid of the market.

The world of start-up businesses, which rapidly are born and die, produces a social wealth that is often based on the virtual exchange of stocks. We know that in certain technological districts, such as the California of electronics, the number of nouveau riche is now a grave social problem. Sudden wealth interconnected with other sudden wealth within a closed system of societal connections produces a parallel economy without real money, and therefore a relational, virtual, reversible, and often irregular wealth. This wealth is difficult to quote on the stock market precisely because it is not linked to a real and stable economy.

This is a matter of a seasonal, district-bound wealth that is fruit of a new form of weak and diffuse political energy within society.

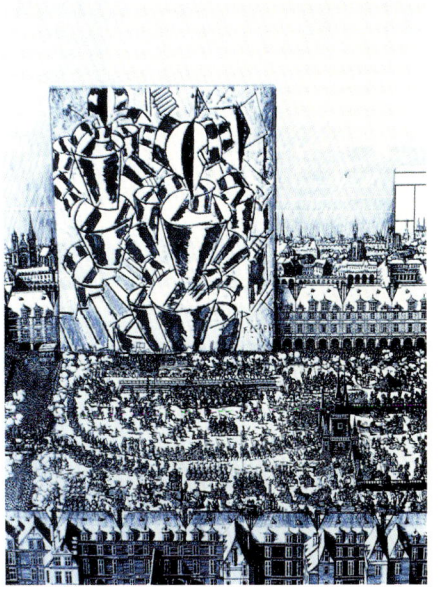

Innovation is born of a critical ability aimed at the limits of the extant world and the ability to imagine a different, technically better, functionally freer, aesthetically more beautiful, or less expensive world. This world does not exist, but could be built now, beginning with a new software, or product, or service. This aptitude belongs to an antagonistic, young, creative culture, and with Business Art, for the first time in history, wealth is produced by the freaks earlier than by the conformists.

This political ability to work starting not from programs and manifestos, but from small business and the world of products, domestic economies, and subsystems of the market does not modify society's structures, but does produce a slow, evolving energy, a perennial mutation, and an incessant reformism that are weak and imperfect instruments—the only ones capable of avoiding dangerous crises within the system.

Urban Dismissal

To modify according to one's own living, productive, commercial, or promotional needs the space inherited from earlier processes of dismissal produces a sort of urban metabolism. This metabolism is difficult to predict or govern because it is linked to the interrupted currents of this new relational economy. A very similar situation is now occurring in many cities of the industrial world; under an apparent normalcy, over the course of the past ten years an unstoppable process of dismissal of all foreseen functions has been produced, and contemporaneously the inappropriate use of almost all extant functions has spread.

Factories have been abandoned, offices have been emptied; schools and university campuses have been created in industrial areas; historic buildings have been transformed into banks and information technology centers; artisan sheds have become ateliers for design and fashion; industrial deposits have been recycled to create shopping malls; warehouses have become homes or theaters; offices have become art galleries or hotels; garages have become recording studios; basements have become research laboratories. One works at home and lives in the office.

The list is long and provisory because this type of sliding with respect to functional zoning upon which the cities were (even recently) designed and built is only at the beginning.

It seems as though there isn't an end-use, function, or predicted specialization that has not in the past few years been contradicted, transferred, or restructured according to new (and provisory) programmatic uses. The same traditional functions of living, buying and selling, producing, and promoting have been transformed and made more fluid, dispersed in new places or concentrated in television (and similar) services.

Many of the new economy's typical activities have found a home in dismissed areas, entire creative districts set themselves up in abandoned industries, finding in this submarket prized spaces, adequate services, and evolved forms of "incubators." Something similar, even if on a much smaller scale, had happened during the nineteenth century in the cities during the Napoleonic campaigns; ecclesiastical goods were suppressed, causing a great number of convents, abbeys, and Carthusian monasteries to enter the market and later be transformed into barracks, prisons, and schools. It took almost one hundred years for this vast and difficult patrimony of buildings to be absorbed, and many of those old dismissals from use still have not been completely resolved.

Just as the urban setting does not seem altered, the cities function better; the dismissals create new opportunities and lower the market values, producing a sort of updating of the city with respect to its new functions, and a greater freedom to use the extant structures.

Not always, though, are the existing norms ready for this type of creeping revolution, and the urban government now has great problems understanding if a building is used as a home or office. In both cases, there are chairs, tables, files, sofas, computers, and services.

In some American cities, new types of building regulations are being studied; ones that no longer try to set in stone the fleeting activities that happen in a neighborhood—for instance a neighborhood of docks transformed into one of incubators of various activities—and proceed instead with definitions of energetic layers.

Archizoom Associates (1966–1974), group photo, studio on Via di Ricorboli, Florence, 1968. From left to right: Paolo Deganello, Lucia Bartolini, Massimo Morozzi, Natalino Torniai (collaborator), Dario Bartolini, Gilberto Coretti, and Andrea Branzi

The city of defunct buildings and diffuse work becomes a large unified organism that surpasses the fractured dimension of architecture; it is a single, large interior space, with no external alternative, which corresponds to the territory of a global market where all activities are carried out in a differentiated and transitory manner.

Archizoom Associates, Competition for the International Artisan Fair at Fortezza da Basso, Florence, 1968

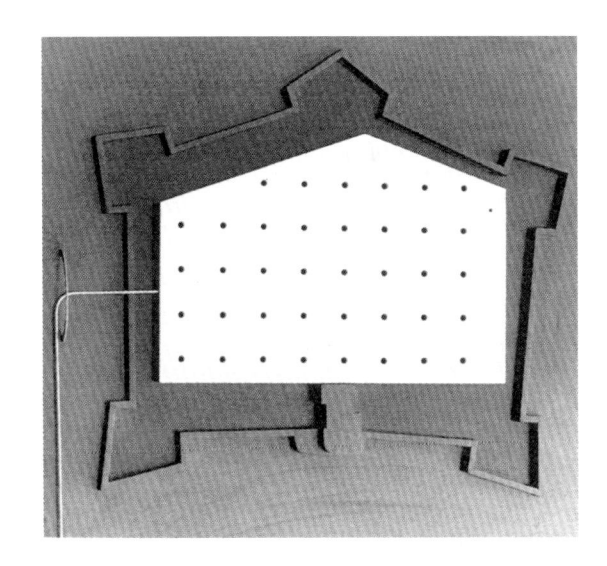

Bernard Tschumi, Le Fresnoy, 1991

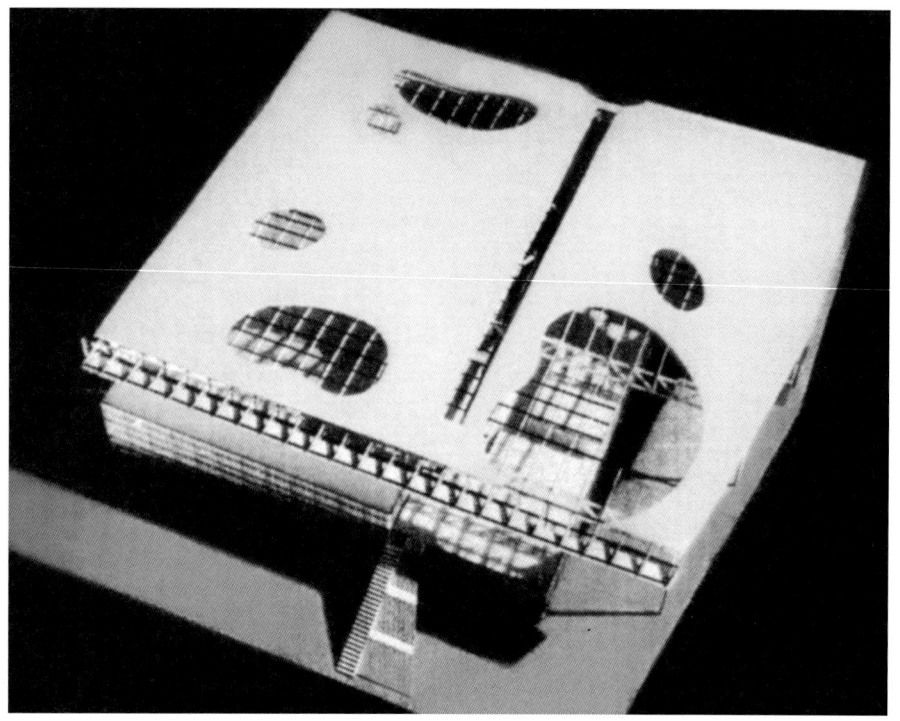

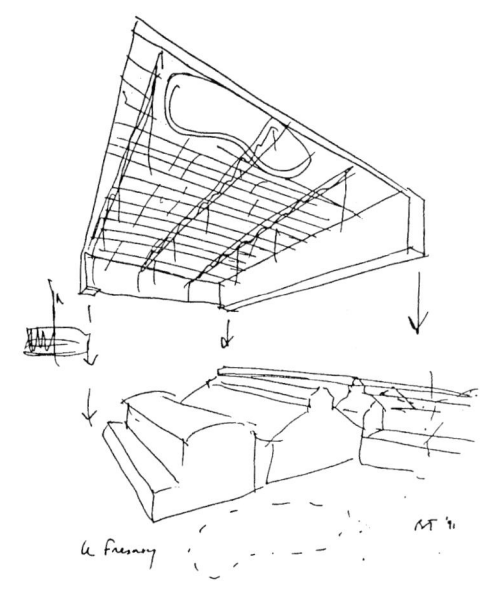

In other words, a determined function can no longer be assigned to a space. Rather, a space is classified in light of its energetic regime, which allows for any type of activity to occur as long as it is limited to a certain number of computers. In this way, a sufficiently elastic range of use is created, and while this guarantees an overall control of urban standards it also leaves great freedom in a given space's use.

This new internal function of the city surpasses typologies and resolves everything through the use of computers and furnishings. This universe of microstructures resolves from time to time the dismissal and substitution of functions, allowing cities to promptly readapt to their changing needs. This is like an extraordinary ductile plankton that allows for the renewal of form and function of interior spaces within the immobile containers of architecture; this also allows the use of construction from one or two thousand years ago without problem.

This creates a sort of lubricant that prevents the city from sticking, allowing it to readapt continually to the new. When we now speak of cities without architecture, and architecture without cities, we are not indicating anything dramatic, merely a natural condition that has matured through the long process of modernity, but which modernity has kept hidden or denied. This condition that now clearly emerges originated in the uncontrolled growth of the metropolises, and above all in the fall of the presumption that the culture of design were capable of positively recomposing the interests of millions of citizens, with those

In the contemporary city, underneath an apparent normality, a profound tectonic change is underway: not a single activity corresponds any longer to the architectural structures it was made for. Factories house universities, gasholders are museums or residences, people work at home and live in the office, banks are made in churches, galleries in garages, and gyms in laboratories. But the city used in this apparently undifferentiated manner seems to work better. New, unforeseen activities spontaneously find a home and convenience within an inherited real estate that would otherwise have been destined to become defunct or be destructed. The city of the future is therefore realized in the interior spaces of the contemporary city.

Silos Dorrego in Buenos Aires transformed into apartments (from Rui Roda, Master's research, Politecnico di Milano)

that produce objects, those that build houses, and then with those that program and govern a city. This unity of interests has perhaps never existed in history, but the criterion for judgment of the constructed world still makes reference to this type of utopia. Now, on the other hand, an era of deregulation is beginning, where each design gesture converges to create the conditions of a flexible, polycentric system; this system is reversible precisely because it is disarticulated in its own interior. It is also a system able to develop at different speeds, producing competition between the different dimensional circuits it is made up of.

This is a fuzzy, relative, and opportunist design system that creates possible local equilibriums, but does not presuppose more extended syntheses. It foresees the possibility of autonomous experiments and the multiplicity of developmental models both local and global. It is, therefore, a serene, weak, diffuse design, uniting single "logo" architectures of great communicative charge because they correspond to large commercial, museum-related, or institutional organizations. These objects of architecture do not hark back to an idea of city or a unity of setting, but to a new Middle Ages without cathedrals, a medieval period connected into a network within which the jewels of a commercial, secular, and global culture are grouped and act on the urban context through irradiation instead of induction. These are objects to look at more than architectures to live in.

This is a civilization based on objects, information technology, dispersed and lacking synthesis. One could say a civilization without theoretical metropolises other than the various Disneylands spread around the planet and which therefore completely coincide with reality. This is an experimental and reformist society that, as opposed to the twentieth century, no longer looks for strong foundations upon which to build stable systems and shared codes—foundations and codes that would immediately be refused by the society because they pose a threat to its incessant search for freedom.

The mediocrity herein derives chiefly from the fact that the optimal, the definitive, and the perfect must be seasonal values because otherwise they become a limit to the constant freedom to look for them. When we speak of a society without cathedrals we mean precisely this refusal of eternity on earth. And when we speak of an architecture made of isolated trademarks we mean a relative, provisory, and reversible eternity.

Cities without Architecture

This urban subsystem renews itself approximately every five years, adapting with no problem to the changing needs of the market, supplying a constantly updated functional system, and creating an ever-current aesthetic film. Contemporary architecture suffers from this new urban centrality of its subsystems and their ability to intervene in the functional processes of the metropolis. It also suffers from the predominance of commercial communications applied to the façades, which in the form of a promotional system are able to define the aesthetic qualities of streets and neighborhoods. In other words, these weak, reversible, diffuse subsystems have become the real protagonists of the continuous reorganization of functional and perceptible qualities of the contemporary metropolis. This new alliance between objects and territories, between communication and the urban scene, seems to have begun by bypassing architecture and its complex composite system. A disconnect has come between city and architecture, and between architecture and the system of objects. These categories, which Rem Koolhaas defines as small, medium, large, and extra-large, no longer define a structural continuity, and no longer do they belong to the unity of design; rather they indicate conflicting logics that do not find their re-composition in the Plan. Interior design, architecture, and urban planning follow autonomous logics that cannot be reassembled; these belong to autonomous layers, each of

Ludwig Hilberseimer, New City, 1944

which vindicates its own centrality. Beginning with each of these categories it is indeed possible to develop designs that differ from one another, not because they are based on different instruments, but because they aim to affirm absolute, different, irreconcilable priorities.

This crisis of the discipline's unity is a great cultural chance because it opens up new spaces for design. Design is no longer set within a logical chain that from small brings it without contradictions up to extra-large, from micro to macro; instead it causes design to intercept all the contradictions of the constructive processes, bringing to light all the potentialities that each dimensional category can offer with respect to the whole.

In other words, with the fall of the rapport that positively joined the city to architecture the unifying path that always entrusted metaphysics with the verification of physics' efficacy has been interrupted. This gave the greater good the right to pass judgment on the lesser good, the large over the small, the general over the particular. This system of evaluation has always produced rigidity, and in the world of architecture made it practically impossible to reform the typologies, go beyond the concept of building and the processes of territorial integration. In other words, it rendered the foundations of the discipline indestructible, transforming them into an obligatory route of connected responsibilities often foreign to the transformations of society and technology.

Ludwig Hilberseimer, New City, 1944

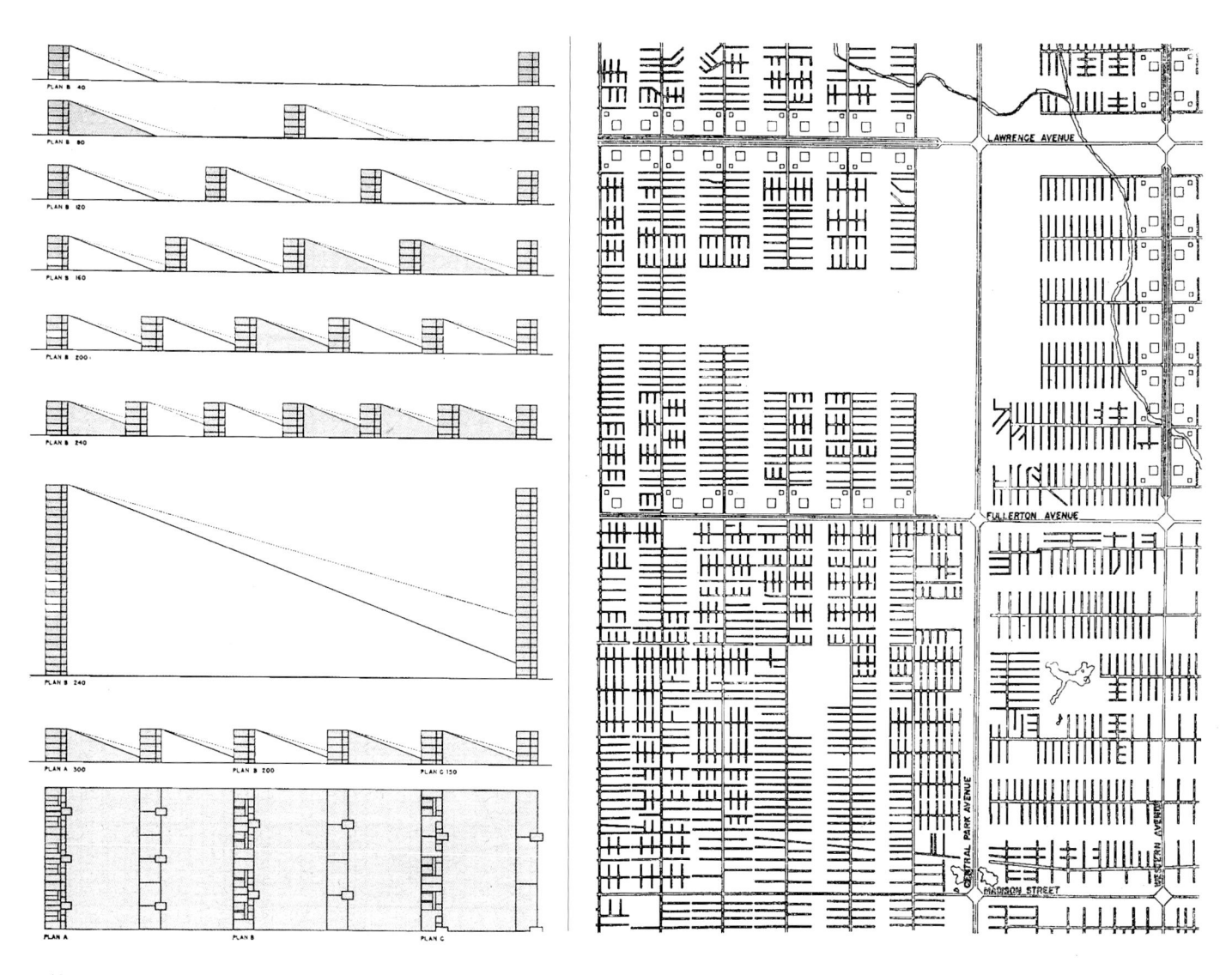

"The city without architecture" is the city whose functions no longer occur through the devices of architecture, but now occur through systems of electronic instruments, products, information, and above all through the componential approach to interior design, which permits the refunctionalization of its interior spaces in real time. This is, therefore, a city whose external image no longer corresponds to the activities carried out in its internal spaces; such activities are now done in an independent fashion, separated from the architectural backdrop.

Robert Musil in his study

Mark Rothko, 1952

Mark Rothko, Light, Earth, and Blue, *1954*

No-Stop City

In 1969, with the radical group Archizoom Associates (Andrea Branzi, Gilberto Corretti, Paolo Deganello, Massimo Morozzi, Dario and Lucia Bartolini) we opened a reflection on the contemporary city, seeking to rid from our research all those questions regarding linguistic, formal, or composite problems that are so typical of the discipline. Following the line, then, that began in the theoretic designs of Ludwig Hilberseimer, passing through the works of Mark Rothko, Richard Hamilton, Andy Warhol, and the music of Philip Glass, this arrived at the large warp and woof of current territorial agriculture.

In other words, we were interested in bringing to light a knowledge of architecture in exclusively quantitative terms, eliminating the qualitative question from the debate on the contemporary city, as it inevitably implies the limits of building and the urban layout as a visible form of a metropolitan reality that instead requires a completely different theoretic approach.

The term "cities without architecture," which we use very frequently, indicated a preliminary refusal of all the design criteria still linked to figurative codes, characteristic of the fragmentation of pre-industrial architecture. This was an architecture where the respect of standards tied to natural illumination and ventilation determined the process of interruption and articulation of the constructions (in order to allow natural light and air to enter the building), which is at the very base of the concept of architecture and the figurative formation of the historical city.

Even the modern city is still the sum of single figurative episodes, single buildings, and an intertwining of paths. The modern city, in fact, still has not removed from its core the respect for those natural standards of light and air, in an era where air and artificial light are universally spread. Against this conventional nature of the contemporary city, which continues to present itself as a natural reality, an unrepeatable result of an unrepeatable history, we wanted to affirm the technical and artificial reality of the urban construct, defining the city as a concave space, a territory of exchange and information.

We were interested that in the twentieth century, brusquely interrupting that historical logic, the industrial revolution had introduced large factories and commercial malls in the city; these were organisms that were artificially ventilated and lit, and therefore endowed with theoretically infinite dimensions. Applying this criterion of totally artificial spatial organization, in all the other civil functions (living, studying, exhibiting) there emerged a form for concave, inexpressive city, totally adherent to the quantitative logic of contemporary economics. This was, therefore, a city freed from the aggressive structures of architecture, following the dimensions of the market in an unlimited world where form, value, and meaning had become impediments and chains for design and economics.

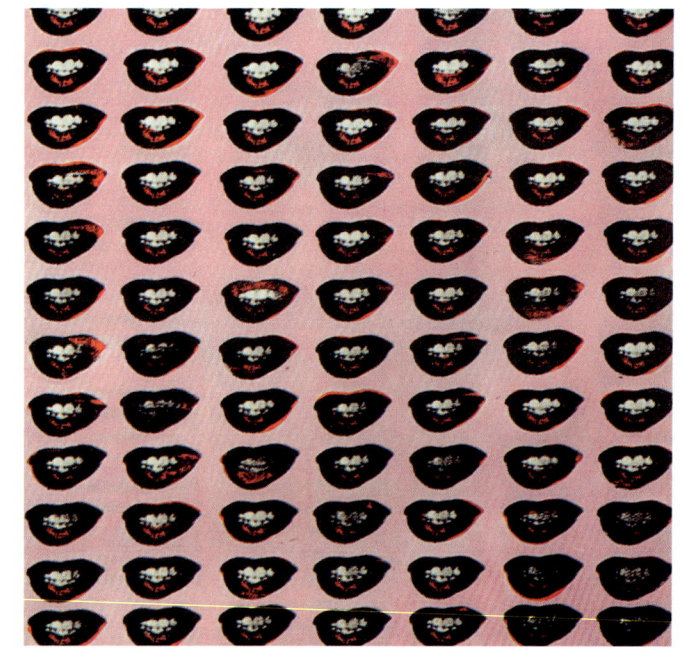

Andy Warhol, Marilyn Monroe's Lips, *1962*

To the right and on the following pages:
Andrea Branzi, For a Non-Figurative Architecture, *1968, typewritten diagrams in preparation for the project* No-Stop City
Centre Georges Pompidou Archive, Paris

Philip Glass

In 1968, the No-Stop City—a non-figurative architecture, for a non-figurative society that no longer had an external form, but had infinite interior forms—prefigured the central role of industrial products, merchandise, furniture, and services in the construction of fluid settings of the contemporary metropolis. This was the city seen as a conglomerate of habitable parking lots, as a system of typological storages and free residential forests; this indicated a global system already lacking external space, where the city corresponds to the dimension of the global market and the system of networks spread across the land. The citizen is not he who lives in the city, but he who uses the industrial products and information supplied by telecommunications.
Refusing that tradition of vanguards who still thought that the architecture of industrial society must resemble a motor (from the futurists to Archigram), the No-Stop City thought that the only logic of the industrial system had to be sought out not in mechanics, but in that quantitative utopia that is the only morality of a consumer society that has internalized the global and catatonic dimensions of the market, corresponding to a neutral sound as the sum of infinite sounds, and a gray color as the final result of infinite colored signs. This was a city without qualities for a man (finally) without qualities—that is, without compromise—a freed society (freed even from architecture) similar to the great monochrome surfaces of Mark Rothko: vast velvet, open oceans in which the sweet drowning of man within the immense dimensions of mass society is represented.

ARCHIZOOM ASSOCIATI
DIAGRAMMA ABITATIVO
OMOGENEO

IPOTESI DI LINGUAGGIO
ARCHITETTONICO NON FIGURATIVO

struttura montante.

maglia dimensionale.

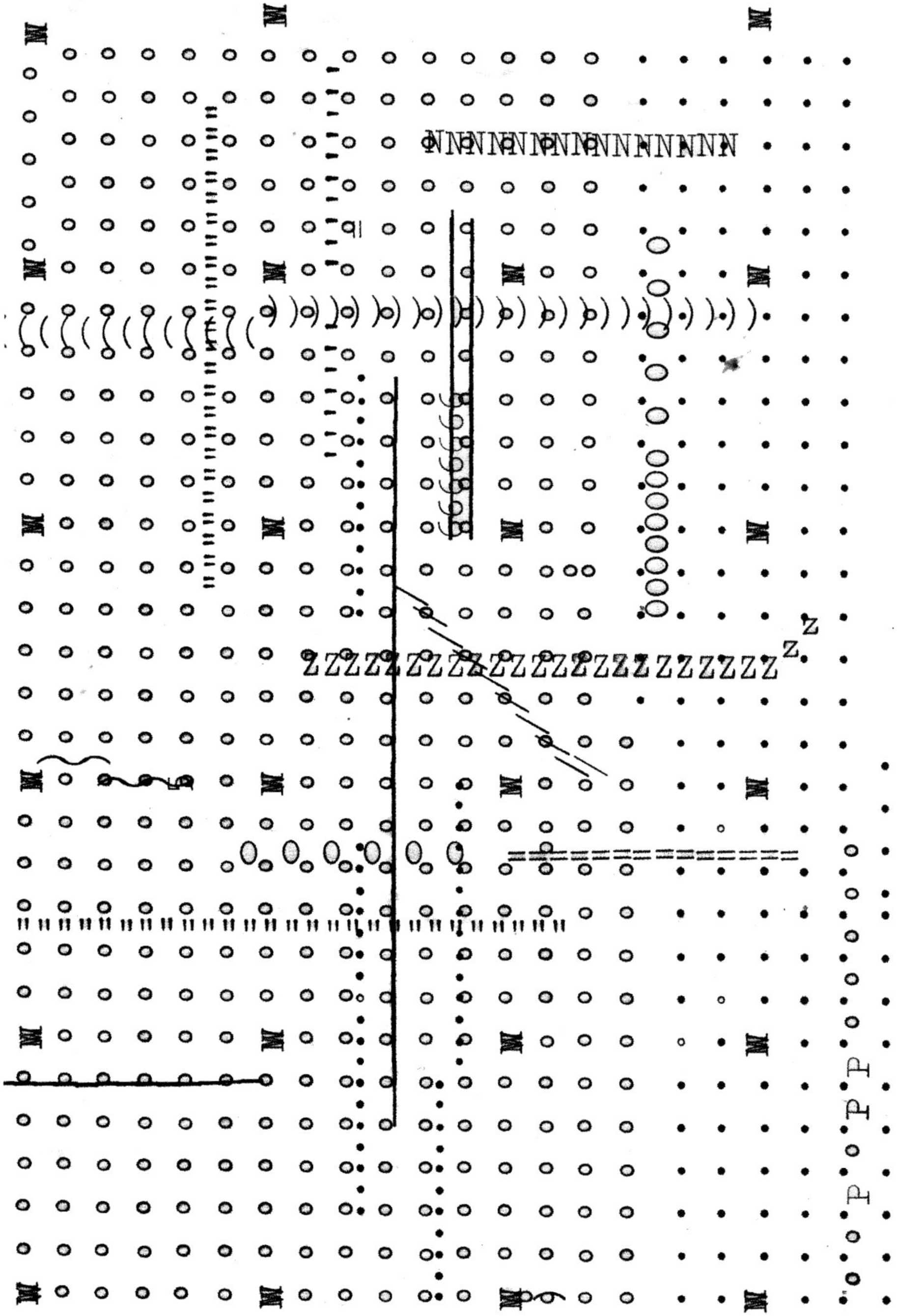

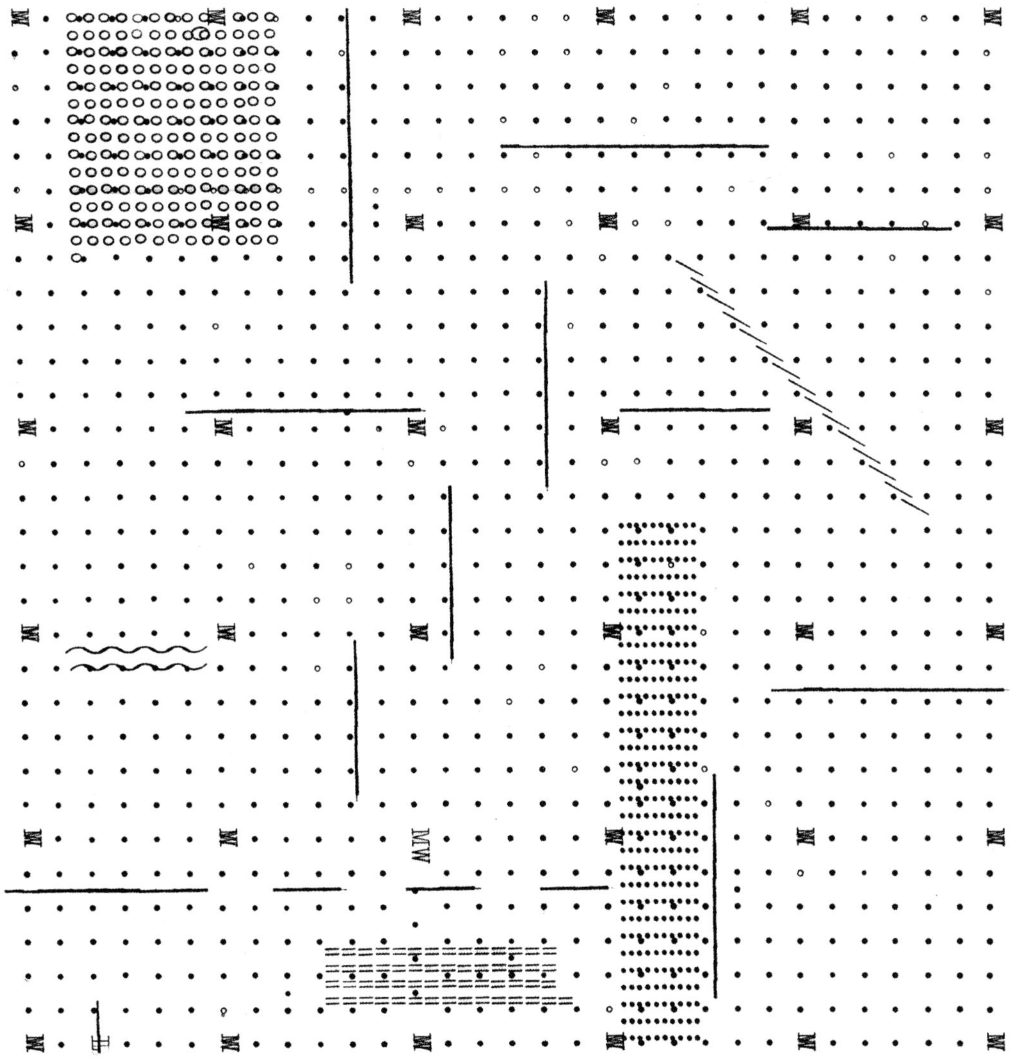

74

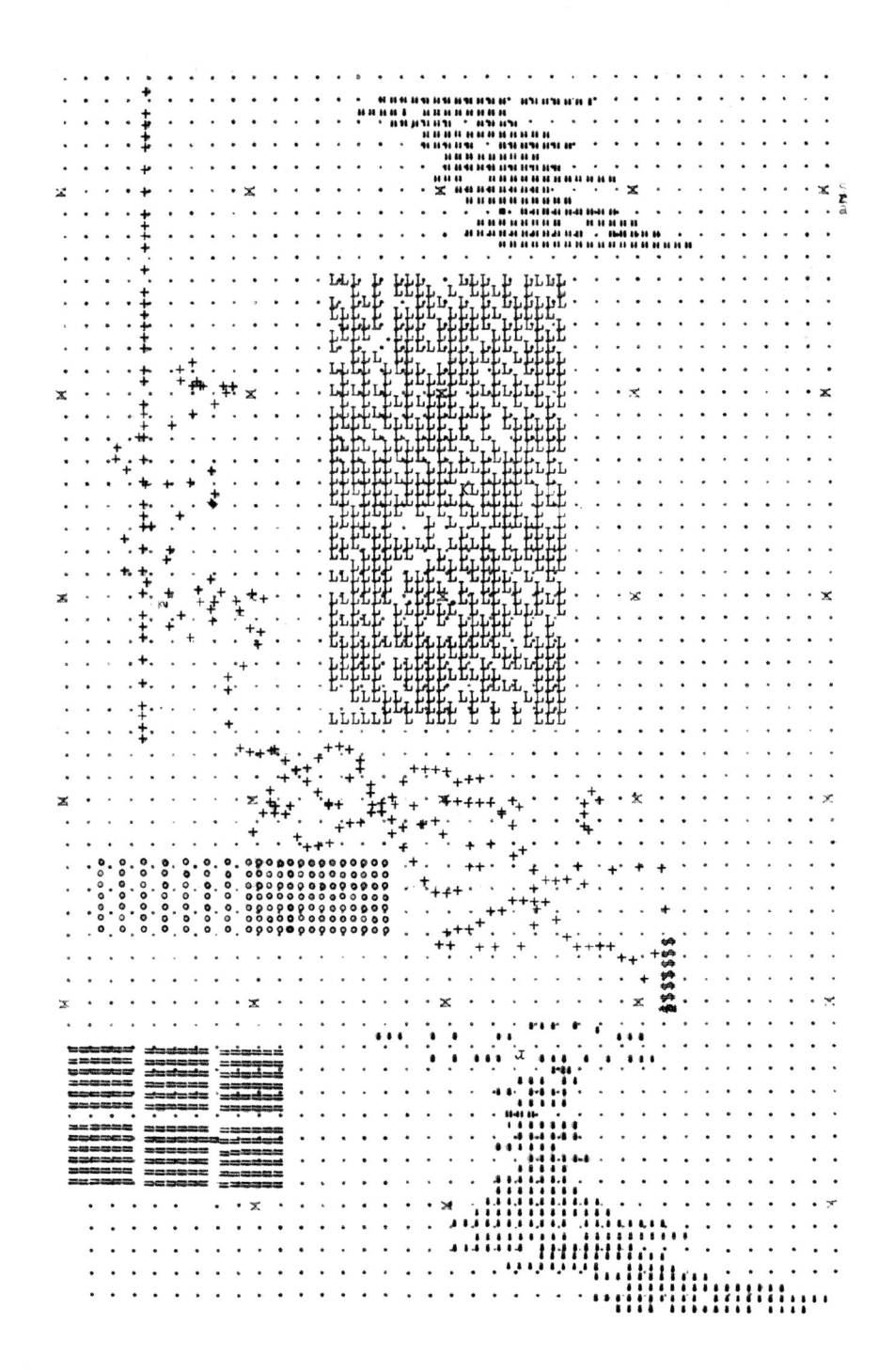

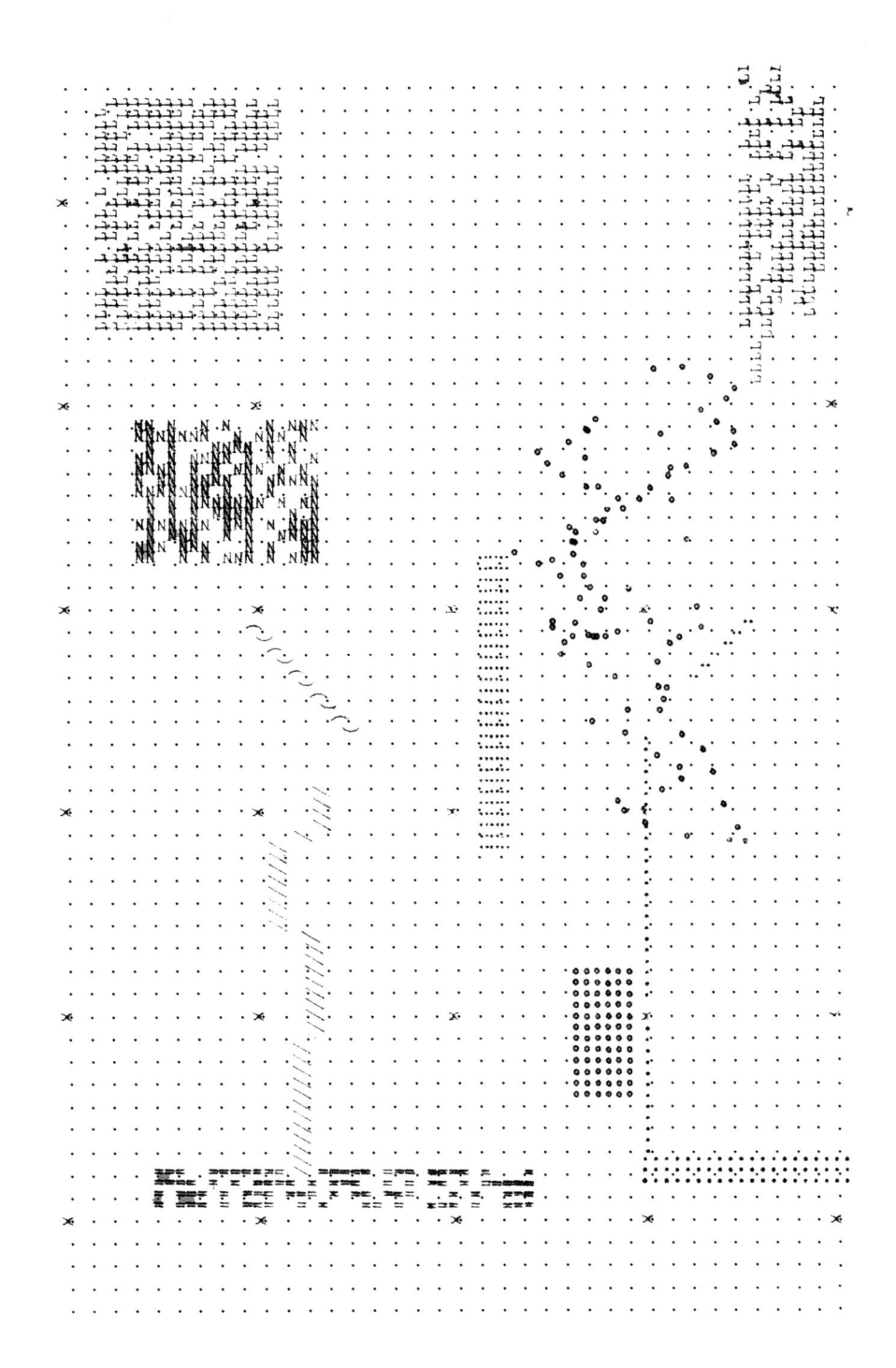

The preceding drawings are preparatory layouts for the No-Stop City design by Archizoom Associates and were typed up (given the absence of computer availability at the time) as "hypotheses of non-figurative architecture." The idea was to represent the urban territory as a vibrating surface, crossed by varying flows of information and products that create an open, temporary system of sensorial and perceptive structures: the city as an "experiential," rather than formal, reality, outside and through the perimeters of architecture.

Archizoom Associates, No-Stop City, 1969–1972
Centre Georges Pompidou Archive, Paris; CSAC Archive, Parma; FRAC Archive, Orléans

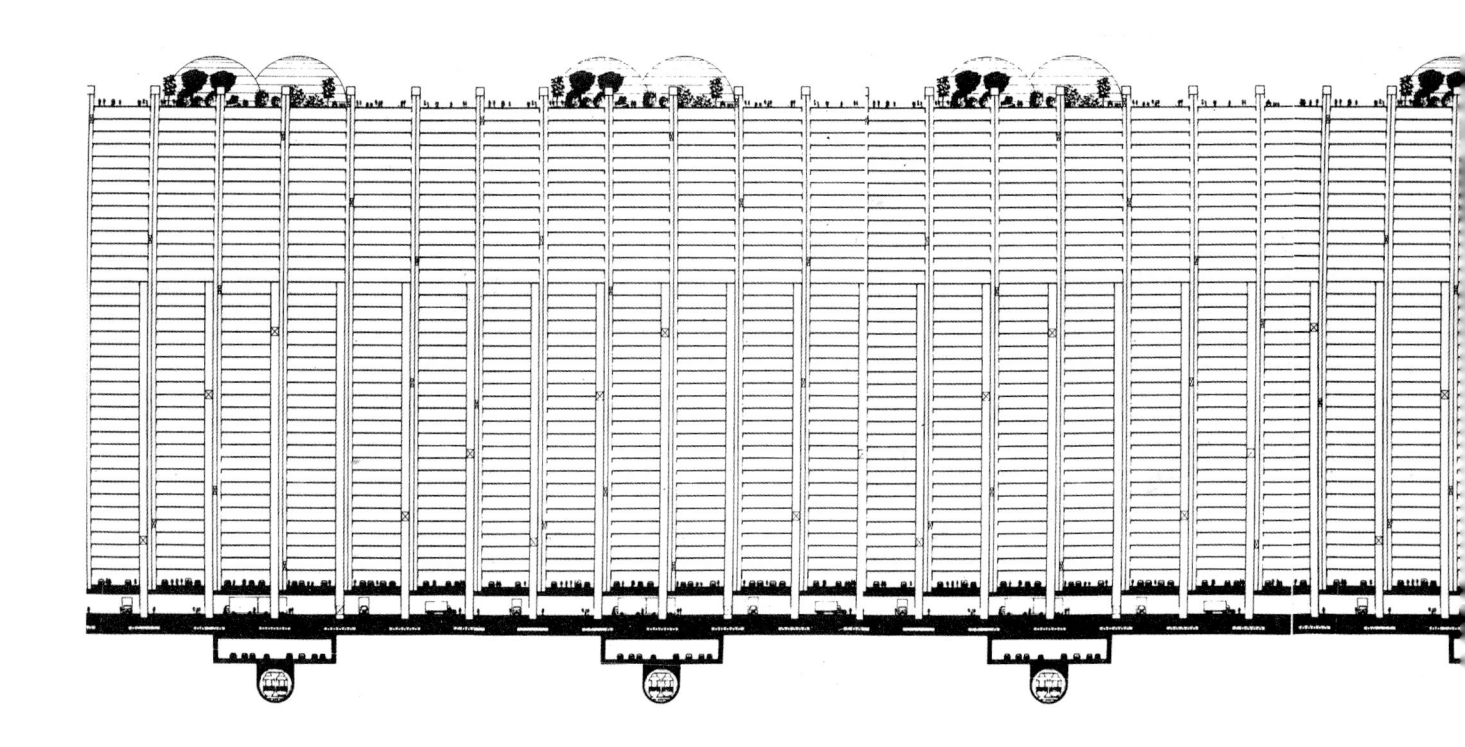

Archizoom Associates, No-Stop City, 1969–1972, *mirror simulator, 2002 reconstruction*
Centre Georges Pompidou Archive, Paris

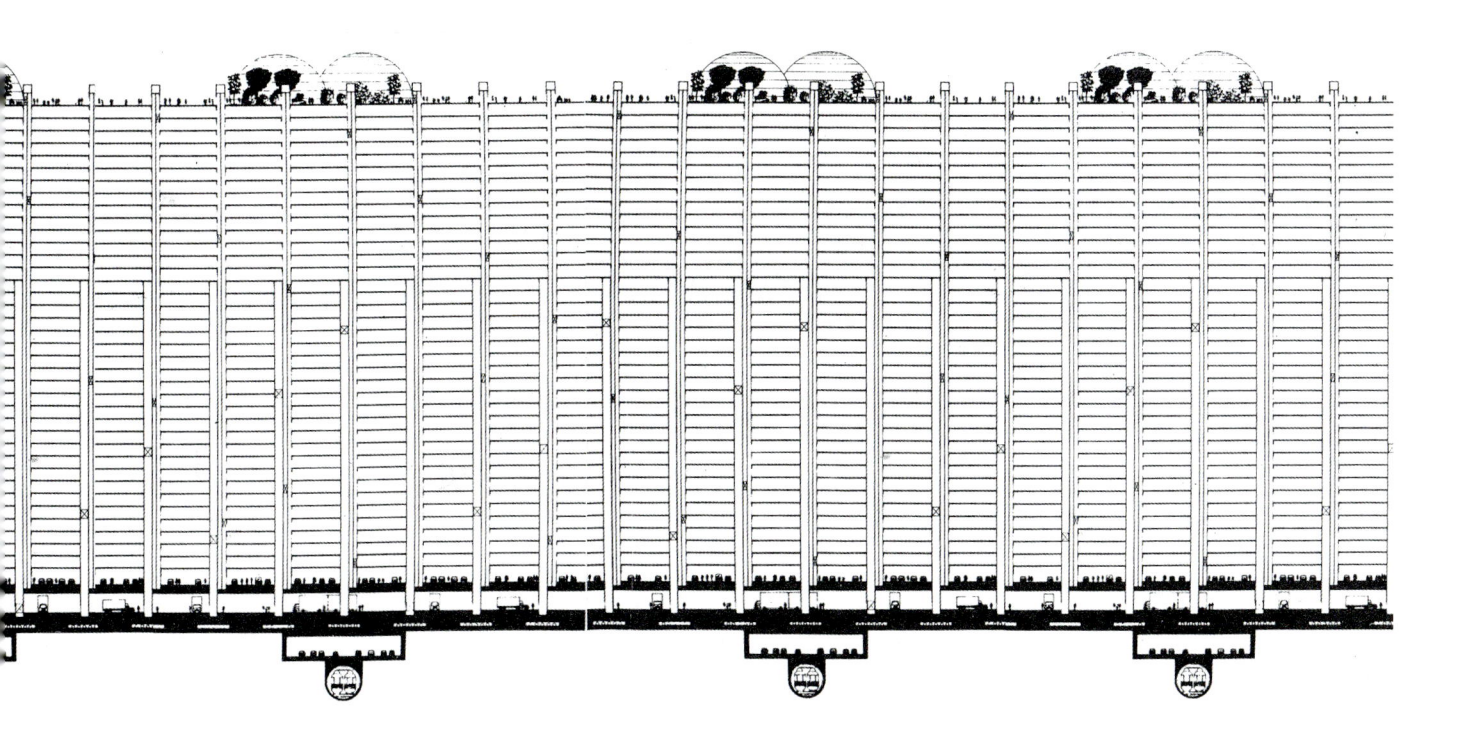

The No-Stop City is not a design, but rather a radical level of representation of the contemporary city as an apparently hyper-expressive reality that is, actually, substantially catatonic because it is the result of the infinite repetition of an alienating political system without destiny. In these neutral spaces, within large interior spaces, an uncontainable social energy develops, which in turn pollutes all functions, creating a highly complex, lowly specialized hybrid passage. The "city without architecture" presents itself as an agricultural territory that is structured, but does not change according to the unfolding of its life cycles.

Archizoom Associates, No-Stop City, *1969–1972*
Centre Georges Pompidou Archive, Paris; CSAC Archive, Parma; FRAC Archive, Orléans

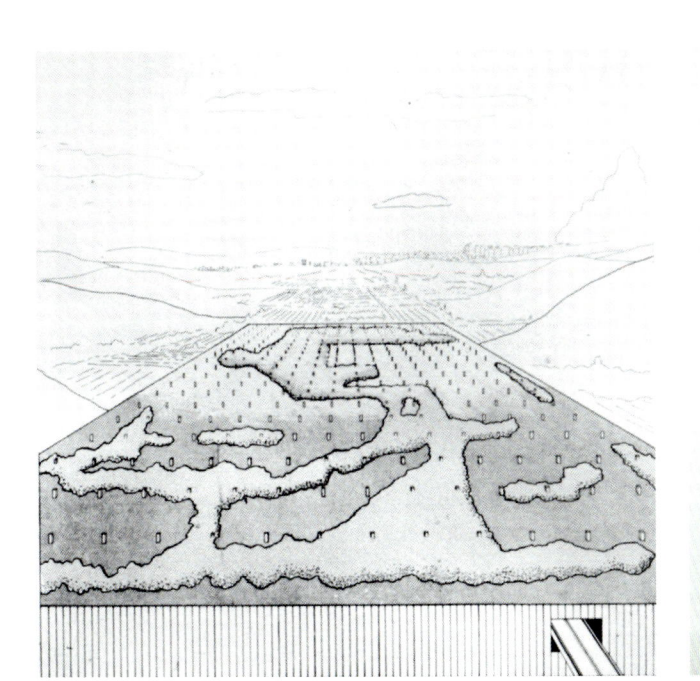

Archizoom Associates, No-Stop City, *1969–1972, mirror simulator, original CSAC Archive, Parma*

Archizoom Associates, No-Stop City,
1969–1972
Centre Georges Pompidou Archive,
Paris; CSAC Archive, Parma; FRAC
Archive, Orléans

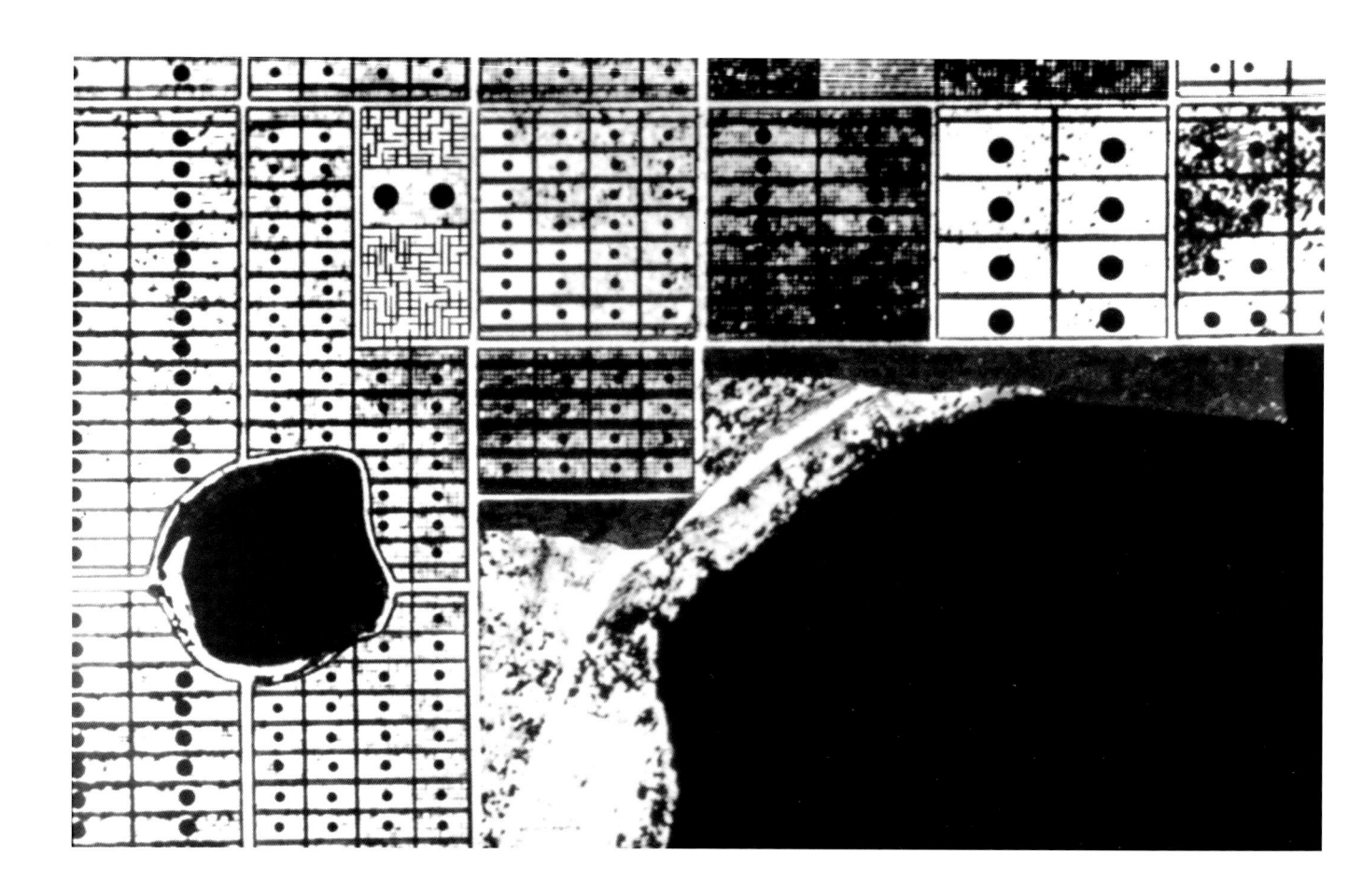

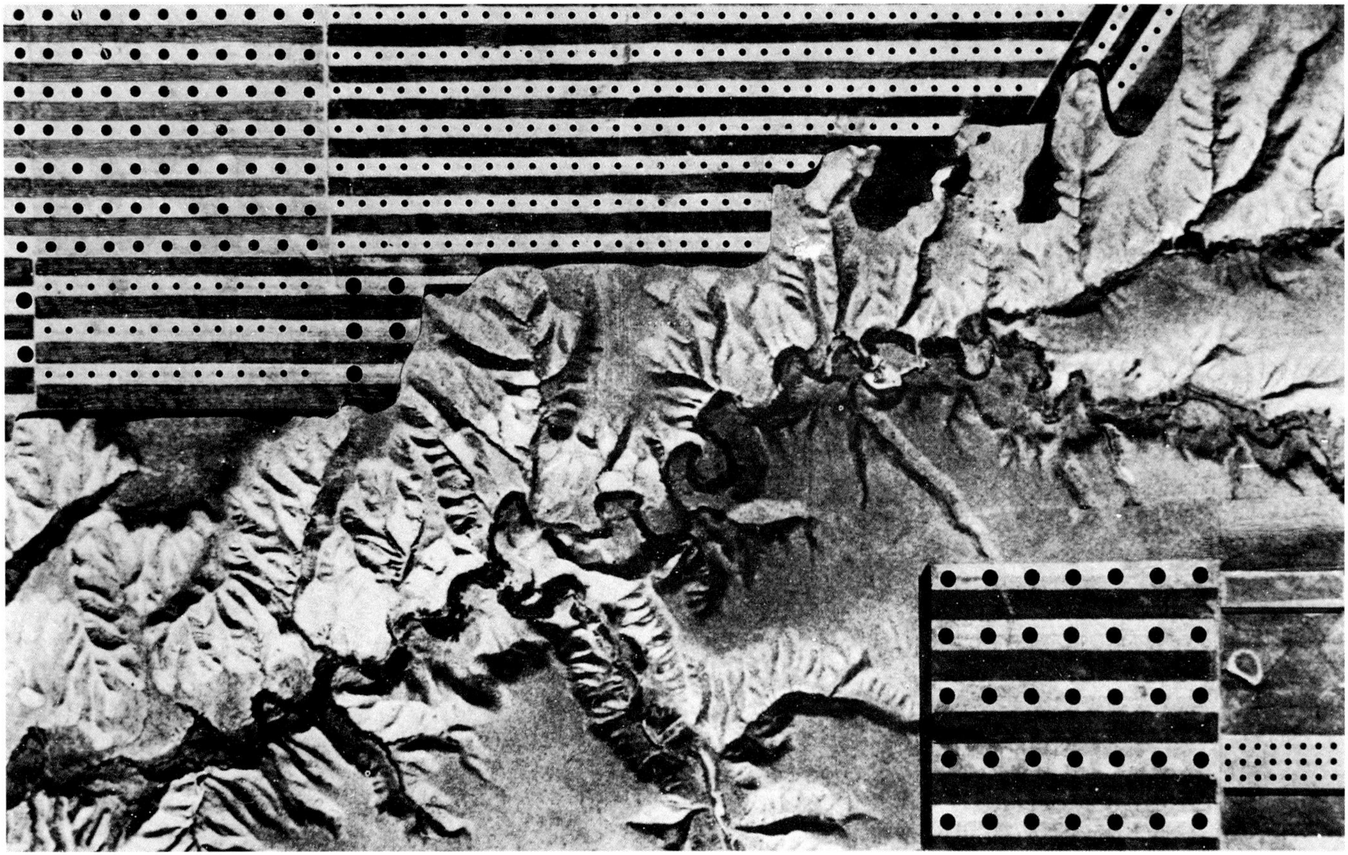

Residential and Commercial Center, San Donato Milanese

Competition for the urban design and architectural improvement of the central area of the Town of San Donato Milanese

Client
Town of San Donato Milanese, Milan

Year
2000

Design
Tullio Zini, Andrea Branzi
with
Soichiro Kanbayashi, Lapo Lani, Francesco Messori, Rita Neri, Mattia Parmigiani, Dante Sangalli, Michele Zini, Claudia Zoboli

The design starts with a hypothesis of unification of the park and the city following a model of weak urbanization, focusing, in other words, on the creation of an intermediate form between an inhabitable park and a productive agricultural structure, in the presence of diffuse urban services. The lot is crossed by a long covered street bordered by two buildings. These buildings—articulated and facing one another—define a protected urban passage that, connected to the traditional covered galleries of Lombardy, offers the possibility of a multifunctional exchange.
On this mall the commercial structures and residential services conglomerate, viewed as spaces that correspond to the diverse programmatic uses of a large available structure rather than formal typologies.
The extant viability is to be confirmed. The parking lots are on a subterranean level with three types of spots: those for residents, traditional short-term parking, and long-term parking with automated storage and return operated on request by a card, such that the space of exchange between the public and the cars is safe, comfortable, and close to the points of interest.
The design corresponds to an idea of the relational, unified city, all made up of interior spaces, with a density similar to that of historical city centers, where there is a maximum concentration of exchanges in the presence of a dense but traversable structure.

Studio model

General plan

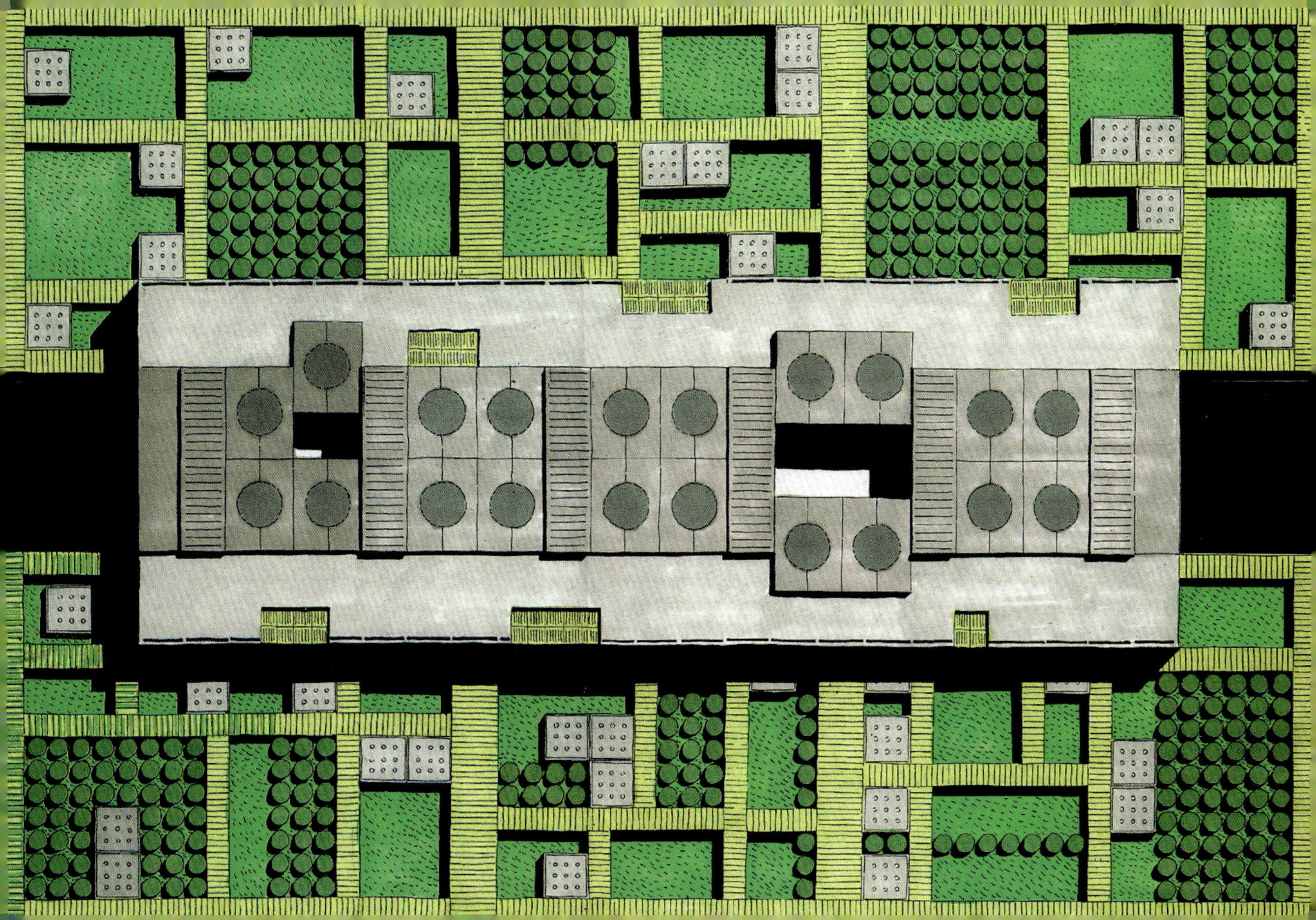

This type of "urban aquarium" is born of the attempt to overcome the architectural fracturing and typological limits of the compositional tradition through new, integrated organisms where a sole, undifferentiated function is carried, allowing one to live in a shopping mall according to the theoretic modalities elaborated within the No-Stop City. The traditional typology of the historic quarter (with residential, commercial, and artisan areas) is disassembled and reassembled following a logic of maximal indifference to functional distinctions, like an electronic circuit that contains devices for a multiplicity of activities not previously programmed.

Main section

Studio model

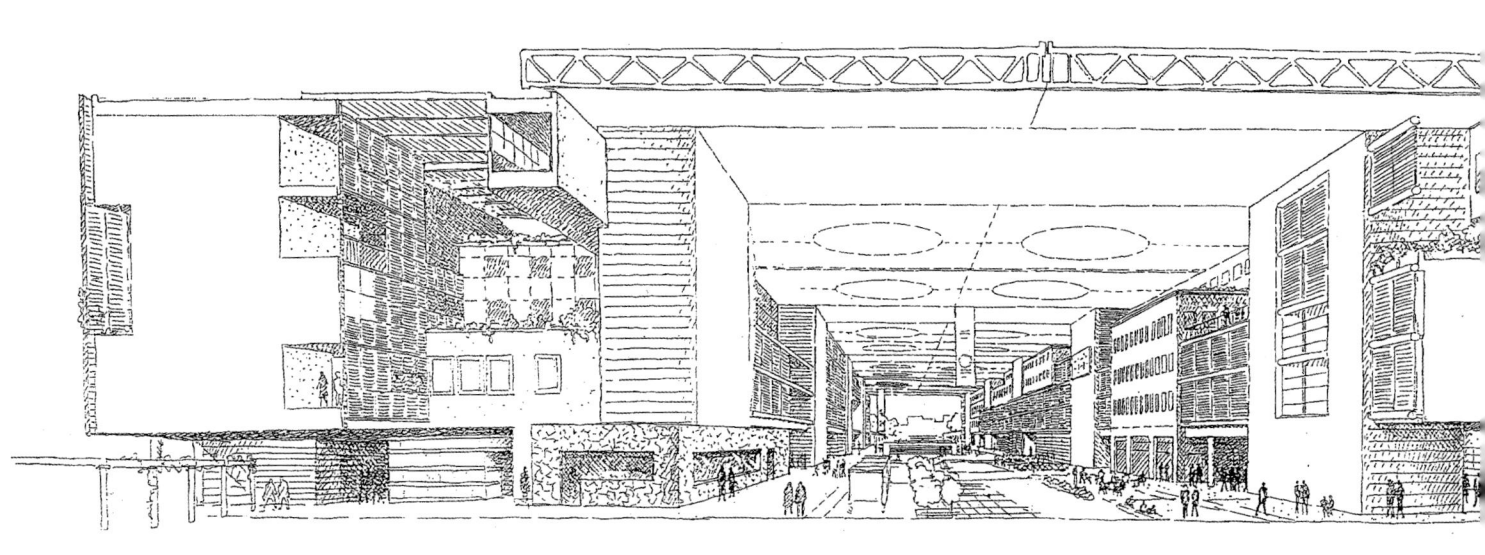

85

Time and Network

Andrea Branzi, Erwan and Ronan Bouroullec, installation at the exhibition Blossoming the Gap, *Spitz and Rendl Gallery, Cologne, 2003*

Western architecture originated from the classical tradition, a tradition deeply rooted in the pagan myth of *Kronos* (Time), father of all the gods who ate his own children, continually destroying his progeny. To save architecture from this fatal destiny it was necessary to define a space outside of time. Graeco-Roman architecture rested on this foundation, produced by the separation of time and space. The monument was the best testimony of history, but did not belong to history.

Classical architecture did not, in fact, evolve; it repeated itself outside time. History, natural, cyclical time was human time, the scenario of a repeating destiny, where everything was false and deteriorated as if in a theatrical scene. Classical time was therefore twofold: the eternal time of myth, and the circular, human time, in which development did not exist, merely an eternal return. Only with the fall of pagan culture and the advent of Christianity was time divided into a before and after: beginning with the creation of the world up until the Incarnation, and after this up until the end

Infinite gardens produced by mirror simulators correspond to an idea of the "infinite" that belongs to all objects and industrial flowers as part of a "series" without end and without perimeter.

of the world and the Resurrection of the dead. Time thus became a linear concept, with beginning and end, and was no more an elliptical succession of scenes, but rather a continual process of evolution. Even taking part in this evolution through its various styles, Western architecture still maintained its classical statute of eternity, of a presence that challenges time, perforating seasons and history while remaining intact. This is quite different from Shintoist Japanese architecture, which, not belonging to the Roman-Catholic tradition, positively participates in time, with its temples periodically disassembled and then reconstructed with new materials. The problem and stimulus towards the future pushed modern architecture to accentuate its contradiction of eternal testimony, but was also destined to guide us towards a different future. The refusal to demolish modern monuments proves this.

Modernization has happened, and progress no longer corresponds to a linear process, but rather to a dispersed galaxy. The future is no longer one, but manifold, diffuse, and its force of attraction is becoming weak. From the age of great hopes we have moved into an age of permanent uncertainty and stable transition. This is an age of crises that is not an intermission between two seasons of certainty—that of the past and that of the future—but an age subject to a process of certainties—that of the past and that of the future—an age subject to a continual process of updating, change, and innovation without end and without a goal. The future is no longer a destination, but a reality that works for the present. In a certain sense, time once again becomes elliptical, reversible, seasonal, and space becomes unlimited, natural, and traversable in all directions. Boundaries and limits belong to history and geography; they no longer belong to our culture, virtual spaces, and the real time of web-based culture. Web culture develops, abolishing history and geography; the Internet allows the retrieval of information in real time, accessing a state of availability that nullifies distance. From any point on the Net another point on the Net can be immediately accessed; the Net rests not on the ground, but in virtual space. Because of this history and geography are not structural parts of information, but rather elements of appreciation, accessories. The Net is traversable in the sense that internal perimeters do not exist, only distributing portals of organized information. The perception of time and space are therefore destined to change according to the original methods, involving the modes of designing as well.

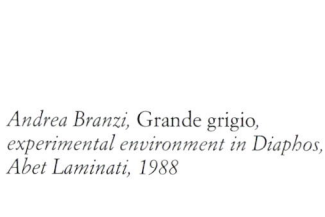

Andrea Branzi, Grande grigio, *experimental environment in Diaphos, Abet Laminati, 1988*

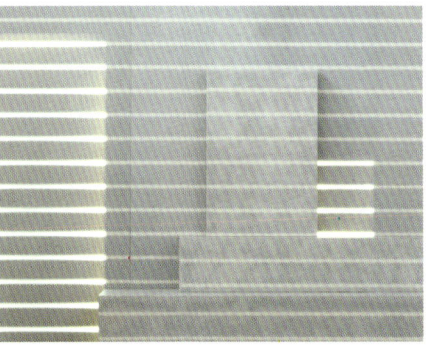

Opacity and nebulosity belong to the post-illuminist visual culture, where vision is no longer the instrument that allows for the investigation of profound mechanisms upon which reality is based, but becomes a more complex perceptive instrument, independent of any recognizing function and producer of more delicate, poetic experiences that are less clear, but richer than other information.

Lamp with vase from the Blister collection, Design Gallery, Milan, 2004

New York Waterfront – Architecture as New Territories

International competition held to reorder the western coast of Manhattan presently occupied by commercial piers

Client
Municipal Art Society, New York

Year
1987

Design
Andrea Branzi
with
Tullio Zini, Rhea Alexander, Dante Donegani, Giorgio Ferrando, Corrado Gianferrari, Giovanni Levanti, Ernesto Spicciolato

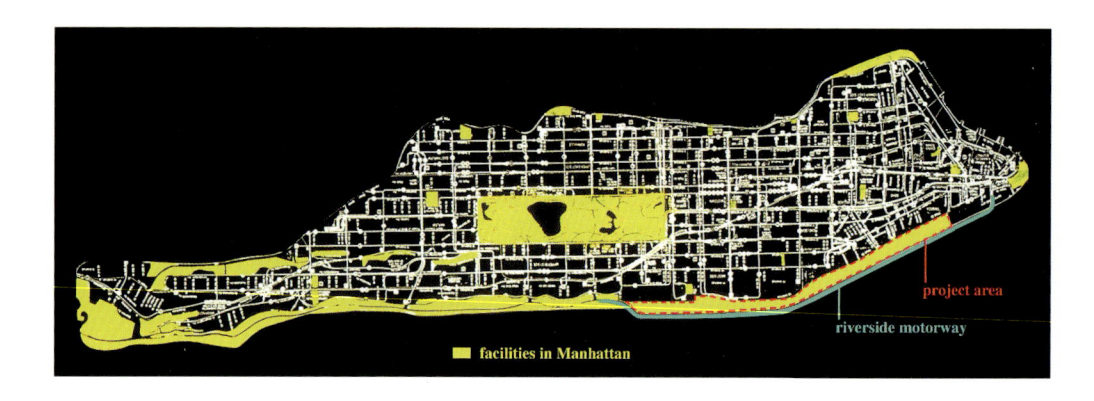

The basic idea of this design was to create an artificial territory along the western coast of Manhattan connected to the other large green spaces of New York City—Central Park and Riverside Park.
The artificial park consists of an underwater basement that contains general city and area services (parking, offices, theaters, museums, stadiums, meeting points, restaurants, cafés, and sporting facilities) in a structure nine stories deep, for a covered, ventilated, and artificially lit surface with a total area of 11,000,000 m². The platform is circled on its exterior border by an urban highway, while the interior border is connected to the extant roads. The cover of this large pier includes a park with hills, forests, lakes, paths, covered spaces, and large graffiti murals.
The goal was to give Manhattan a shore facing the new frontiers of the third millennium: a large horizontal platform, open to the sun, which emits strong skyward signs representing a humanity that lives in the artificial nature of twenty-first-century New York. These signs are similar to that which for a century America, through the Statue of Liberty, represented to the world.
This design responds to New York's need for growth and life, while at the same time hopes to go beyond the mental and constructional limits of the composite tradition of modern architecture and its (fragile) myth of vertical development that was so well represented by the Twin Towers.

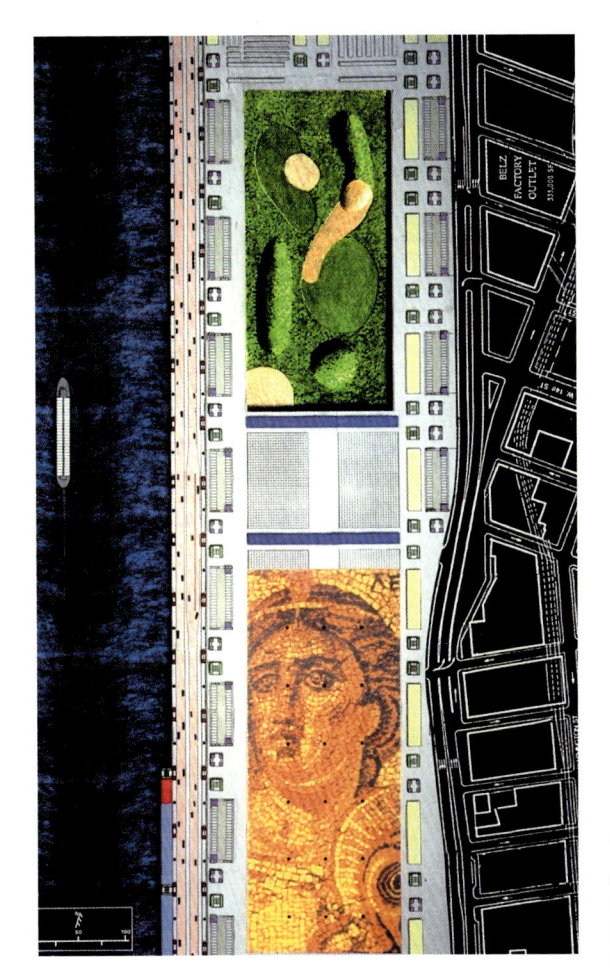

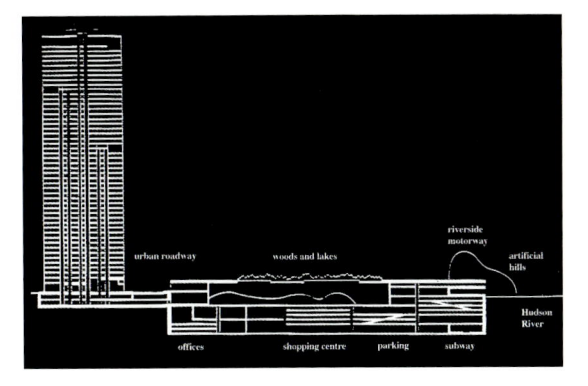

This project refers to the idea of a possible "non-figurative" architecture that constructs new horizontal territories that therefore no longer belong to the excessively exhibitionist and vertical tradition of modernity. This is an architecture made up exclusively of unlimited interior spaces suitable for any use whatsoever, from parking lots to large libraries, which become a sort of tectonic plate of a new geology upon which an artificial landscape with large figurative signs is propped.

The platform of Manhattan is in large part artificial and has had a progressive development through the application of Dutch technologies for constructing new land on marine areas. The hypothesis of a new phase of planar expansion of New York over the surrounding water belongs to the tradition of this city, and would allow for the optimization of its circulatory infrastructures and the creation of new services along the external border of the geologic platform.

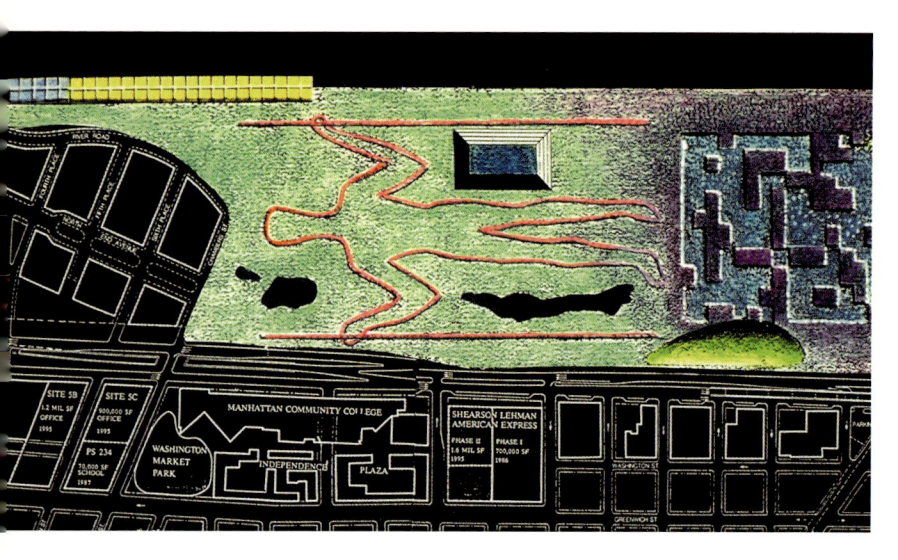

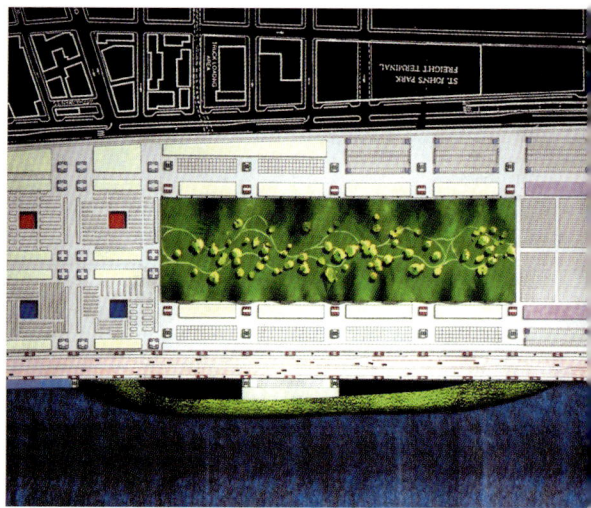

93

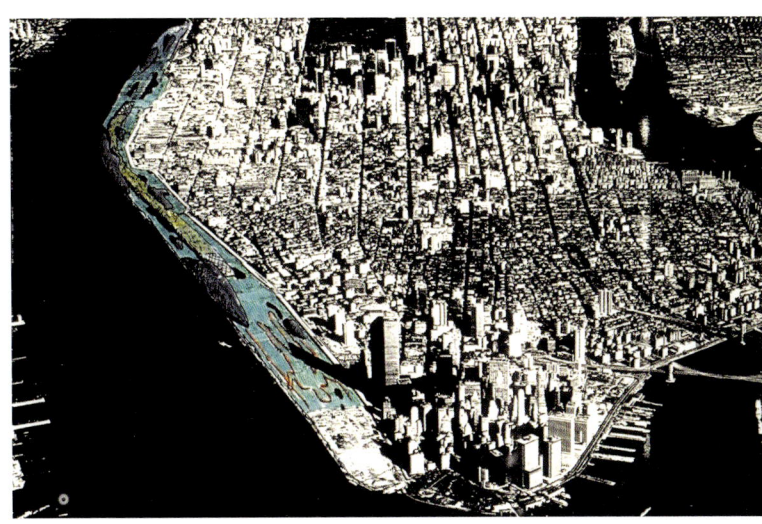

"La Certosa" Real Estate Complex, Sesto Fiorentino

Client
Nikol

Year
1991

Design
Andrea Branzi
with
Studio Astypalea and Studio of Roberto Banchini and Massimo Meli

Sesto Fiorentino's residential quarter is in a peculiar suburb, at the back of the western hills surrounding Florence, in an urban setting characterized by a mixed typology that combines common buildings in vertical residential blocks and a vast fabric of small garden villas.
It is an urban setting where vertical models alternate with typical typologies of horizontal expansion according to mixed criteria of intensive and extensive urbanization.
This design was born by *overlapping* these two logics, creating a sort of new *hybrid* typology, where atop the large volumes small garden villas are connected, all linked to a pedestrian walkway at elevation. Thus the quarter loses its typological uniqueness in order to become a sort of territory upon which various scenarios and autonomous-use devices are set up.

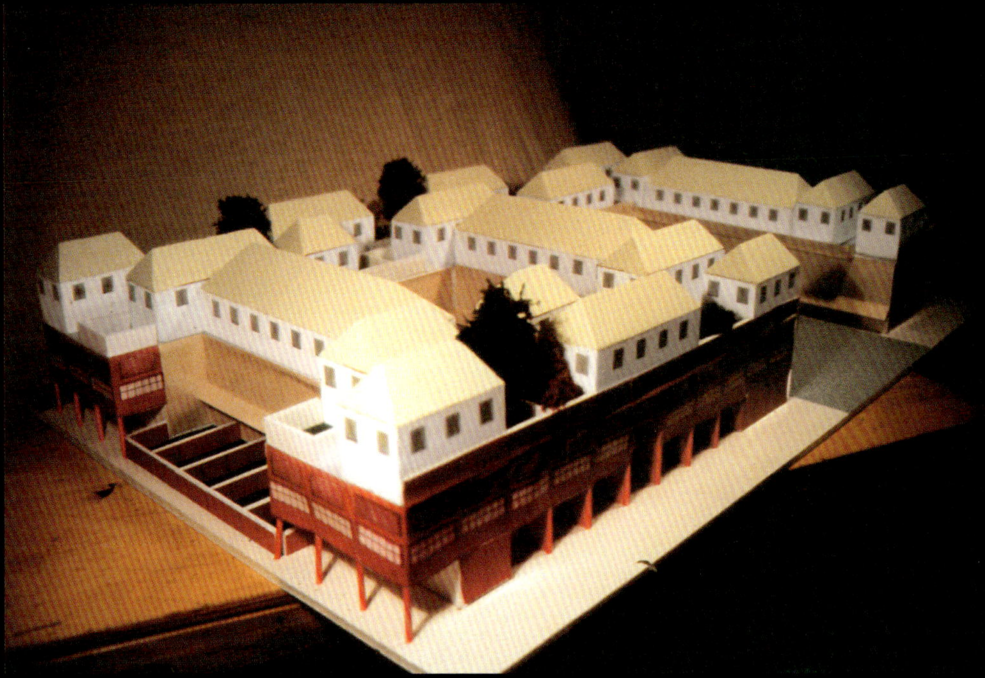

The conception of the city as a system of territorial sandwiches and different typological and functional layers, set one atop the other and not harmonized, makes up the fundamental reference of this design, with autonomous logical and formal systems that run on different levels without creating a true typological unity. Like a sectioned geological layering where one can visibly see faults and rock strata emerge, layered upon, but independent from, one another. In place of the compositional tradition, which always works to create a formal unity among different components, a pure logic of montage is experimented with: one thing atop another, something within another thing, all while preserving their reciprocal autonomies.

97

Master Plan Tokyo City X

Meta-design of an 800,000 m² multi-use installation in Tokyo Bay on a 27-hectare area of the old Mitsubishi iron works

Client
Mitsubishi Institute of Research, Inc. Urban Planning and Consulting Dept.

Year
1989

Design
Andrea Branzi
with
Clinio Castelli, Isao Hosoe, Tullio Zini

The design aims to define only the qualitative parameters of the internal spaces, leaving the external form of the large building to the growth processes of its own internal functions. This is an anti-composite and anti-typological design, in the sense that Tokyo City X acts as a large, undifferentiated, dynamic container as a single large system; in other words, a single large metropolitan interior. Within it the space is organized in luminous planes that can be installed differently (the system of setting) and used differently (the goods system). Its interior fabric must include large warehouses, historic urban networks, great *ramblas*, the *calle* of Venice, high-rise luxury residences, parking for metropolitan nomads, offices for large companies, and private professional studios. It must also contain hospitals and free time, depending on criteria that can change over time.
Within Tokyo City X there must not be any synthetic materials—only artificial ones. A large part of the internal and external structures of this design will be monolithic and made of a single material.
The design can describe percentage-based relationships between materials of differing specific weights, and the relation between parts in stone and paper, between wood and composites, between glass and metal are divided according to categories and percentages relating to their aging—artificially aged, nobly aged, their exteriors, etc.
This is a central quality of Tokyo City X as a sweet enclave, and silence is its impenetrable citadel: a soft, counterfeited silence upon which the great noise of parties, markets, and crowds is constructed in planned places and occasions.

Centre Georges Pompidou Archive, Paris

General section

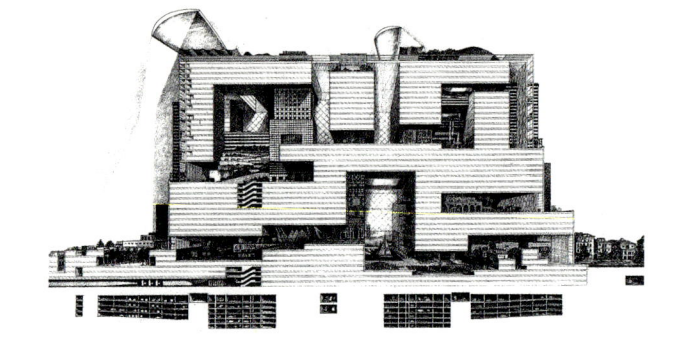

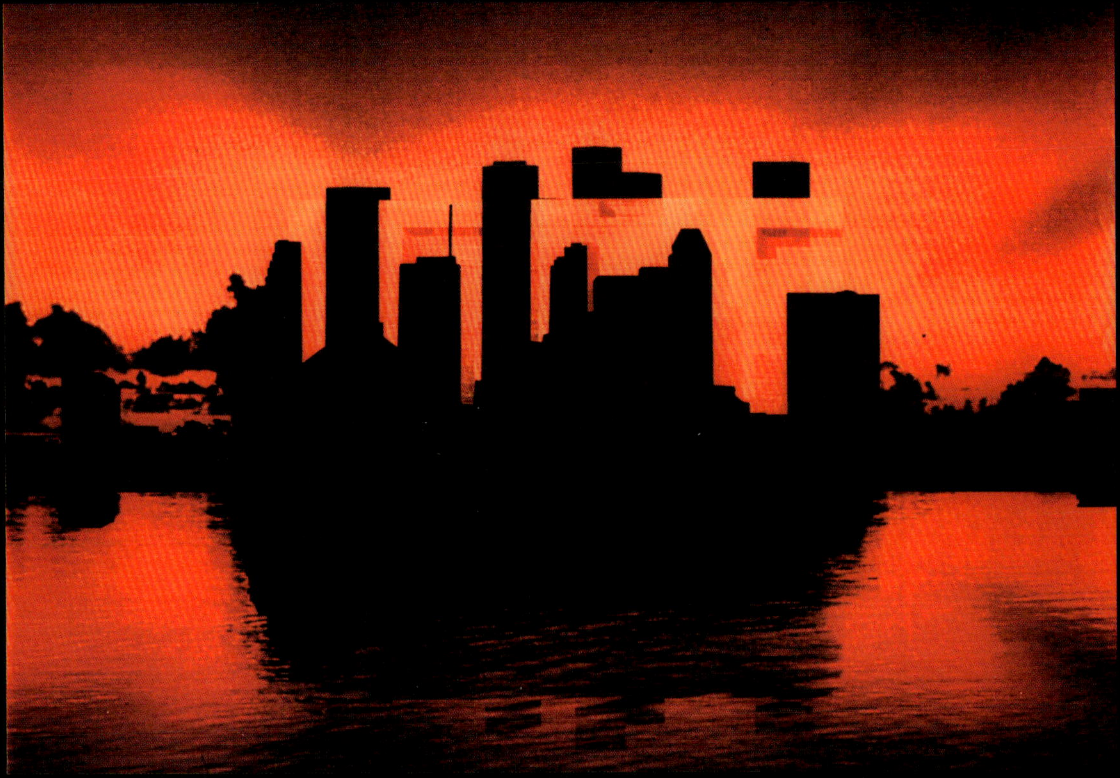

A large greenhouse with conditioned microclimates contains architectural volumes in free expansion; above the greenhouse a large spoiler reflects the sun's light and removes the building's shadow on the surrounding territory.
The complex form of the design, system of interior spaces, architecture (without shadow), and territory are considered completely separate realities.

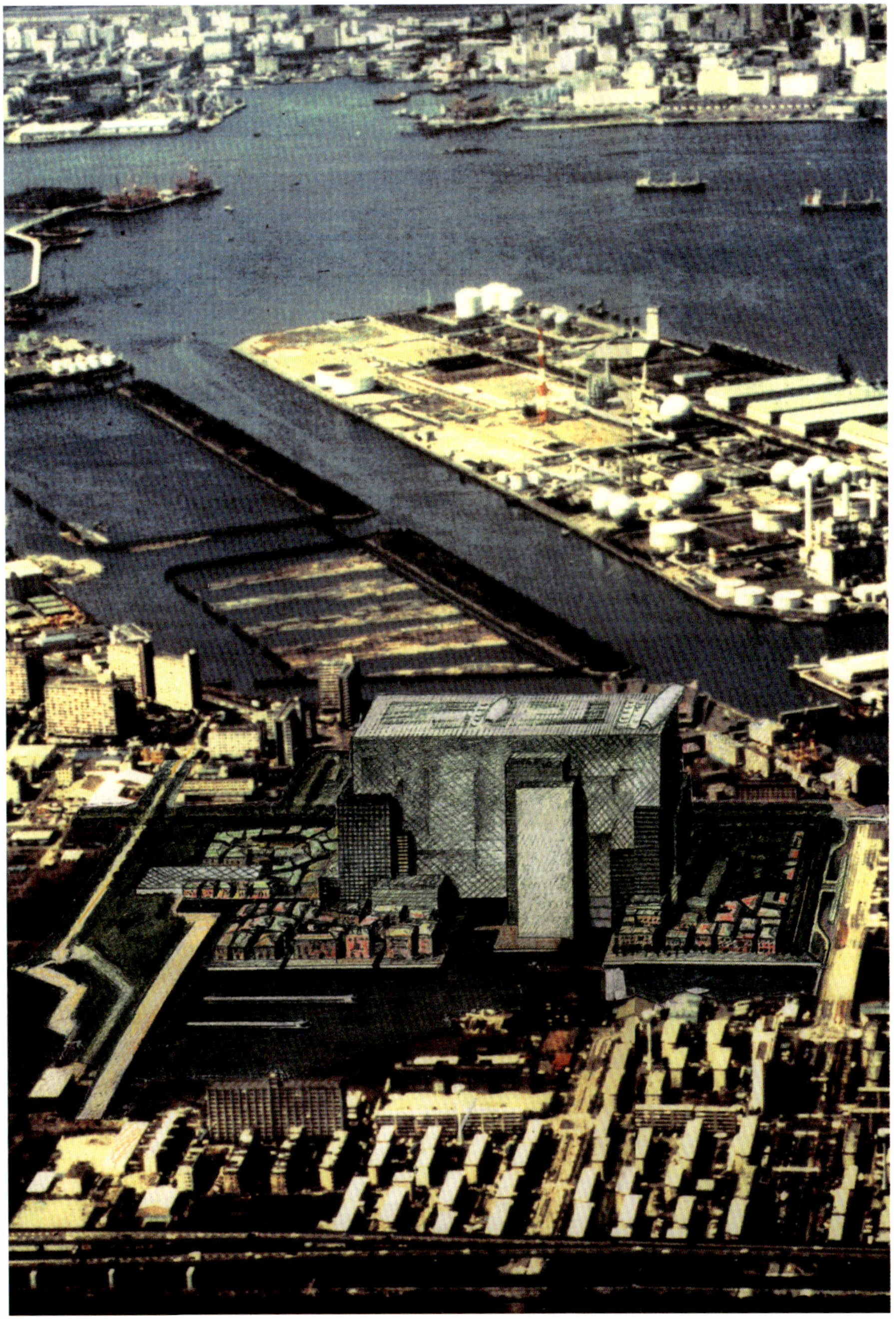

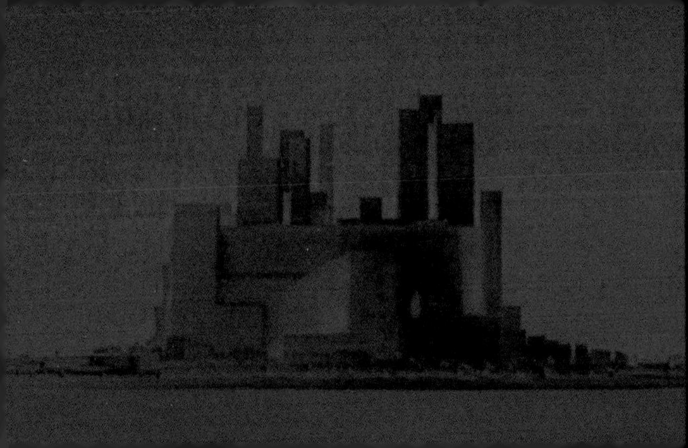

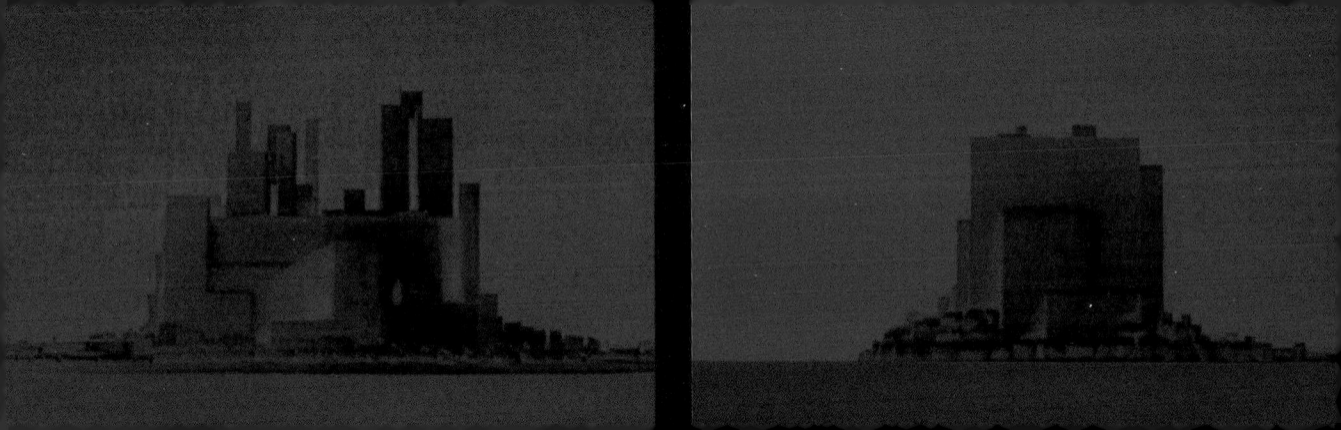

Domus Academy Master's – Incubators

Year
1995

Teachers
Andrea Branzi, Francesco Messori, Michele Zini

This project investigates the possibility of overlapping the traditional city with a serviceable, reversible, and temporary level of architecture that is activated depending upon the needs of space for temporary activities, thereby creating a changing and incomplete architectural profile.

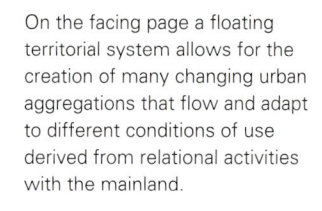

Ekrem Ali Parmaksiz, Interface, *1995*

On the facing page a floating territorial system allows for the creation of many changing urban aggregations that flow and adapt to different conditions of use derived from relational activities with the mainland.

104

Yasmin Lari, Fless-Growing Floors, *1995*

House-boats at Soochow Creek, Shanghai (from Bernard Rudofsky, Architecture without Architects, *Academy Editions, London, 1981)*

105

The Sensorial Revolution

The material world that surrounds us is quite different from the one the modern movement had imagined; in place of an industrial, rational order, the present metropolises present a highly diversified setting, where productive logics and opposing linguistic systems live together without contradiction. This is a world crossed by continuous stylistic tensions and uninterrupted formal innovations. Design, design culture, and the culture of style follow more or less critically this tempestuous world that seems to renew itself and seems to remain always the same.

A sense of saturation begins to diffuse: everything seems to have already been thought of, designed, and produced, and the continual demand for new qualities that the market produces finds answers ever more difficult to come by. Technological research calls for ever higher investments, and the productive application of the results of this research calls in turn for an ever more sophisticated imaginative ability. The industrial system has an ever greater need of fantastical strategies: that which designers are now asked for is no longer the simple form of a product, but the indications of new imaginative territories that respond to the growing fantastical output of the consumers. Thus we are witnessing the progressive movement of the center of gravity of growth in the post-industrial system—from the search for material technologies to the search for imaginative technologies—all the while capable of finding new strategies for industrial production and technological research itself.

This means that in the future there will be a large growth in human ability to produce and consume imaginative and immaterial goods. The result of this growth cannot be reached through social, technological, or cultural change; rather it will be reached through sensorial change.

For some time a silent but radical Sensorial Revolution has been occurring. When we speak of Sensorial Revolution, we mean a sort of genetic mutation that the advent of new media has produced (or is producing) in society.

For the rationalist culture of the modern movement, "understanding" reality was more important than "perceiving" it, analyzing it through its elementary components, discovering its dynamic mechanisms, and never stopping at the surface. Those who did not know how to lead these in the right direction were "fooled by the senses"; they were inferior, untrustworthy, and substantially obscure perceptive instruments. They provided accessory, intuitive, superficial, and therefore substantially misleading information.

At the end of the sixties an immense haste for information and stimuli to determine that which we call the Sensorial Revolution developed, and consisted in an unchecked growth of sensorial information and consequent development of all the perceptive sensitivities of man. This great informational, musical, and behavioral sensitivity is based on a new perceptive hierarchy: the senses are no longer a simple instrument that transmits inert information to reason, which only reason can then transform into organized conscience. The senses have become a refined, vibrating, cognitive instrument of reality and an element of the individual's political formation.

The reality produced by music, fashion, and social behaviors, but also by electronics and new materials, is a reality of surfaces, which imposes a knowledge of surfaces.

If modern man's sensitivity was analytical and mechanical, that of contemporary

Andrea Branzi, Studies on the theme of the ear, *1989, Musée des Arts Décoratifs, Montreal*

man is synthetic, electronic, and resonant.

The Sensorial Revolution displaces some of the old codes in order to introduce new ones; it does not produce a new Vanguard. It is rather a matter of a series of filters, additional lenses, and sonorous amplifiers that tend to revisit existence, displacing knowledge towards a world of absolute immediacy. This is not a spontaneous, simple world; quite the contrary, it is an extremely sophisticated universe, where, however, there no longer exists a critical and ideological distance between man and the phenomena that surround him.

The perceptive ability capable of instinctively choosing useful elements of the complex stratification of informational fabric that reaches the individual through space is growing.

This new "auditory ability" that the metropolitan inhabitant is developing consists in the integrated use of all the perceptive abilities of the body: we could paradoxically say that he sees through touch, listens with the eyes, and smells with the ears. In the sense that all messages, real or virtual, that he receives imply a whole, sensorial deciphering. A film on television is not only a question of seeing and hearing; it moves an appreciation and secret connections of other senses, like touch, smell, and taste. On this mechanism all advertisements produce sensorial short circuits: a color smells, a brand scratches, a sign makes sound.

The eye was the illuminist symbol in the mechanical age, when a glance allowed a deep inquiry into the logic of reality's movement, similar to that of a large clock.

The hand was Le Corbusier's symbol that, through "Le Modulor," gave the modern world a chance to recover a human dimension in the act of making.

The symbol of man in the post-industrial world now is the ear, that strange, enigmatic organ perennially open to the outside, and within which simultaneously millions of complex information bits are input, allowing us to perceive within the great soundtrack of the metropolis the light hum of the computer, a bird's song, or the sound of a jingle.

The ear represents quite well the Sensorial Revolution, where "understanding" the internal mechanisms of phenomena no longer counts, rather "perceiving" the effects of these mechanisms, choosing the sounds and information, transforming into culture the gray mass of sounds present in space.

We are in contact with these sounds; we are not in contact with who and what produces them. Only war, the voice of human tragedy, the important music of our culture reaches us, but it is the ear that chooses and finds them mixed amid all the slag and useless choruses floating around space, transforming them into political sensations, emotions, and anguish.

One single view of the world is no longer enough if there is not any sound information to act as its key: do those images come from a film, or are they real scenes from the Gulf War? Is the chase of those traffickers fiction or a scene from Bolivia? We listen, and we will understand.

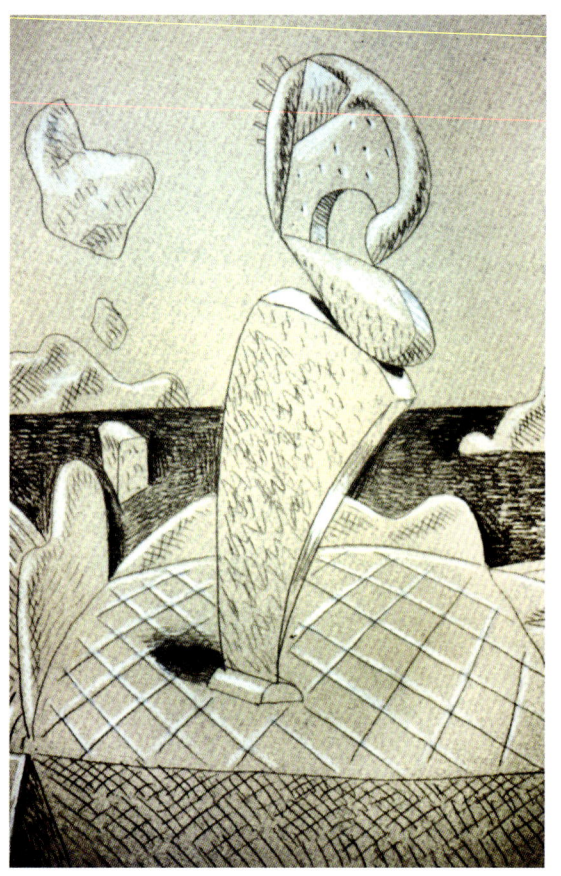

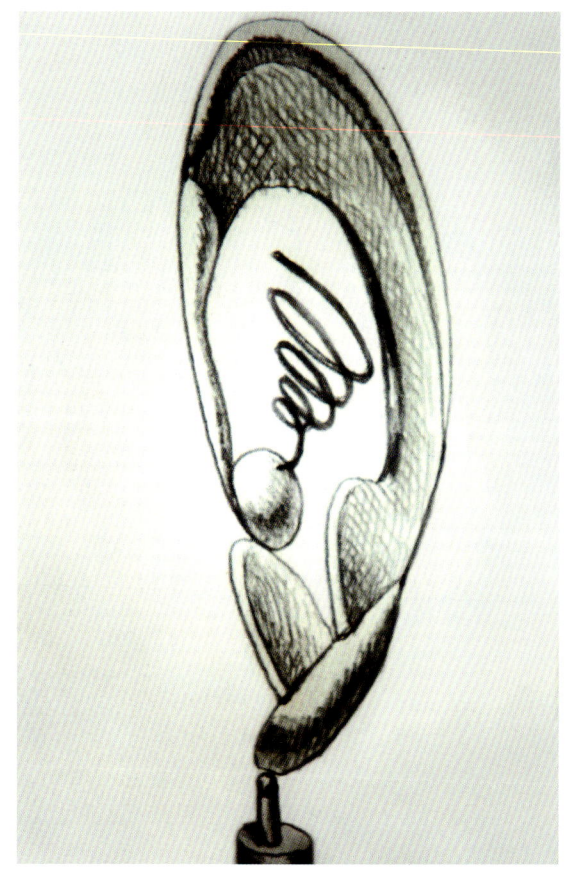

Andrea Branzi, Studies on the theme of the ear, *1989, Musée des Arts Décoratifs, Montreal*

108

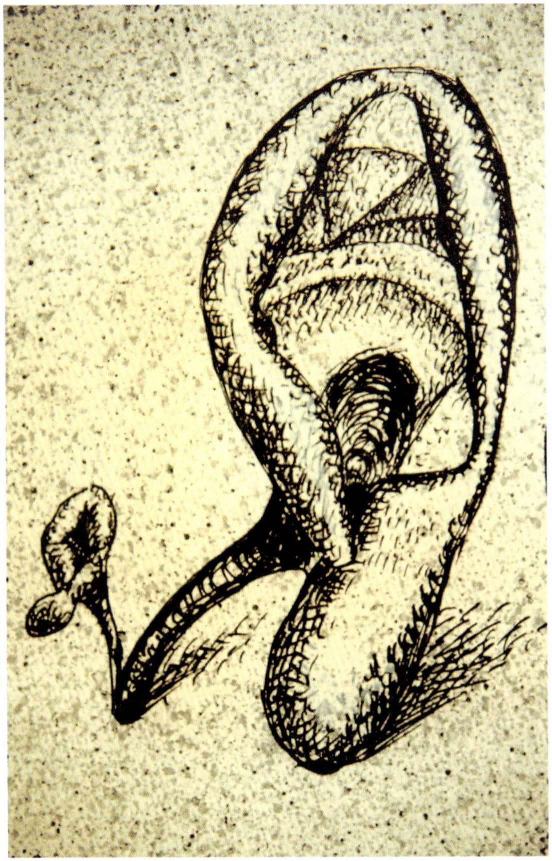

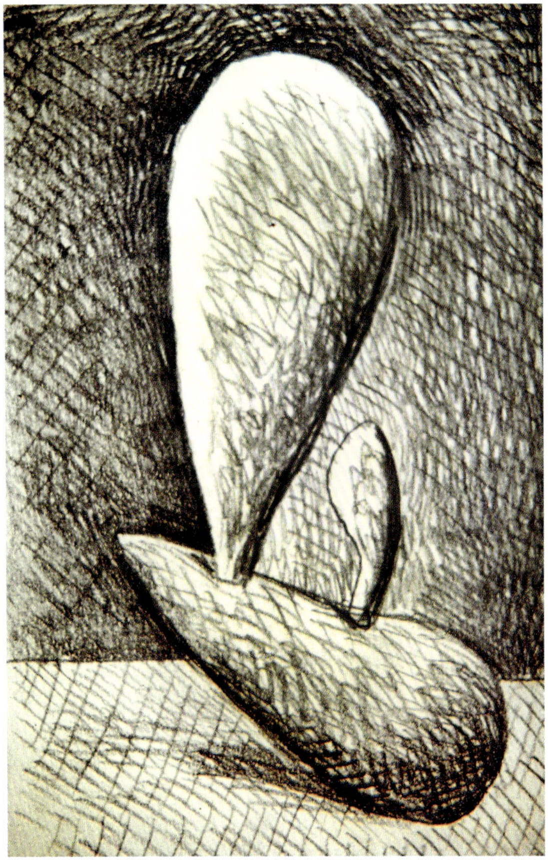

Tokyo Forum

Tokyo International Forum
Competition

Year
1989

Design
Andrea Branzi
with
Tullio Zini and Franco Lani

collaborators
Grazia Franzoni, Michele Zini,
Claudia Zoboli, Daniela Ascari

This design proposes a gray, closed, inexpressive building for the center of Tokyo, surmounted by a large parabola in the form of an ear as a listening center within a space full of information and network tides.
I frequently used the ear symbol for my designs in those years as a sign of the perceptive ability of man within a post-industrial society, immersed in a liquid space of sounds and noises that the human ear successfully selects and interprets.

111

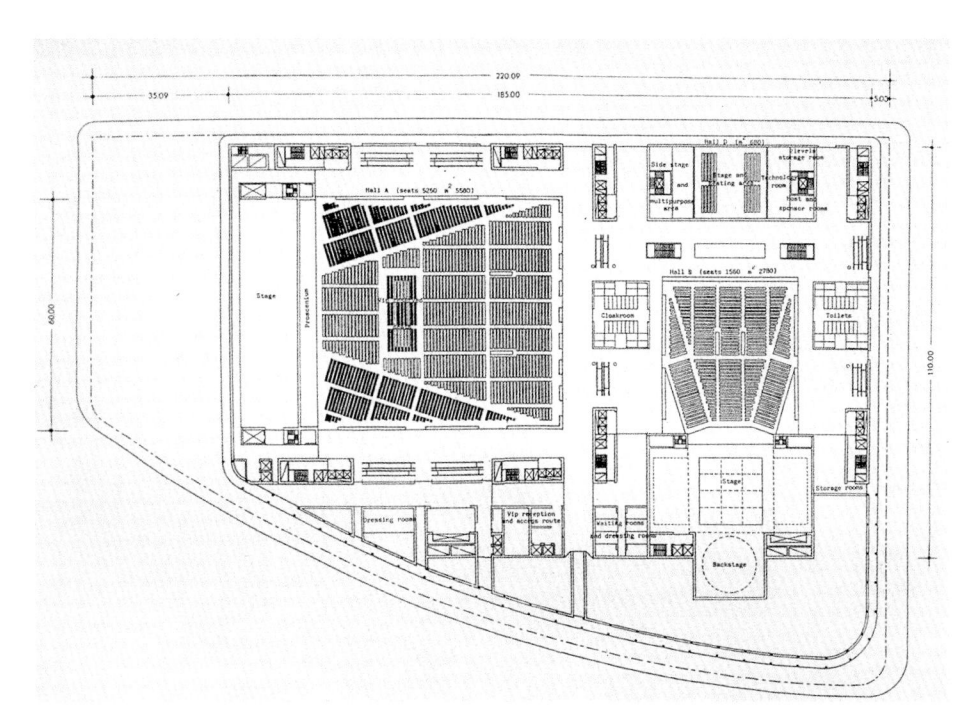

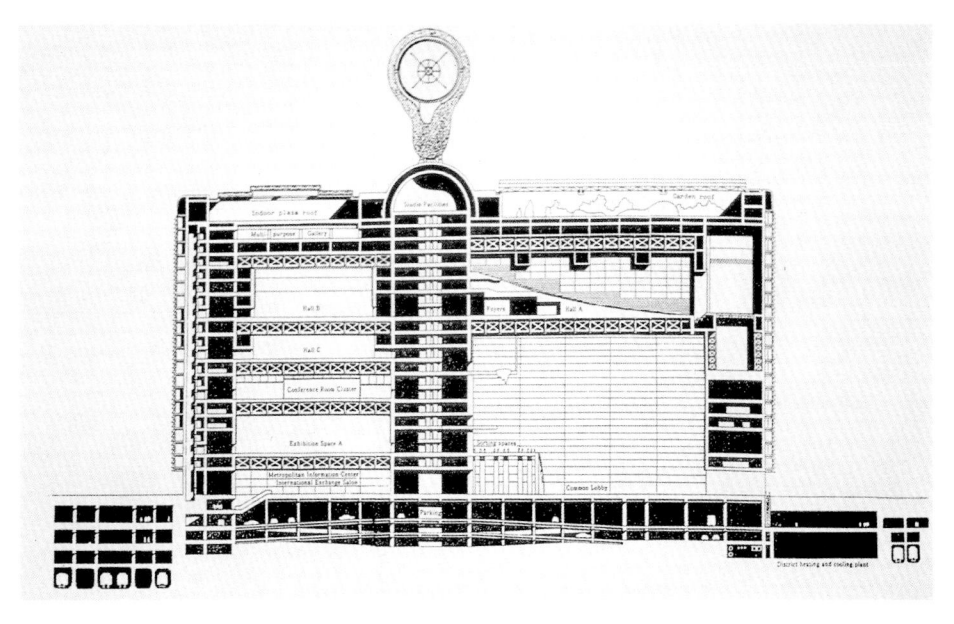

Corporate identities are those sensorial or symbolic structures present in the working spaces of large service organizations that are needed to render a brand recognizable and memorable to the public. Colors, scents, materials, the conditioning of microclimates, and systems of environmental information create enjoyable interfaces that transfer to the user particular levels of sensitivity of the given services. This is a sort of immaterial architecture that creates environmental systems that are perceptible even in subliminal ways, but are also very efficient for communicating a business philosophy.

Andrea Branzi, corporate identity models for the exhibition Citizen Office, *Vitra Design Museum, Weil am Rhein, 1994*

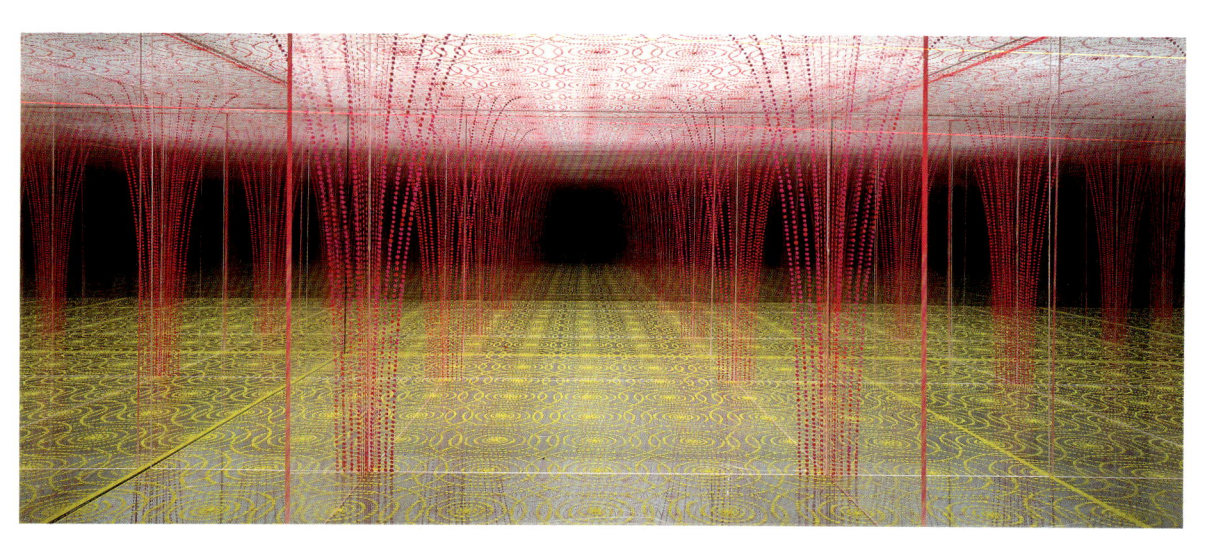

On the opposite page the figure on top represents the visualization of a discontinuous system of air-conditioning or microclimates aimed at creating a sort of sensorial architecture where hot and cold zones alternate in a perceptible manner, avoiding an excessive homogenization of the climate—like when in a cold house there is a lit fireplace that creates a naturally attractive aggregation point. Instead, the other two images are a "physiognomic information system" for service societies where the user recognizes his account's face rather than its name.

Architecture and Agriculture

The architecture of the twentieth century stabilized a preferential axis with the world of industry, adopting its morphologies and construction technologies. The futurist Antonio Sant'Elia spoke of the factory as the new cathedral of the modern city.

This alliance also included the idea of the factory as a concentrated, closed place with respect to the city, as a strong presence of modernization, a place in which definitive choices based on productive reason were made. So the factory, as Zygmunt Bauman would say, is viewed as a place of reconstruction of the solid bodies of modernity.

Virtual products, "informationized" markets, and global construction processes have all transformed the market into a multimedia system where the physicality of the product is a little part of a vast system of relations and services. In this more fluid, more articulated world, the factory no longer expresses the centrality of organized work, but is instead an accessory presence, a backstage of the market that is usually best hidden and sometimes best shipped abroad to distant countries.

The development of industrial districts, born in Japan and greatly developed in Italy in the eighties, originated also from the dispersion of large industrial concentrations, which were transformed into socially sapient territories where a population of small entrepreneurs created designs and innovation in a highly competitive regime.

A large part of mass entrepreneurship and the diffuse research we have spoken of was developed in these districts, or produced new districts. The self-branding of the new economy is a typical phenomenon in a regime organized by district, where each subject produces business and wealth, beginning with its own ability to create innovation.

In this context, it is the territory that becomes the privileged protagonist of the post-industrial economy, acting as a place for working out the weak and diffuse energies of a powder-fine productivity, which perfectly matches the powder-fine and ever-changing reality of the market. The concentrated city and locked-down factory, in the end, become a difficult-to-manage reality because they are both too rigid; only when placed in a context of districts that provide an articulated support and different specialties can the city and factory successfully become a reality adequate and appropriate for the global markets. The economist Giacomo Becattini interpreted such districts as positive examples of imperfect, incomplete, weak, and diffuse industrial processes, but precisely because of this they are able to adjust to all that is new, and to offer something new. In Italy, fashion and design, which represent almost 70% of payment activities, originated in over 100 Italian districts and in their ability to be innovative interlocutors. These new productive orders have many similarities with the territorial systems of modern agriculture: both are diffuse systems, which correspond to a constructive energy fed by the weak energies of nature, the climate, and genetics. This agriculture is no longer tied to traditional techniques, and is able to use symbiotic technologies to intervene in large territories, transforming them into flexible systems of food production. The agricultural enterprise is now, according to management theorists, a self-balancing productive organism, regulated by seasonal cycles, fed by natural energies, and able to spontaneously produce diversified series of edible and biodegradable products. The diversified series actually originated in nature: a grouping of one million apples is always

Irrigation pivot in Arizona, 1980

made up of single apples, one different from the next. In nature, the same form, same leaf, or same apple is never repeated twice. Natural technology is therefore becoming the most sophisticated construction model to which industrial technology looks while seeking to imitate its cycles and services. The artificial world, born in order to substitute an inadequate natural world, is rediscovering nature as an unparalleled realm of technology, as having an extraordinary ability to produce materials, products, eco-compatible services, feeding on the weak and diffuse technologies of nature in whole regions. Agricultural industrial civilization creates a horizontal landscape, without cathedrals, traversable and reversible: the turnover of crops allows the management of the agricultural landscape following a transitory logic, which adjusts to the productive equilibrium of the terrain, the passage of seasons, and the market. Because of these combined motives contemporary architecture should begin to look at modern agriculture as a reality with which new strategic relations can be made.

This is an architecture that completely renews its models of reference, confronting the challenge of a liquid modernity. New relations can be established with a culture such as the agricultural one, which is not a constructive culture in the traditional sense, but is productive in enzymatic terms, and which follows bio-compatible logic and uses highly evolved supporting technologies. This design hypothesis is set within the general reflections made thus far, within a less rigid, absolute way of understanding the transformational forces of the city.

Le Corbusier, Villa Savoye, 1928–1930

Archizoom Associates,
No-Stop City, *New Mexico,*
1969–1972

Walter De Maria, The Lighting
Field, *New Mexico, 1973–1979*

Today architecture and agriculture are two completely opposing realities: where there is one there cannot be the other. But the agricultural origin of architecture (and likewise the architectural origin of agriculture) is easily provable in the areas of the Mediterranean where these diverse land uses cohabit, generating themselves from one another and often living together in a symbiotic manner. This consideration is important inasmuch as it regards the different presence of the component "time," which today has completely vanished from (a rigid and definitive) architecture, and is instead omnipresent in the seasonal cycles of agriculture. In the levels on which these two technologies live together, like in the groves of the Mediterranean coast, agriculture plays a constructive role, and architectural structures take part in the natural productive energy.

Andrea Branzi,
Architecture/Agriculture, theoretic
model, *FRAC Collection, Orléans,*
2005

Citrus orchards in Positano, 2005

Lemon groves on Lake Garda
(from Bernard Rudofsky,
Architecture without Architects,
Academy Editions, London, 1981)

Focus Commercial Center, Munich

Client
Focus

Year
1990, model from the original 1982 design

Design
Andrea Branzi

The hypothesis of a symbiotic cohabitation between architecture and plant elements is a theme capable of modifying the rigid devices of building: façades and plant coverings permit the substitution of the traditional morphology of architectural idiom with natural and changing expressive systems.

Archizoon Associates, building in Champs de Mars, Paris, 1971

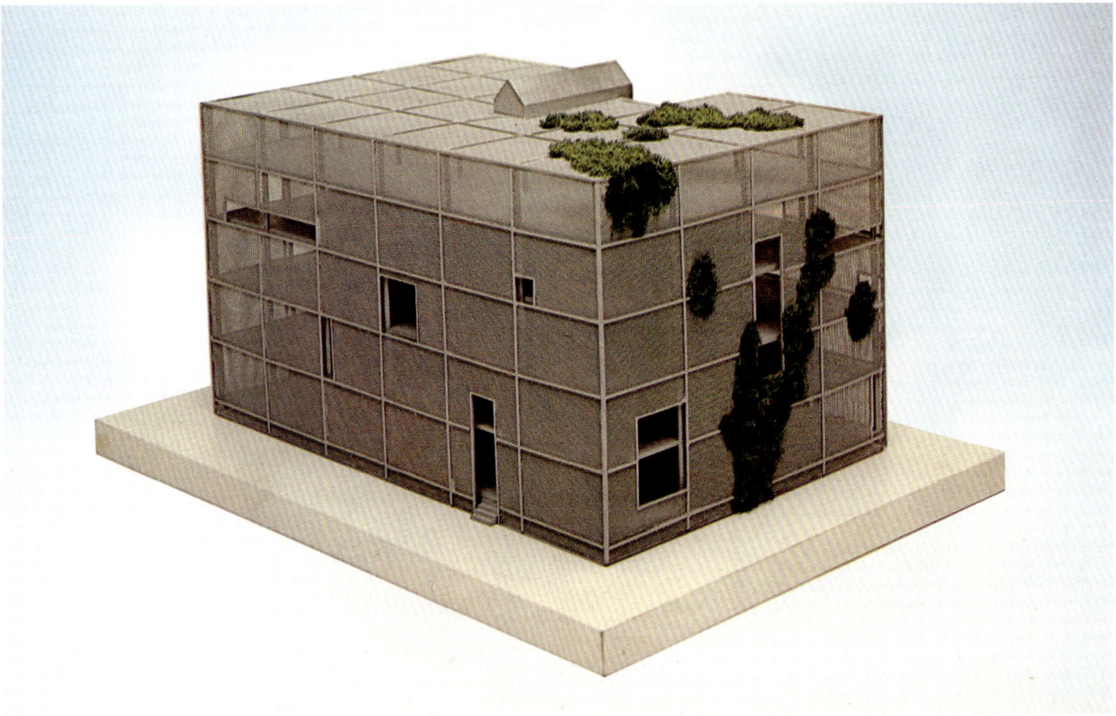

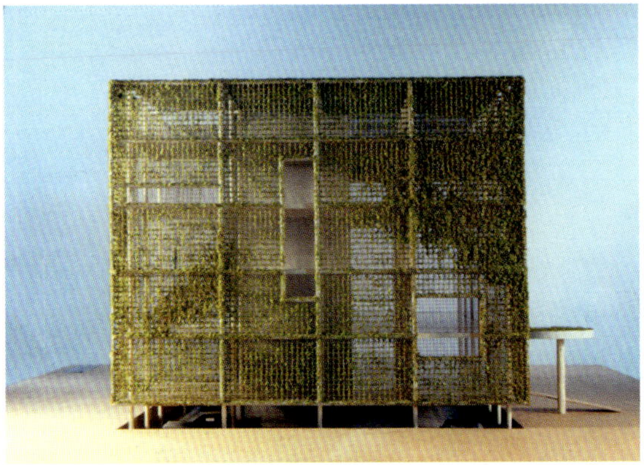

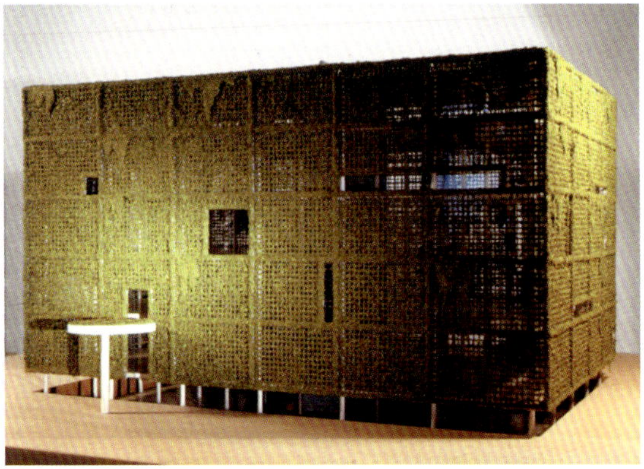

Osaka Pavilion

The pavilion for the international exposition in the gardens of Osaka experiments with the expressive use of the raw elements of nature, set within the divisions of architecture, to verify an increase in expressivity, with the presence of the *other* that magnifies its sign and mysterious weight.

124

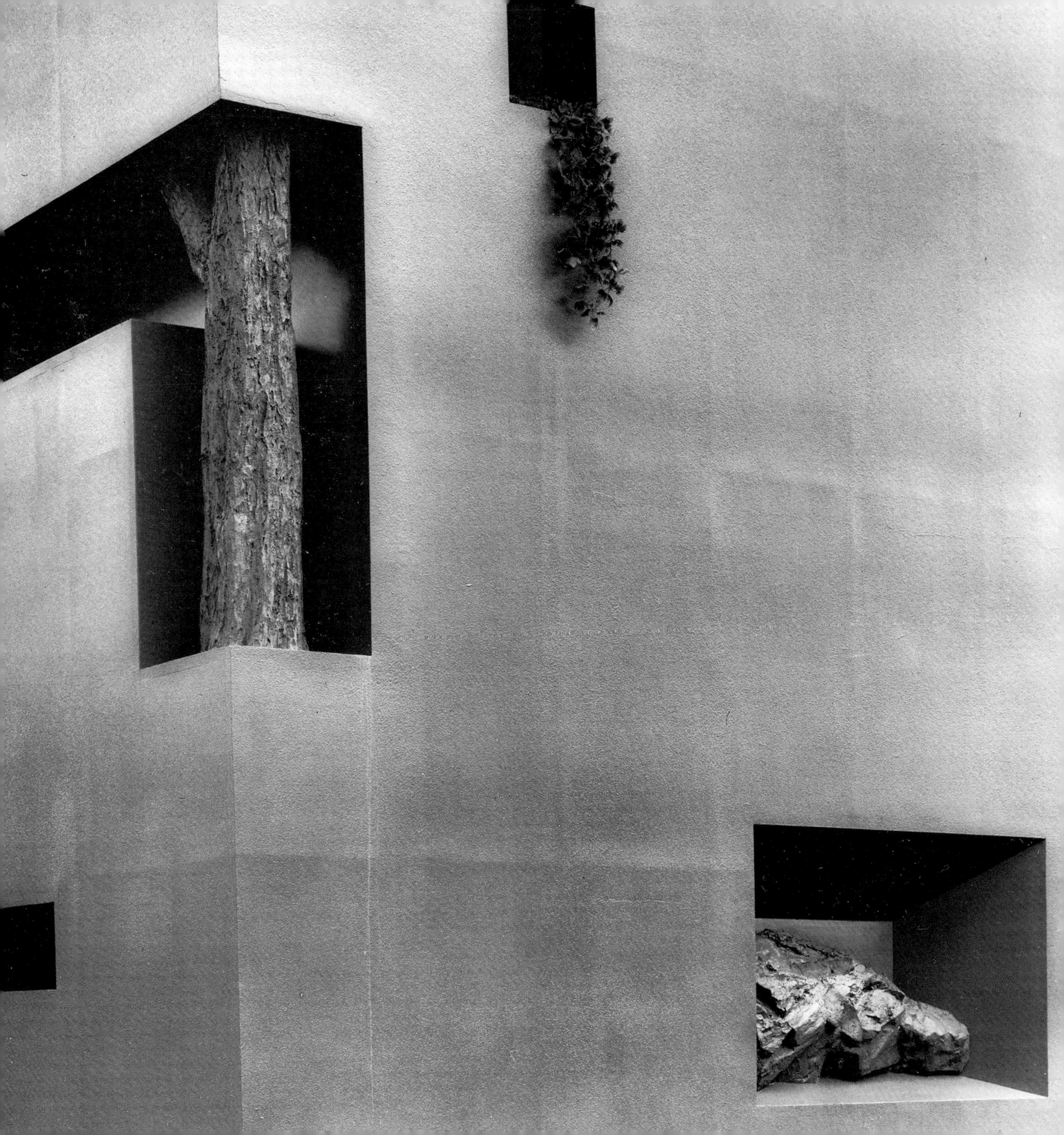

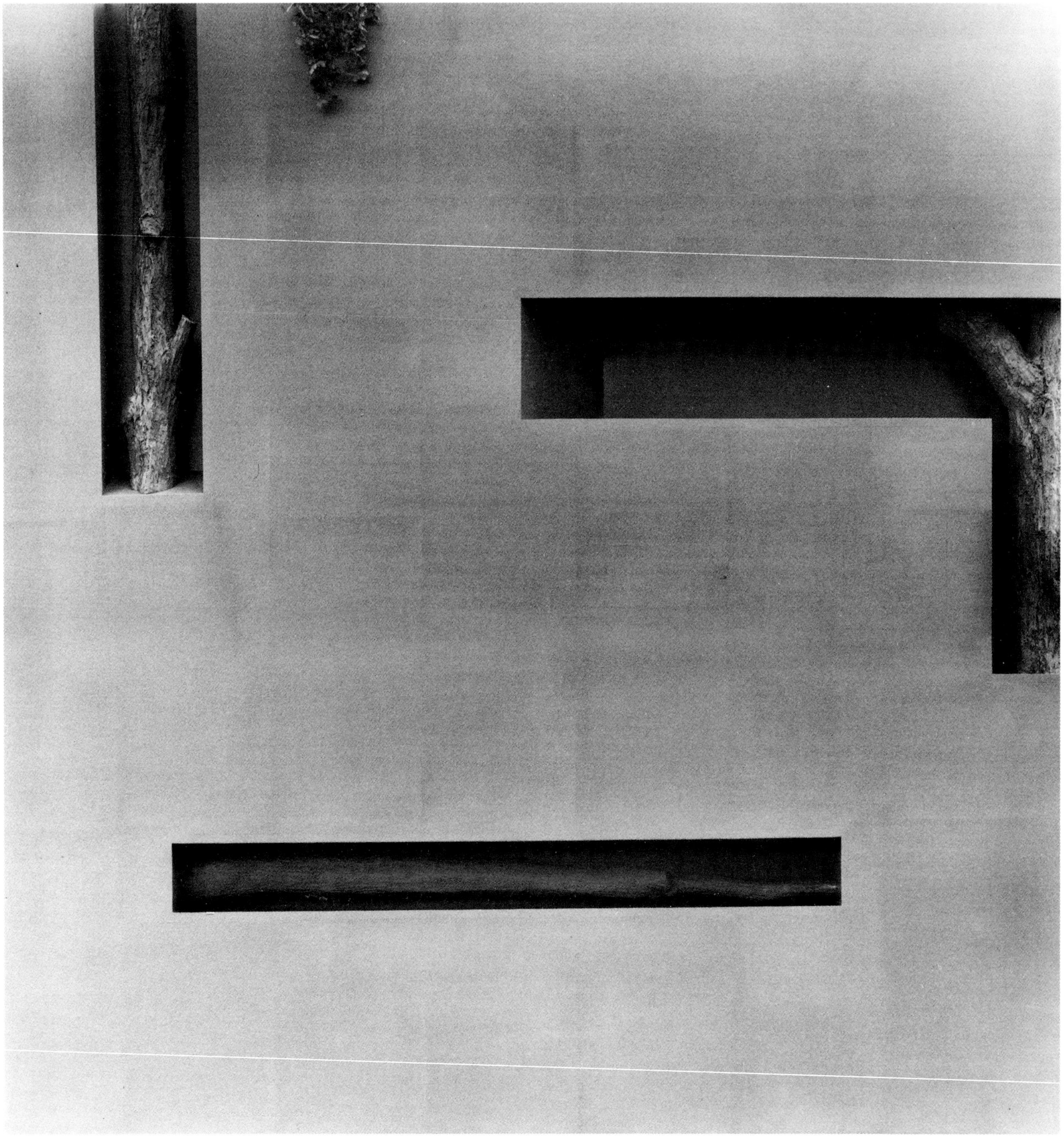

127

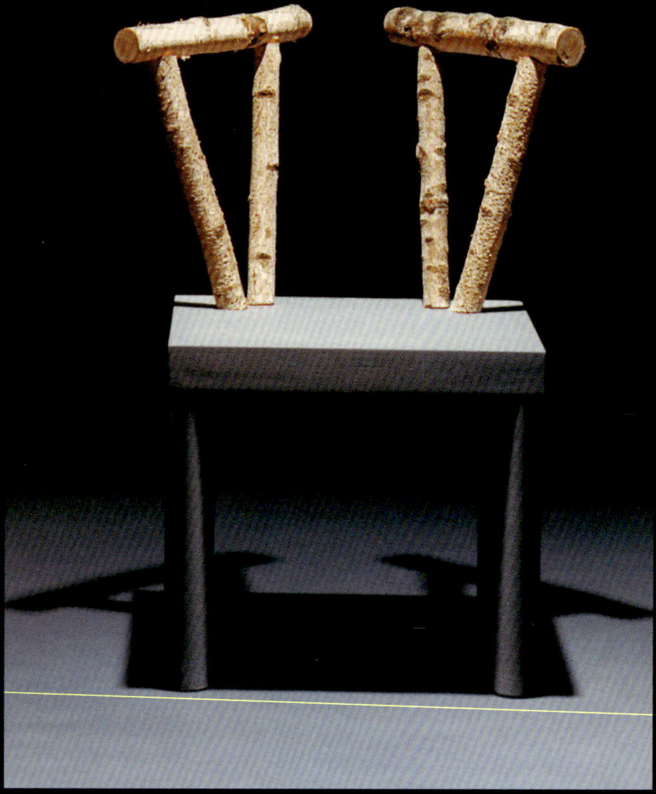
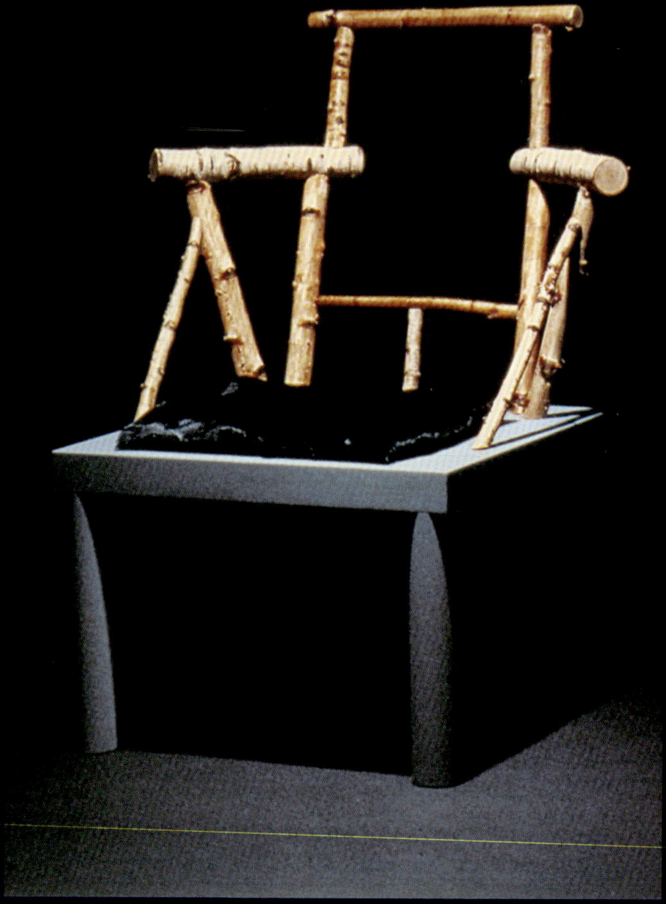

The "Domestic Animals" collection is made up of hybrid objects that are partly industrial and partly natural. The bottoms of the seats are realized with the technologies of industrial carpentry, while the backrests are made of rough birch branches. The idea was to seek out new archetypes that would add value to the identity of the object as an autonomous presence within the environment, not strictly functional, but gifted with its own identity (like pets). The double nature of objects also guarantees the definition of a "diversified series" because each object will always be different from the next, since in nature the form of each branch will always be inimitable.

Andrea Branzi, Domestic Animals, Zabro, *1985*

Today industrial technology tends to reproduce natural technologies. The *Foglia* lamp is made up of an electroluminescent leaf—a surface spread with phosphoric crystals that are excited (becoming luminescent) when placed in a magnetic field activated by electric circuits made up of the leaf's veins.

Andrea Branzi, Foglia, *electroluminescent lamp, Memphis, 1988*

Andrea Branzi, Piccolo albero, *Amnesie collection, Design Gallery, Milan, 1991*

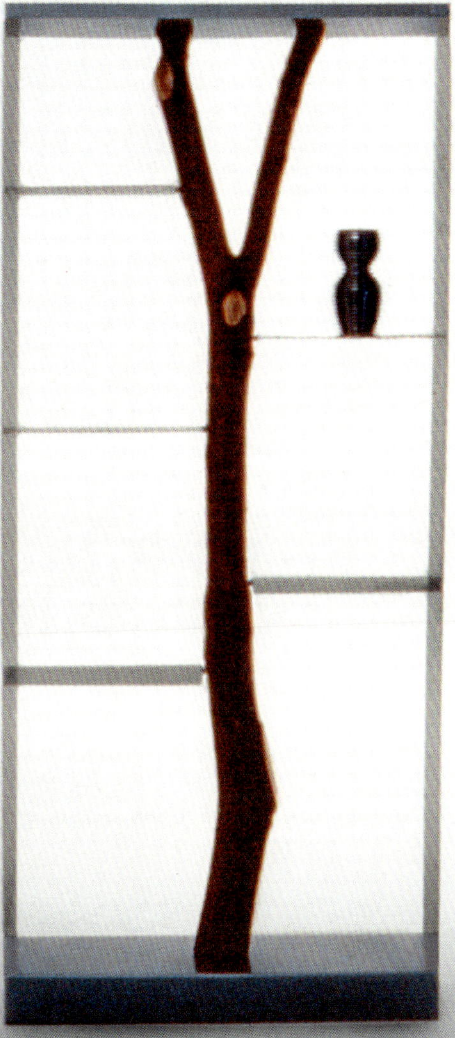

Models of Weak Urbanization

Electronic games allow for the elaboration of simulated territories in which everyone can freely insert constructions and connections, creating a sort of highly complex *favela* in continual transformation.

Urban plan from activeworlds.com

Models of weak urbanization refer to a concept of reversibility and a traversable quality typical of agriculture, and they indicate a way of understanding structures as a temporary, light, elastic reality set within a constructed territory but mixed in with agricultural production as well. Traversable and free of insurmountable borders just like agricultural production, weak urbanization is where architecture becomes a free availability of components and no longer coincides with the concept of buildings and stable typologies. Models of weak urbanization are for a relational architecture not defined by precise functions, yet like a computer available for many different activities; a functionoid therefore that responds positively to the changing of necessities, even seasonal ones. This is an architecture in which the component of time returns as a variable in an imperfect and incomplete equation that adapts itself to change.

We are not speaking about the city of the future here, but of a new type of integrated agricultural park situated beside historic or modern cities; a sort of high-tech *favela*, and like the *favelas* mixed in with nature this is constructed using light, manageable materials that create a multimedia campus. It is a ductile, open structure that represents a compromise between current agricultural facilities and an urban sub-system.

Western architecture in the twentieth century experimented with very few new typologies: during the age of strong and concentrated modernity skyscrapers and Le Corbusier's Inhabitation Units were born. In the age of weak and diffuse modernity, there is a need to seek out new typologies, diligently analyzing those few that have been spontaneously born.

The *favelas* are among these; produced by a state of necessity and grave social discomfort, they objectively constitute one of the few novelties in the urban setting. These must be evaluated independently of the social groups that constructed them in the peripheries of the large cities in order to understand their innovative potential. Many masters of all that is modern had intuited a dispersed architecture open to nature (Mies van der Rohe, Le Corbusier, Niemeyer), but it was always in terms of a new construction finally definitive and immobile in time, an irreversible typology that perfectly corresponded to the given functions. It is a question, then, of trying, through new models of weak urbanization, the possibility of adapting the design to the bypassing of these historical binds, rendering it more adequate for a time that changes and a society that renews itself.

133

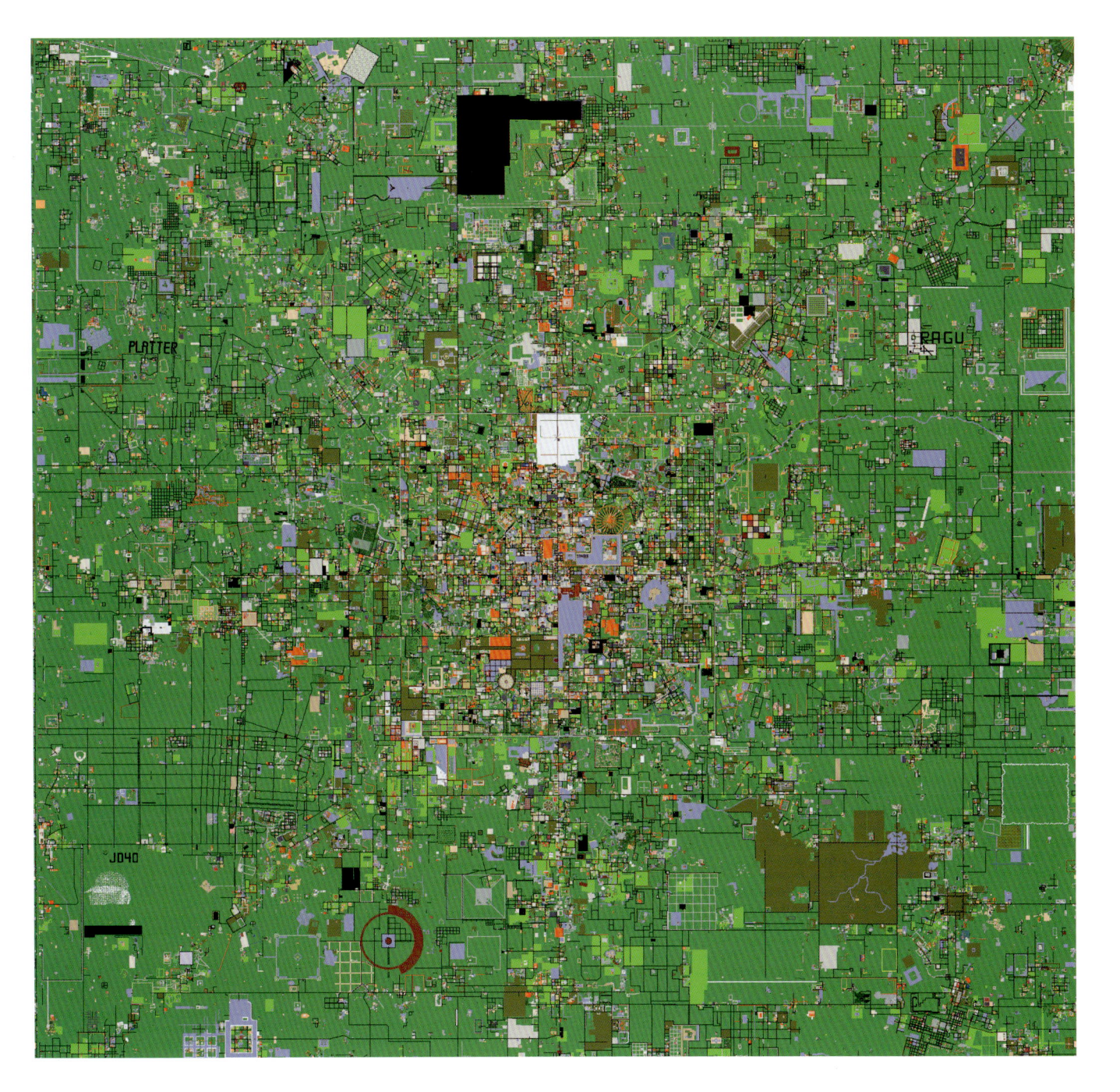

Agronica – Weak Urbanization

Client
Domus Academy Research Center
Philips Design Center
(director Stefano Marzano)

Year
1995

Design
Andrea Branzi, Dante Donegani,
Antonio Petrillo, Claudia Raimondo
with
Tamar Ben David

Agronica is a partial unity because it is set up as "part" of existence, next to, and not in substitution of, the extant. It designs a part of the territory next to the existing metropolis, city, and village; next to the traditional transport system and today's merchandise market. Agronica elaborates on a model of weak urbanization that has not yet been explored, and consists of a system that guarantees the survival of the agricultural and natural landscape in the presence of evolved, but no longer totalizing, urban services. It tends therefore to surpass the old conflict between city and countryside through an innovative mediation, with the certainty that these two realities correspond to sclerotic concepts no longer able to divide the world.
In the preceding phase of the industrial revolution, a strong correlation remained between construction solutions, the land's morphology, and the organizational models of activity: the factory, the office, and the connection networks each had their own expressive form determined by the bounds of technical and functional organization.
For some time now this correspondence has no longer been necessary. The different realities of a place's arrangement reproduce codes that are merely citations of self-referential morphologies that no longer have any real relation to the activities that happen there.
The functions and work carried out in an office building, university, or industrial laboratory could be carried out in a group of farmhouses or a thermoelectric plant no longer in use.
Seven theses are stated:
– separation of form and technology;
– there no longer exists a correspondence between construction technologies and buildings' forms (urban and in use);
– if a tight relationship existed between mechanics and mechanical objects, today there no longer exists a direct relationship between electronics and the form electronic products;
– separation of form and function;
– electronic instrumentation allows for the same functions to be carried out everywhere;
– places collectively lose functional identities;
– the function of places no longer corresponds to a visible stylistic code (home, office, factory), but to a software that changes places' use - in other words, a network program that specializes activities in real time.

Weak Urban Planning
Urban planning continues to follow an objective of physical and functional models' correspondence. The word "plan" itself betrays the illusion of being able to create a system of analogies that allows the structural dimensions present in the metropolitan volume to be transferred to a single level of "metropolicity." Contemporary territory is, on the contrary, a sum of physical and virtual places that respond to different organizational logics that are penetrating one another and constantly readapting. All this renders the metropolis a very dense environment of functions without syntax and structure. The terms and grammar

that are still used today to describe the metropolis (center/suburb, home/work, houses/infrastructure, living spaces/transport systems) are the vestiges of earlier realities (the military city, the industrial city, etc.).

That which we consider the physical form of the city are enlargements, sutures, and concretions of antecedent tissue that had been torn and dissolved. In a new, built architecture, starting from scratch with no historical precedents to refer to, no physical image or frame of reference would correspond to the current functional density.

This is the design-related diagram of the formless metropolises of the third world.

An outline of this new city structure can be found in the traditional concept of the Japanese city, where the distinction between city and countryside has no precise definition.

In the ideogram for city (machi 町), both the rice paddy (ta 田) and grouping of houses (cho 丁) are represented. Similarly, in the term most similar to our idea of countryside (inaka 田舎), again the rice paddy and house (sha 舎) appear, in this case subdivided into two ideograms. Even in the ideogram that defines the village (mura 村), trees (ki 木) and an ancient measuring unit (sun 寸) are represented, placing an accent on the village seen as a grouping of buildings, but also a controlled territorial system. One could therefore say that Edo, ancient Tokyo, was an example of weak urbanization, with rice paddies extending to the shogun's castle walls, interspersed with houses, markets, artisans' production centers, and neighborhoods of pleasure.

Japanese ideograms are taken from The Solid Side, *(ed.) Ezio Manzini and Marco Susani, V+K Publishing, Naarden*

The search for models of weak urbanization began as a theoretical investigation of the possibilities of identifying territorial devices less rigid than those used in traditional urban design, and which would allow for the realization of more nuanced, intermediate, and flexible zoning.

"Agronica" begins with a productive agricultural territory in which, using the system of agricultural posts, single elements of architecture (roofs, walls, platforms) flow and group together or are dispersed according to necessity.

In this way, a semi-urbanized and semi-agricultural territory is created, where temporary service structures can coagulate without creating a permanent passage, setting in motion a dispersed mode of componential building.

In other words, this is agriculture seen as an enzymatic, horizontal, systemic, changing, and inexpressive territory, in the sense that it does not produce "cathedrals" and monuments.

137

Agriculture is no longer the reign of pre-industrial technologies, but an extremely advanced productive system that industry itself now seeks to adopt as a model of reference.
Agriculture uses a mix of biotechnologies based on natural and spontaneously regenerative energies—chemistry, geology, and meteorology—in a spontaneously balanced system of seasonal cycles within a traversable and productively reversible territory. Agriculture further guarantees the production of spontaneously varied series, in the sense that a million apples will always be made up of one apple different from the next.

139

The presence of animals within the biotechnological system of Agronica indicates the possibility of integrating into a unique elastic system realities that are programmable along with those that cannot be programmed—just as in Indian cities where traffic lives alongside sacred cows that circulate in a free and unpredictable manner, creating a sort of speed bump within the functional rhythms of the metropolis.
In the contemporary city, information technologies, nature, the production of series, animals, myths, and religions are no longer opposed to one another, but must instead live together as integral parts of a highly complex service system.

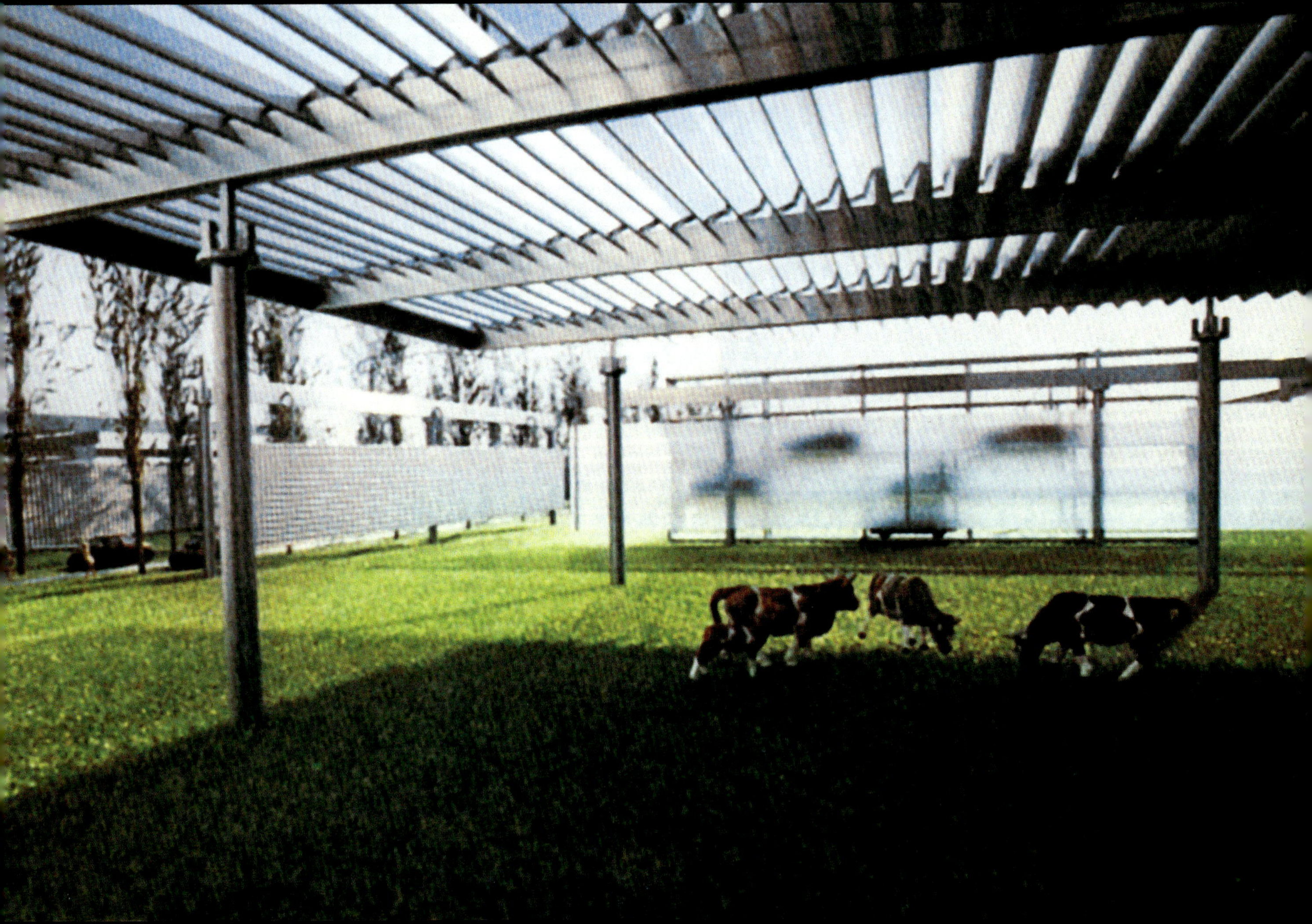

Informational organisms are internally made up of diverse electronic components that, when grouped together, provide a home for various electronic instrumentations. Equally so, in Agronica the architecture is made up of an open system of components that can group together among themselves to create various temporary typologies that respond to the needs of a relational economy and society in continual transformation.

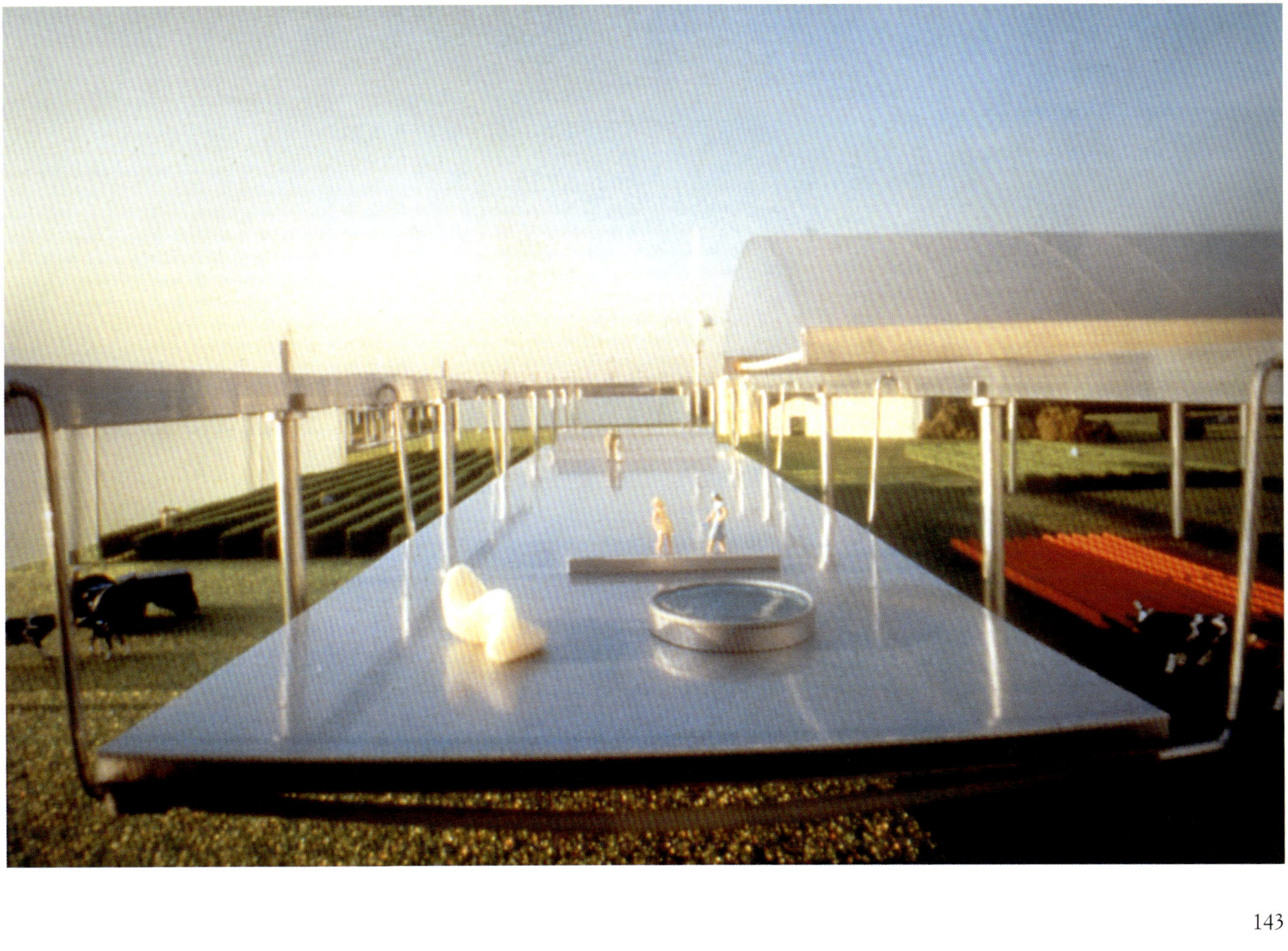

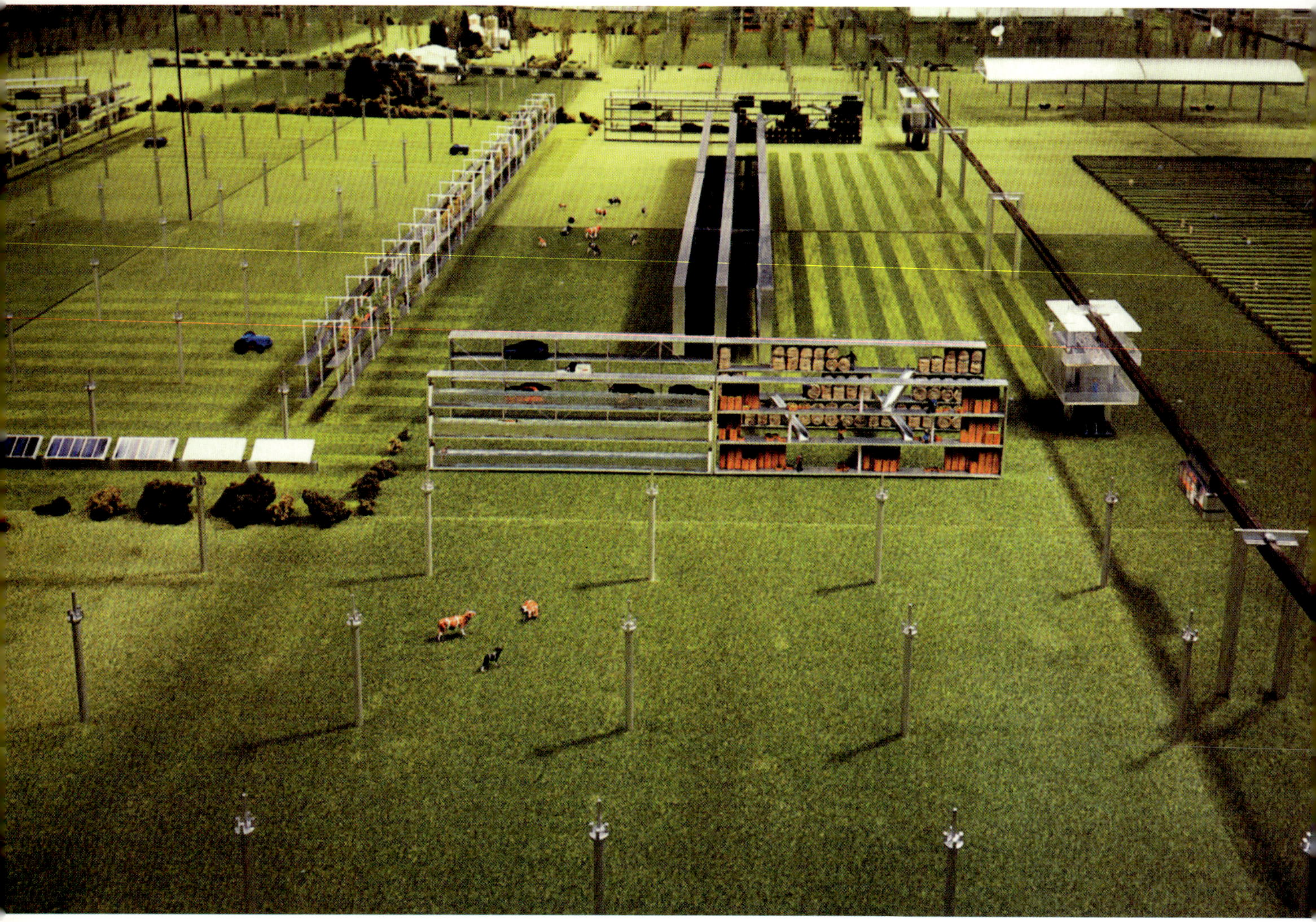

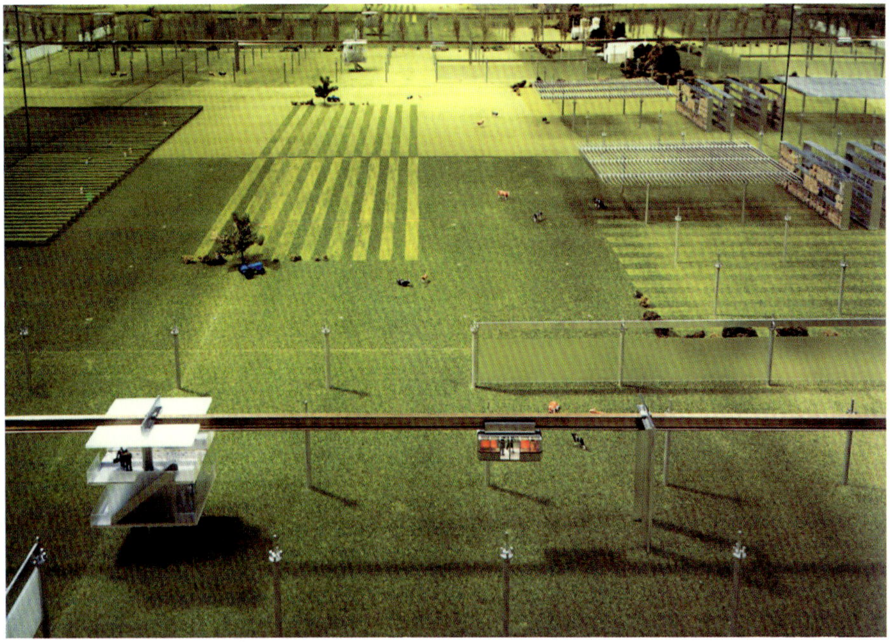

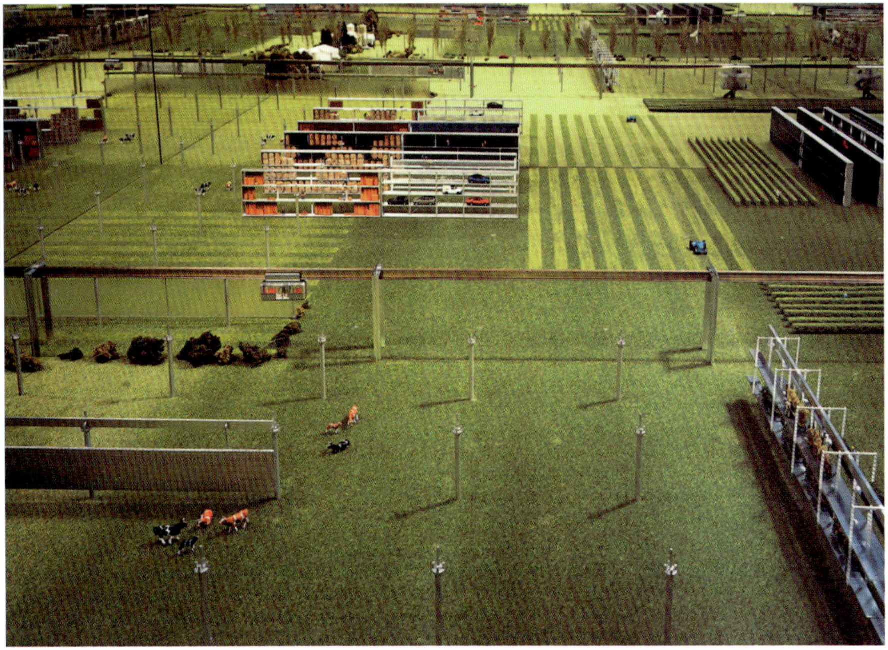

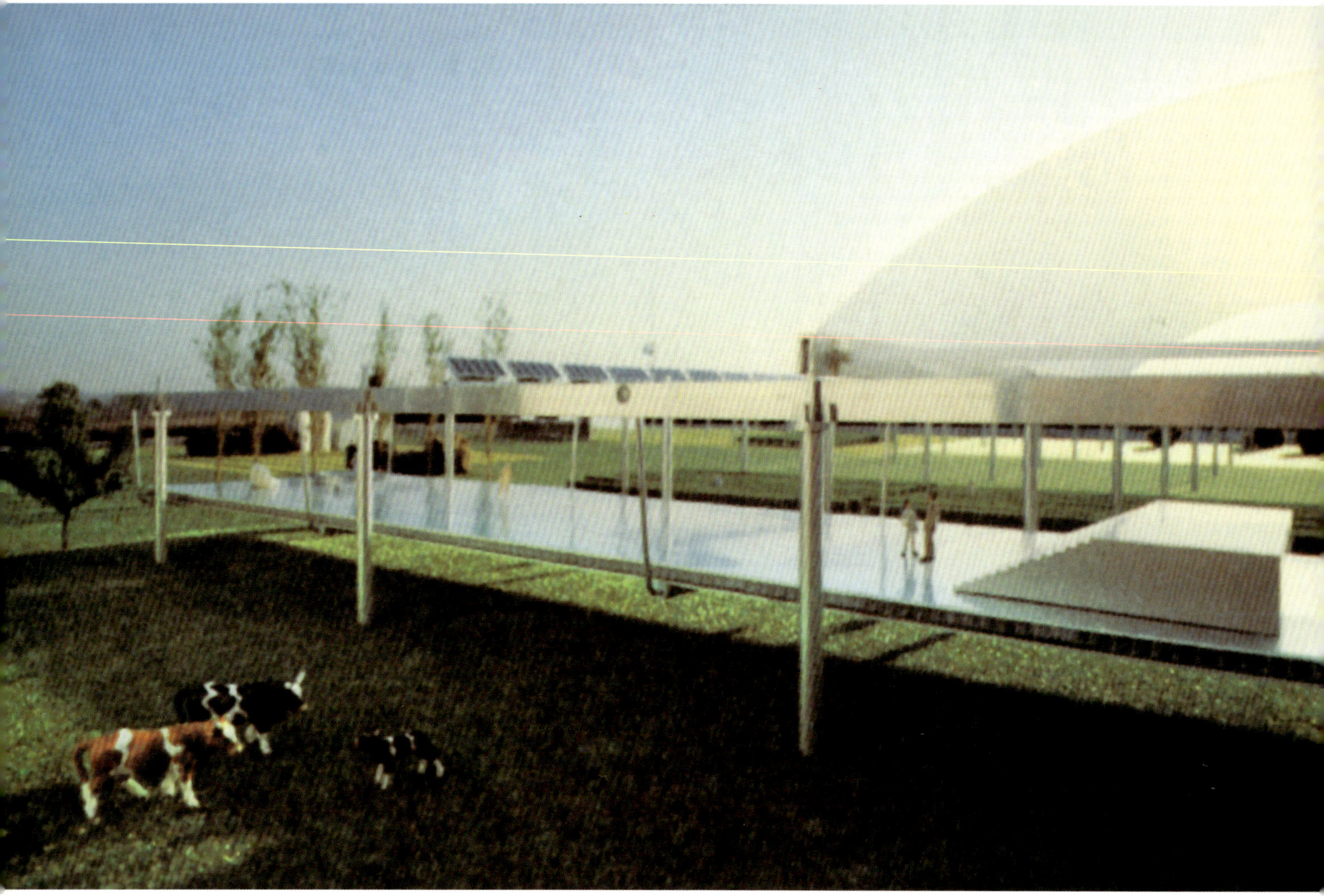

Domus Academy Master's – Flexyroad, Reversible Infrastructures

Year
1999

Teachers
Andrea Branzi, Dante Donegani,
Antonio Petrillo, Claudia Raimondo,
Michele Zini

Students
Aghela Patroula Glytsi, Francisco
Paz Gomez, Frédéric Gooris,
Alon Green, Akiko Horie, Kotaro
Kanai, Pamir Kiraner, Yi-Ling Kuo,
Pelin Fikriye Kurtul, Voraphat
Laokasem, Rafaela Teixeira
L. Macedo, Marco Antonio
M. Fonseca, Gimena Moya
Tonelli

Today's system of streets and highways is very rigid, dividing the land and creating permanent scars. Flexyroad is a system of removable roads for a weak urbanization. It is not an alternative, but flanks the extant system to serve points of reference in continuous change throughout the country while respecting environmental quality. Its characteristics are: flexibility, low spatial consumption, transportability, sustainability, lightness, modularity.
The flexible "ribbon" of the road can be placed on both the ground or on mobile structures.
The structures are self-supporting and can be disassembled for easy removal.
The exits are made with simple ramps from the Flexyroad to the ground.
Flexyroad is moved as a roll. When spread out it takes form through the tension of internal cables that give resistance to the vertical section. It is 3.5 meters long.
The particular warp and woof of Flexyroad allows the system to curve and leaves a transparency along the borders, permitting light to filter through when it is suspended, and allowing the grass to grow when it is set on the ground.

Monumental Cemetery of Carpi, Modena

Expansion of the Monumental Cemetery of Carpi

Client
Town of Carpi, Modena

Year
1989

Design
Tullio Zini

Consultant
Andrea Branzi
with
Clara Bastai, Corrado Gianferrari, Marco Partesotti, Davide Tavani

The old cemetery of Carpi is in the historic city center, so its expansion into the nearby urban park posed a delicate problem because the cemetery addition is surrounded by residential buildings. Our design calls for the creation of two parallel green volumes, similar to river embankments, wherein the tombs are located inside courtyards covered with vegetation and integrated with the park.

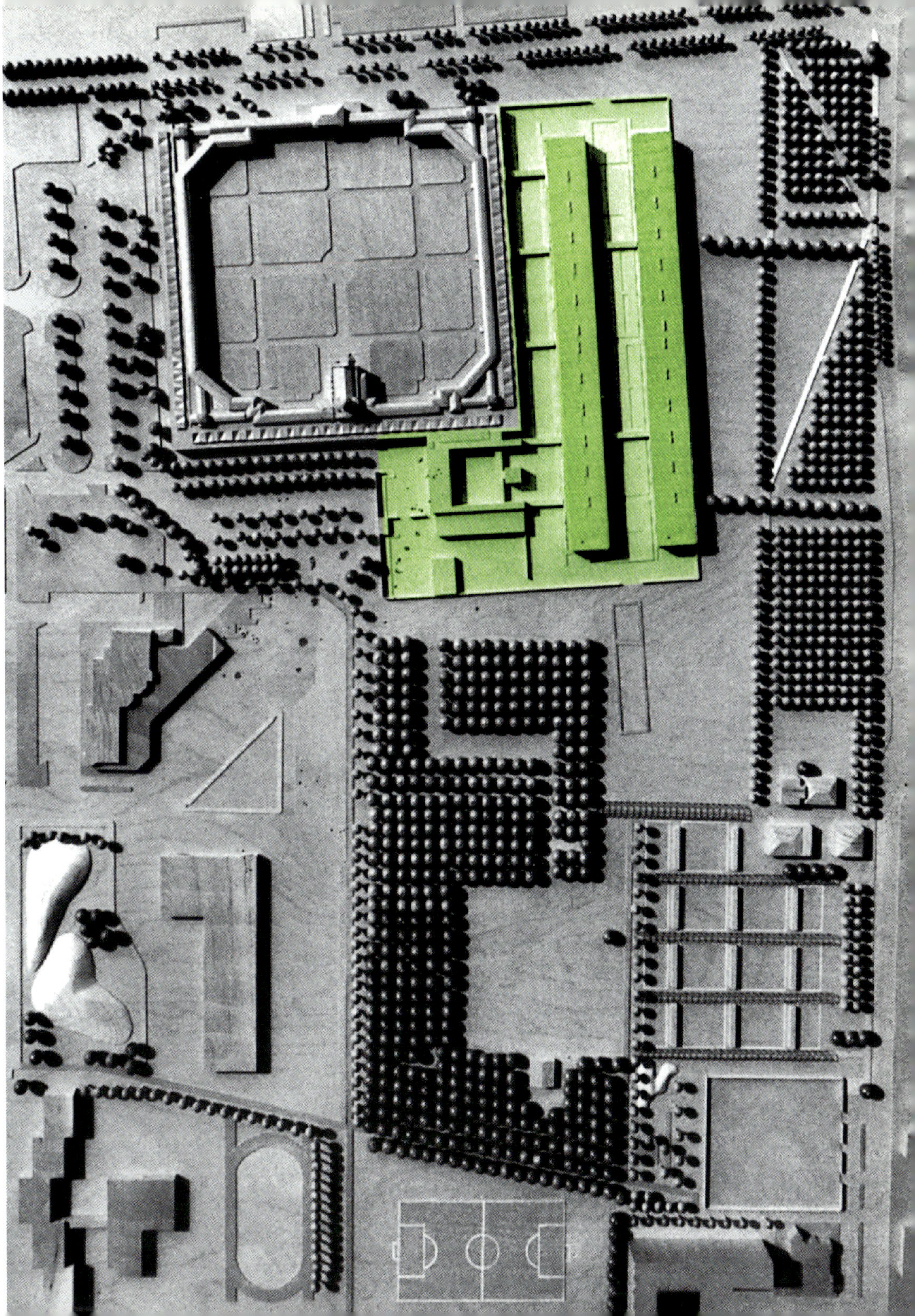

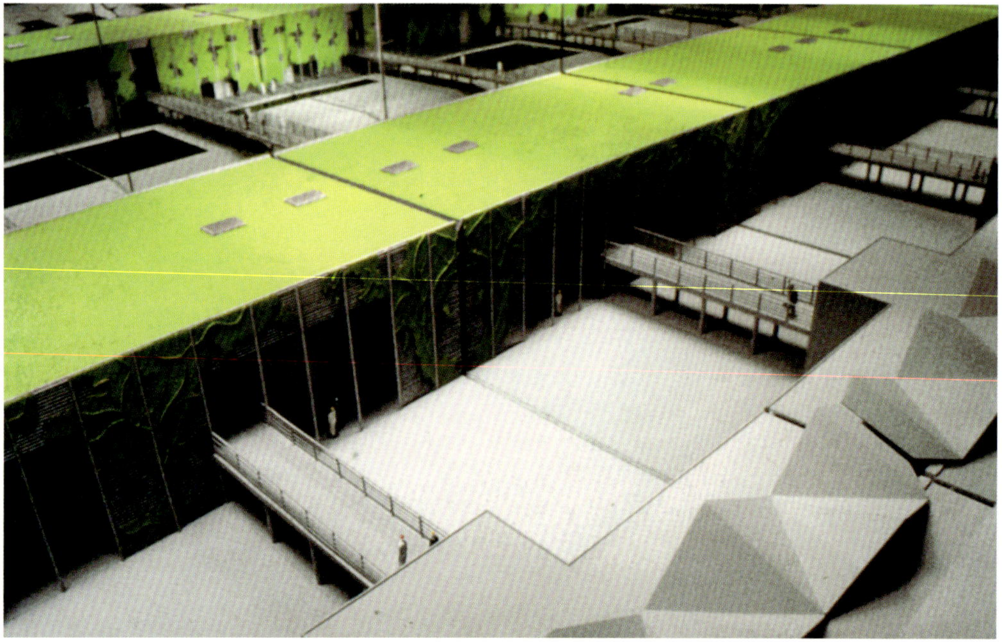

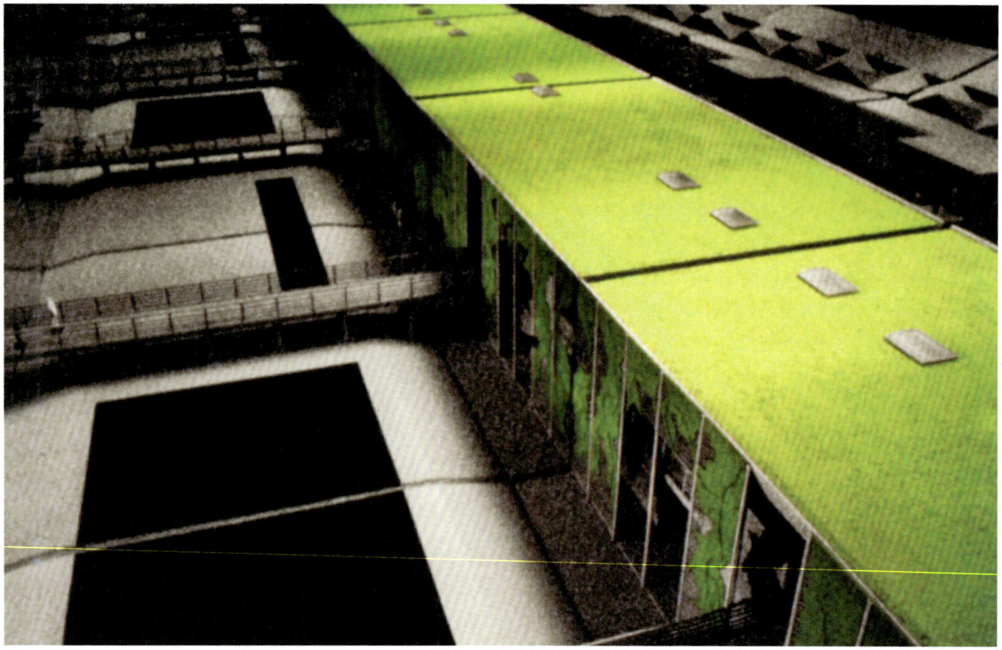

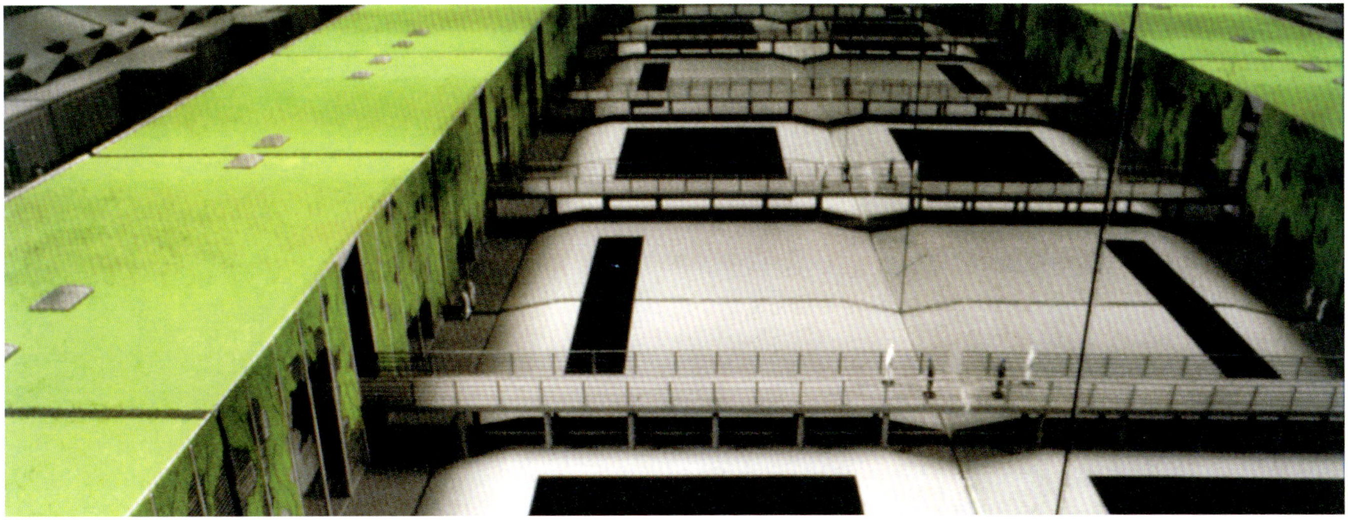

Parco di Fossoli of Carpi, Modena – Architecture/Agriculture

Client
Town of Carpi, Modena

Year
1989

Design
Andrea Branzi, Tullio Zini
with
Anna Allesina, Daniela Ascari, Corrado Gianferrari, Marco Partesotti, Michele Zini, Claudia Zoboli

These "Virgilian parks" came about with the idea of substituting traditional landscape design, which is narrative and romantic, with the orderly and inexpressive fabric of local agriculture alternated with insertions of herbaceous land on which there are small hills shaped like animals or flowers. The expressive tone of the park is lowered, but enzymatic and more orderly textures emerge, along with subtle figurative signs.
The term "Virgilian" refers to the Roman poet Virgil Marone (1st century BC), who praised agriculture and its techniques as a little-seen, but profound part of the literary myths of classicism.

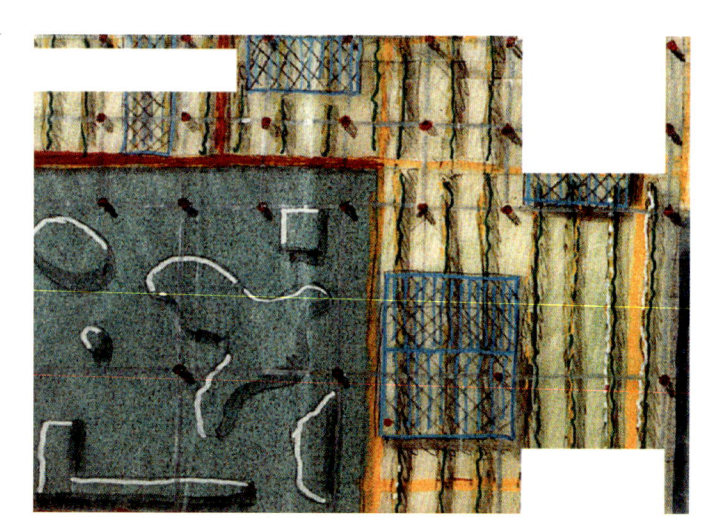

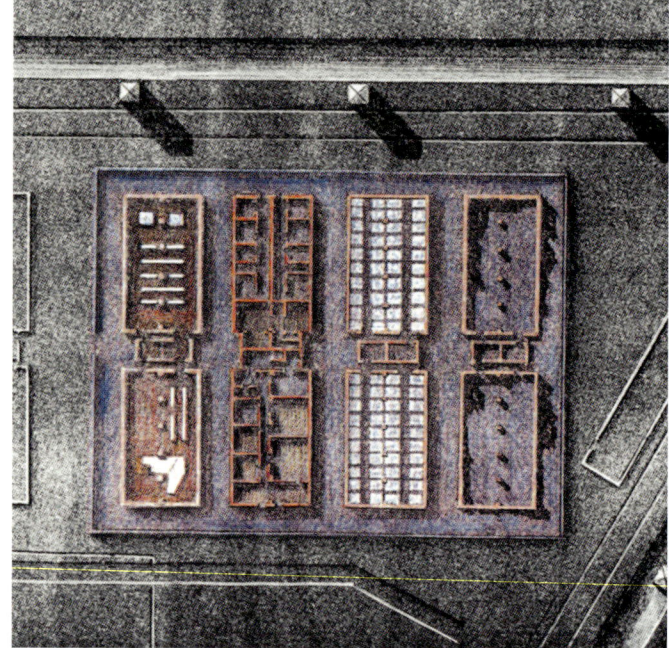

153

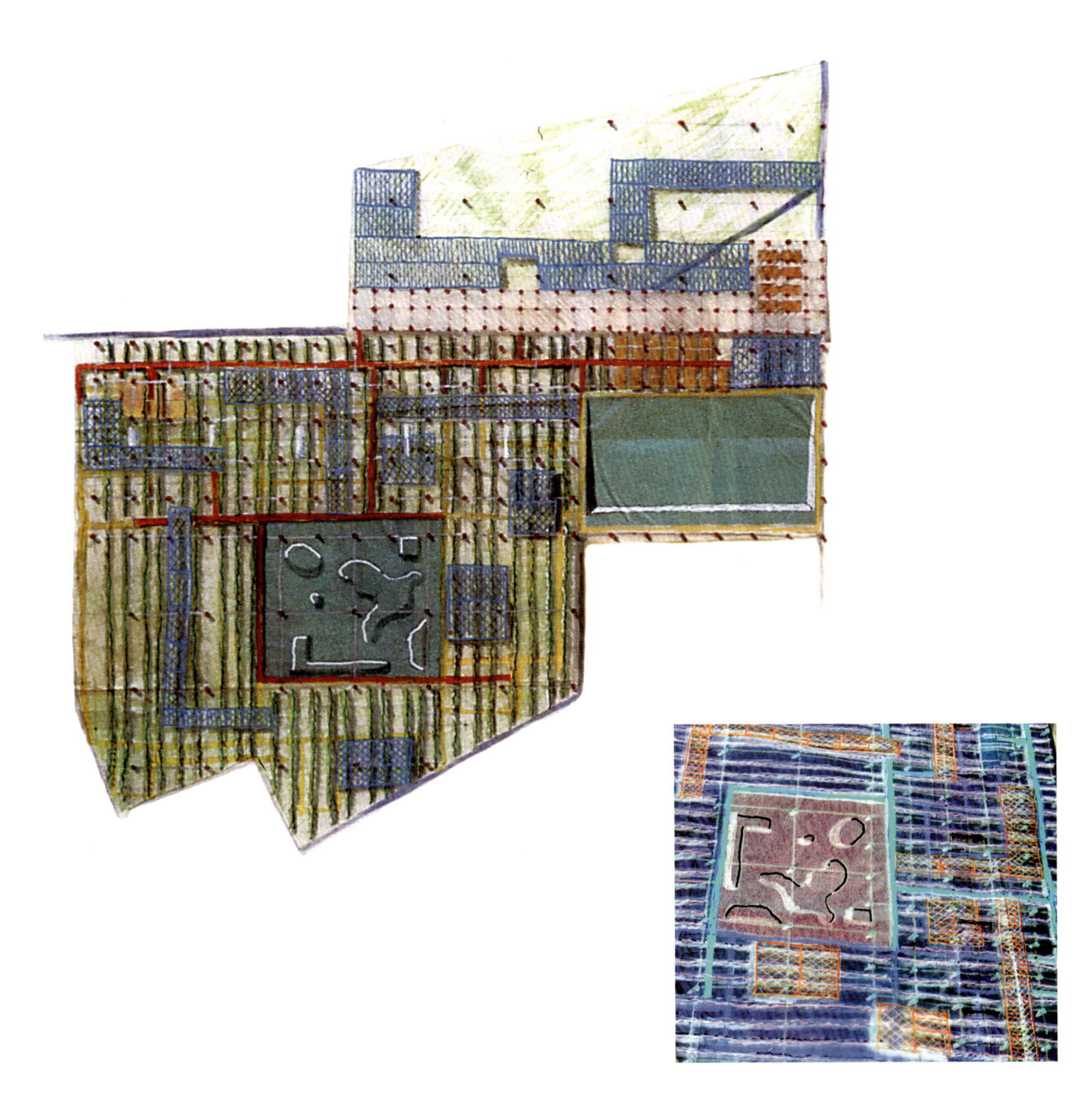

Competition for Fiabilandia Theme Park, Rimini

Design for a private competition for a theme park with children's games

Year
1991

Design
Andrea Branzi

This design is a narrative territory where, in addition to the lake, island, and village, there is a vast (natural) orchard in which small hills are created whose forms are similar to those created by children playing with sand.
In this case as well the morphology of the design as a whole has an origin outside of architecture, and is directly realized through the terrain, in a more sheltered and indirect way.

**Domus Academy
Master's – Agropolis**

Year
1995

Teachers
Andrea Branzi, Francesco Messori, Michele Zini

This is an insertion of mobile architectural elements within the irrigation systems of the agricultural terrain; by connecting among themselves they form alignments and flexible routes.
By connecting, then, the service tools with large irrigational pivots that create fertile circles on the agricultural plane, it is possible to create a mobile network of paths and infrastructures that follow the various phases of productive operations.

Antonio Piscione, Agropolis, *1995*

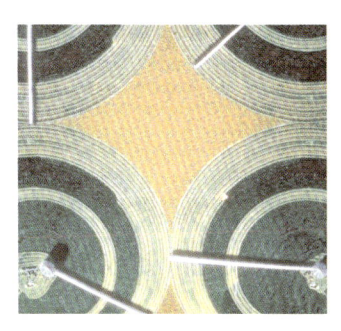

155

Cemetery of Sesto Fiorentino, Florence

National competition for
the design of the new town
cemetery

Client
Town of Sesto Fiorentino,
Florence

Year
1999

Design
Andrea Branzi, Tullio Zini
with
Gracia Franzoni, Rita Neri,
Mattia Parmiggiani, Michele Zini,
Claudia Zoboli

General plan

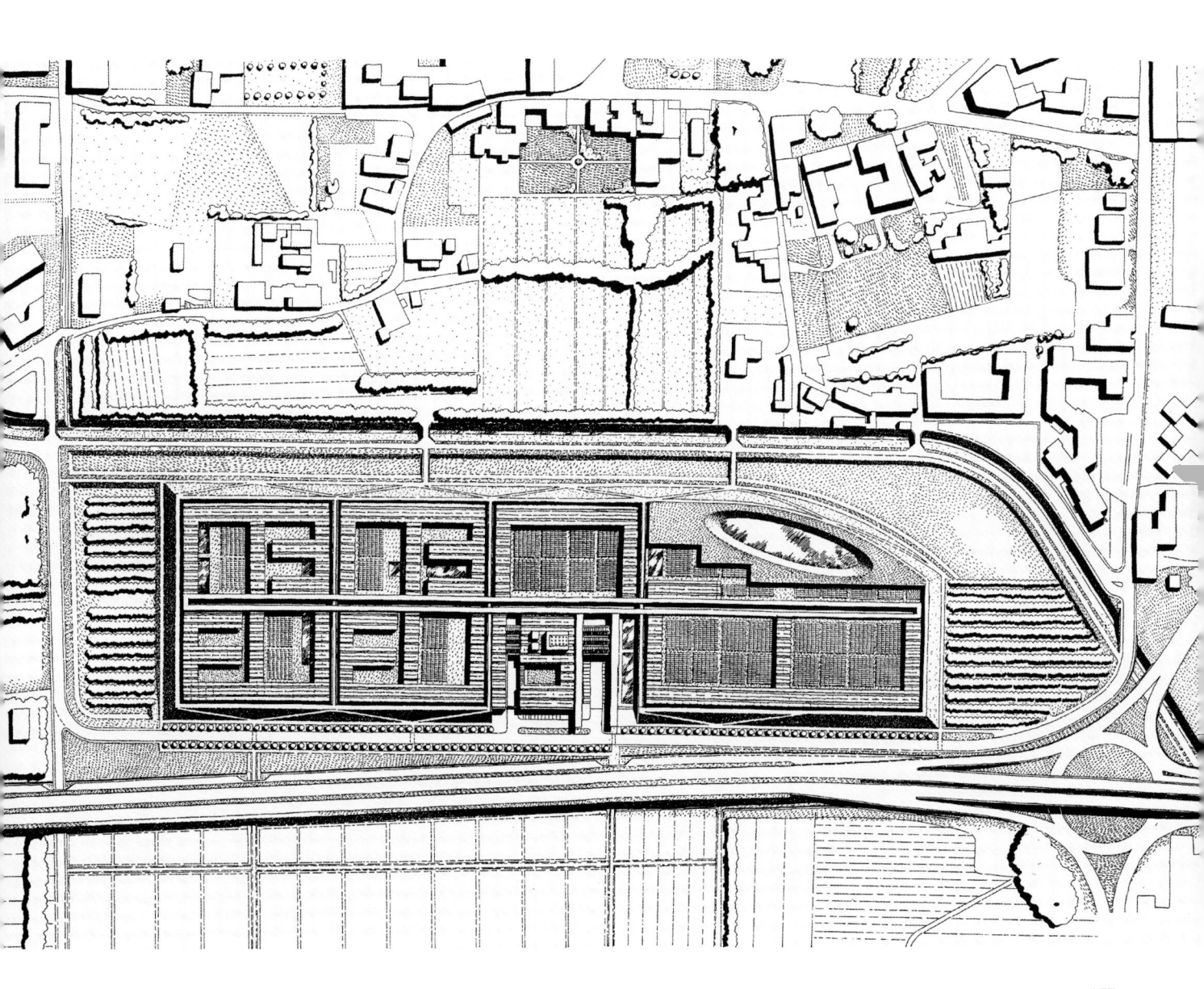

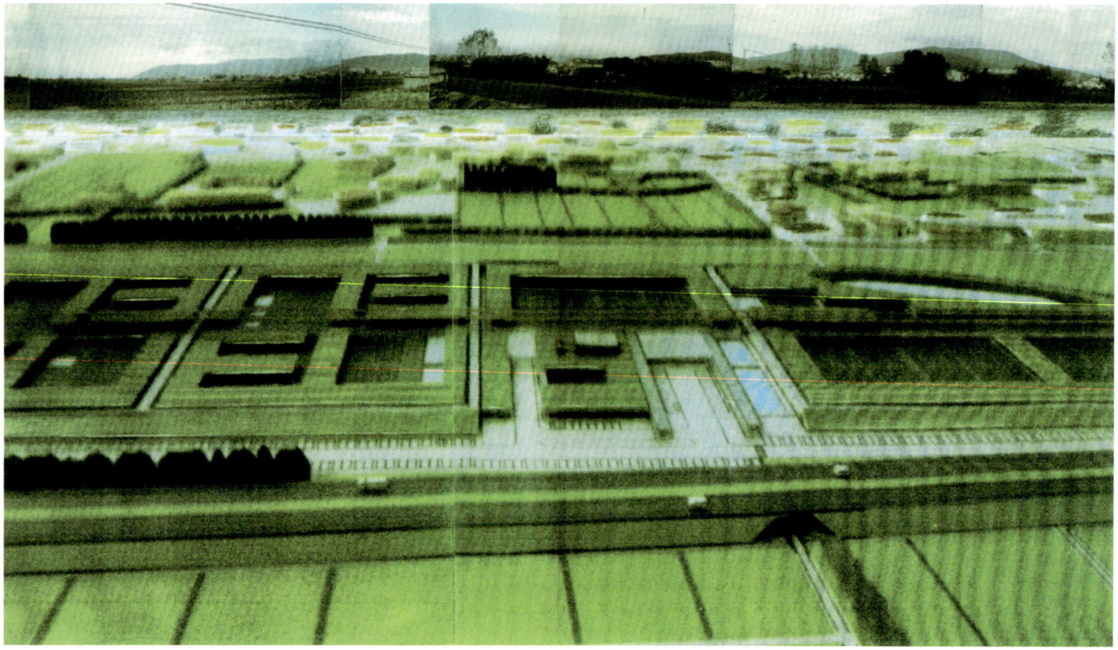

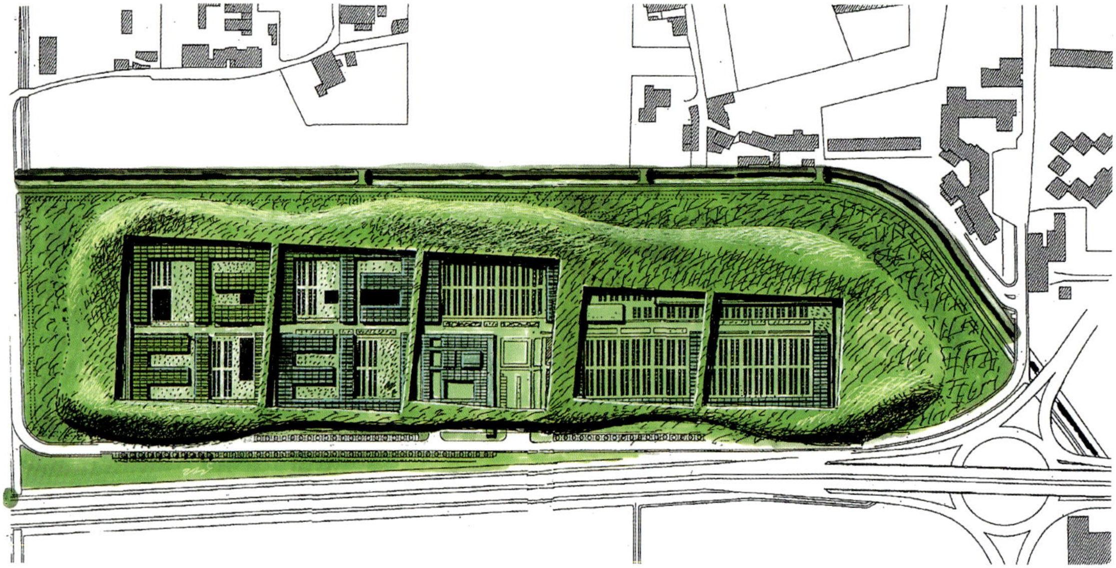

This is the cemetery seen as a way to use an agricultural terrain that is integrated with the horizontal profile of the plane, free of emerging figurative elements, and has a low environmental impact—an ecological model of burial that inserts itself in the productive plotting of the countryside behind low land dykes.

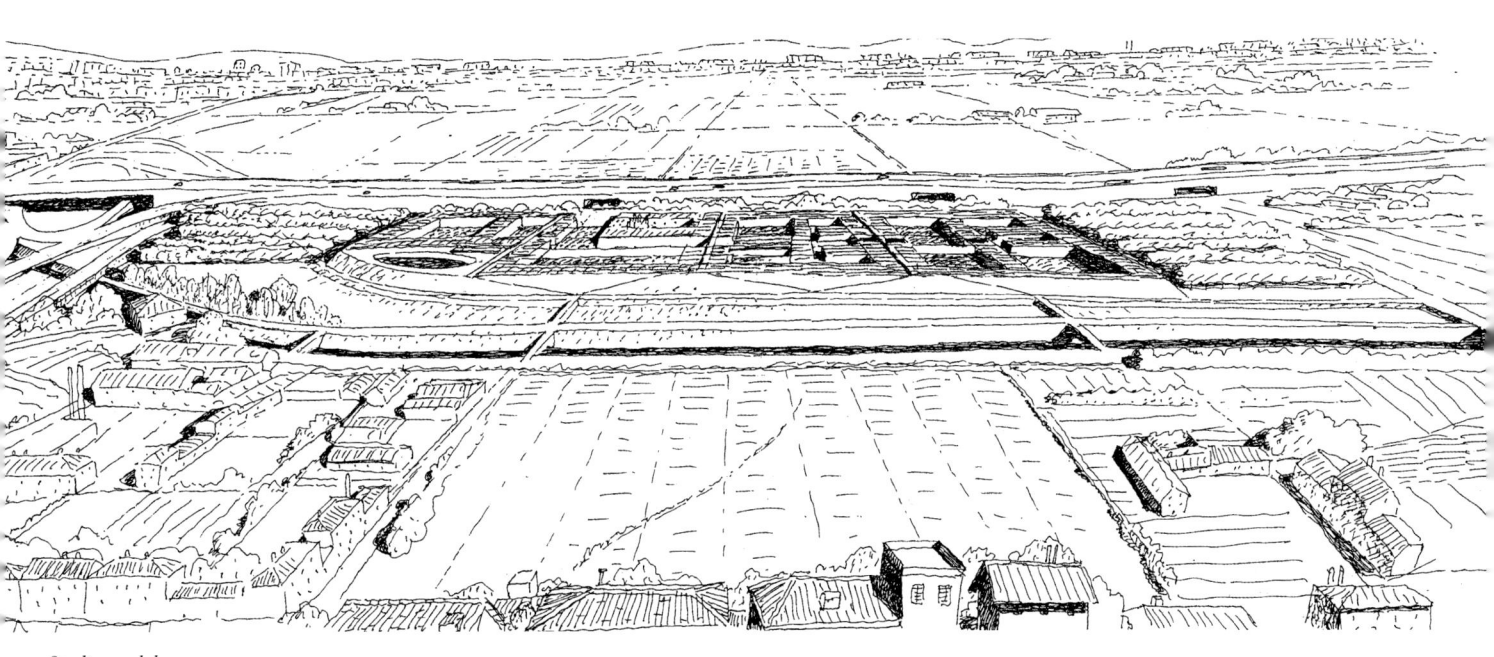

Studio model

Porta Nuova Gardens – Virgilian Park, Milan

Competition for the ordering
of the Porta Nuova Gardens,
Milan

Client
City of Milan

Year
2004

Design
Italo Rota, Andrea Branzi,
Ronan and Erwan Bouroullec

This is an agricultural urban park—
an injection of countryside inserted
into Milan—where productive
areas, temporary structures,
Aeolian structures, open-air
theaters, stalls, animal pens,
and living spaces for the public
are all found.
The park is not a landscape
backdrop, but rather an enzymatic
territory the produces services
and consumer goods.

The park's lighting is made up of lunar penumbras produced by large stationary balls and systems of service lights buried underground. From the high floors of the buildings surrounding the park it is possible to see large luminous signs on the ground.

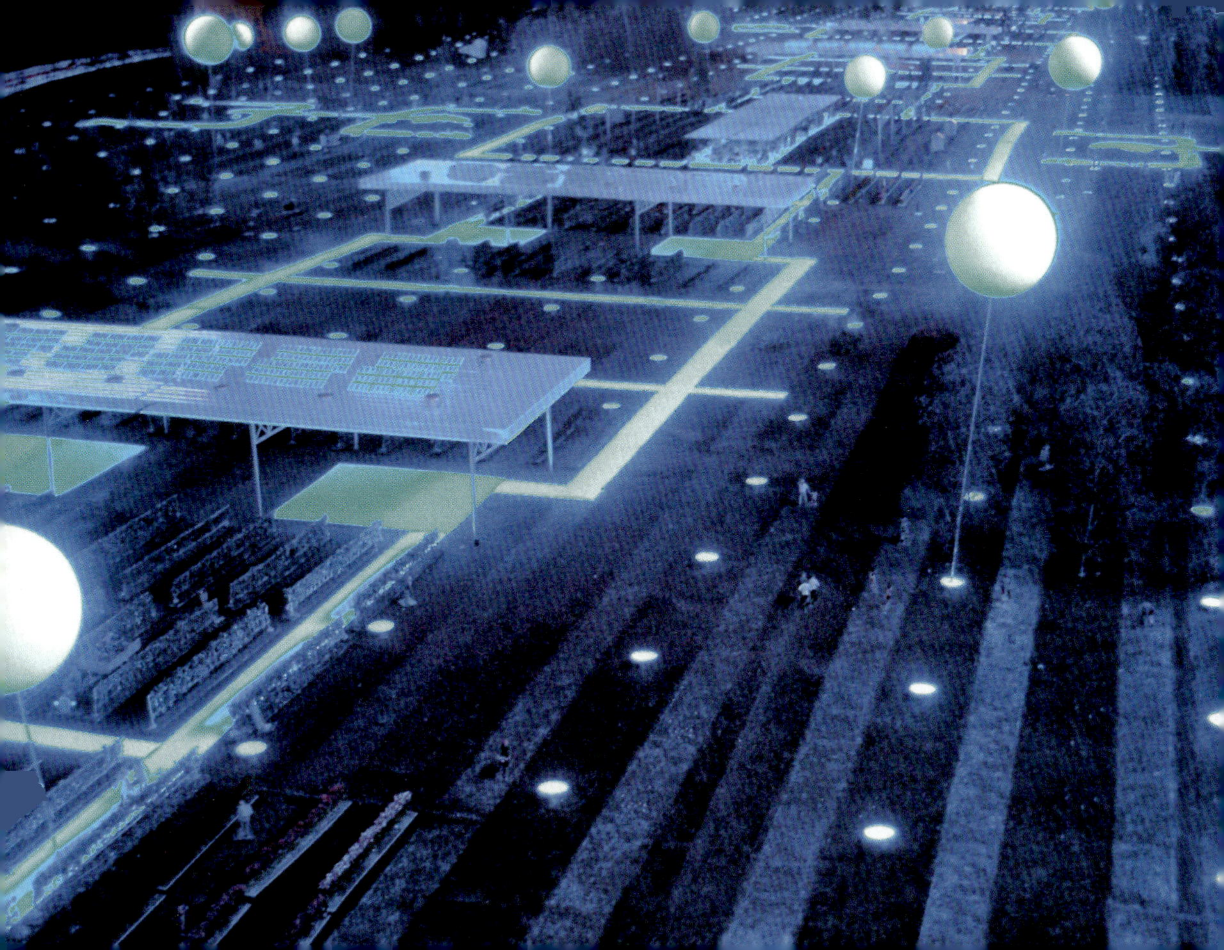

*Temporary game structures proposed
by Ronan and Erwan Bouroullec*

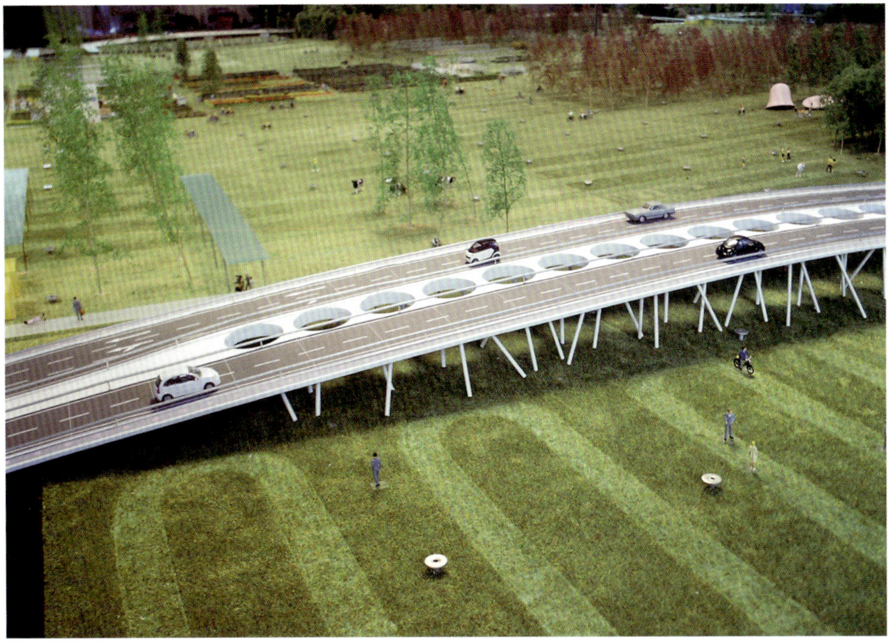

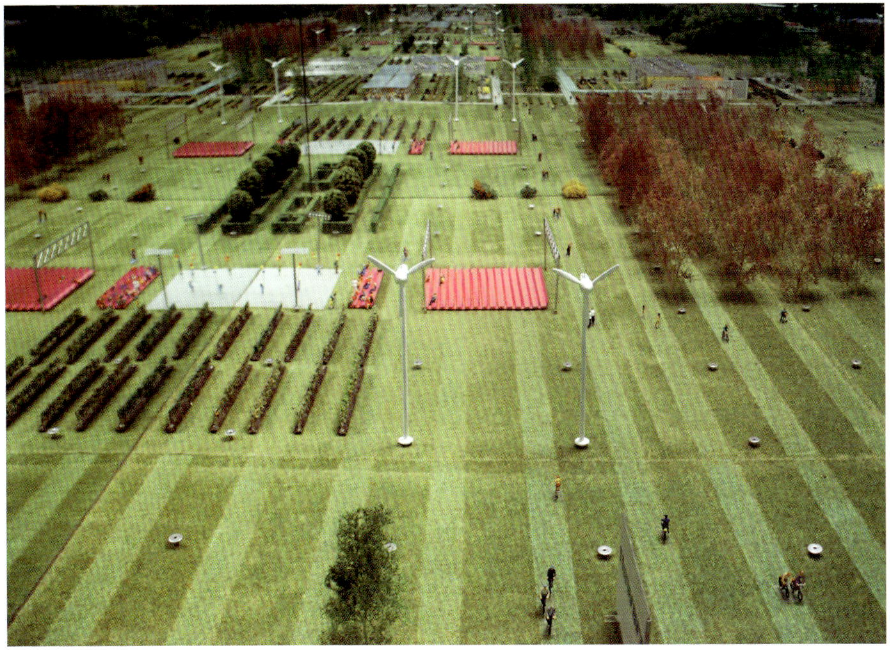

Glass Garden

Palazzo Tursi Doria, installation within the exhibition
Art & Architecture, Genoa

Year
2004

Design
Andrea Branzi
with
Daniele Macchi, Giuseppe Galli
in collaboration with
CIRVA, Marseilles

This small temporary garden in the interior courtyard of Genoa's Palazzo Tursi Doria is constructed by an intermingling of glass, bamboo, posts, and plants, and as such is set squarely between architecture and agriculture.

The design deals with the theme of architecture's perimeter, traditionally rigid and definitive, which separates all that is internal from all that is external; in this case, the walls are made by braiding these two components, thereby creating a hybrid perimeter and softened border that belongs contemporaneously to two opposing realities. Mingling and braiding are technologies rarely used in architecture, as they are based on the collaboration of weak structural components; although they remain autonomous and separate, these components create an elastic surface that can be dismantled and has the peculiar characteristics of lightness and penetrability. In this case, the braid is used to create an architectural garden; in other words, an enzymatic territory, an intermediate between natural energy and construction technologies—an evolving territory that follows the seasons' evolutions within a diffuse, regular system of piles, supports, or columns. This design bears witness to both the agricultural origin of architecture and the architectural origin of agriculture.

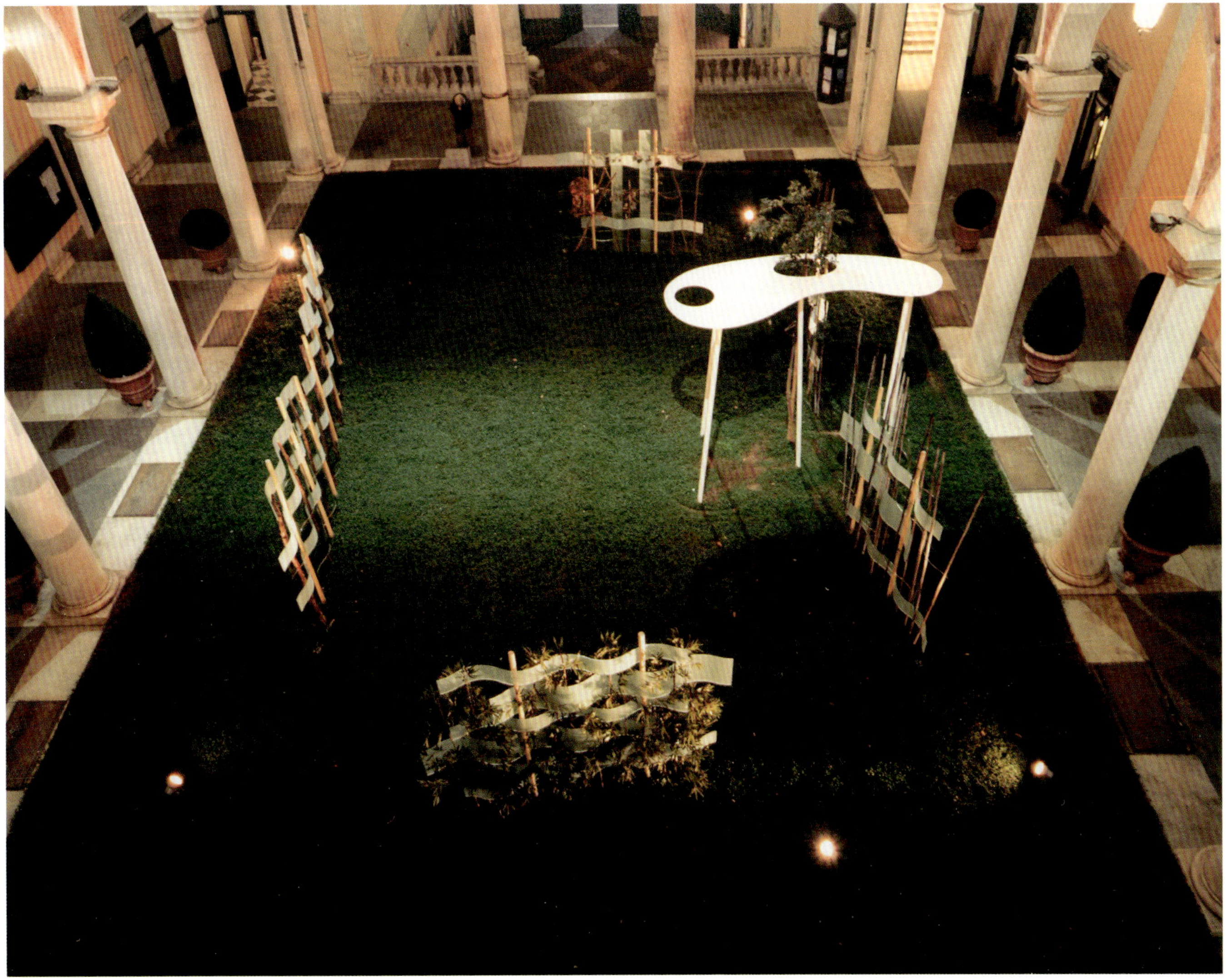

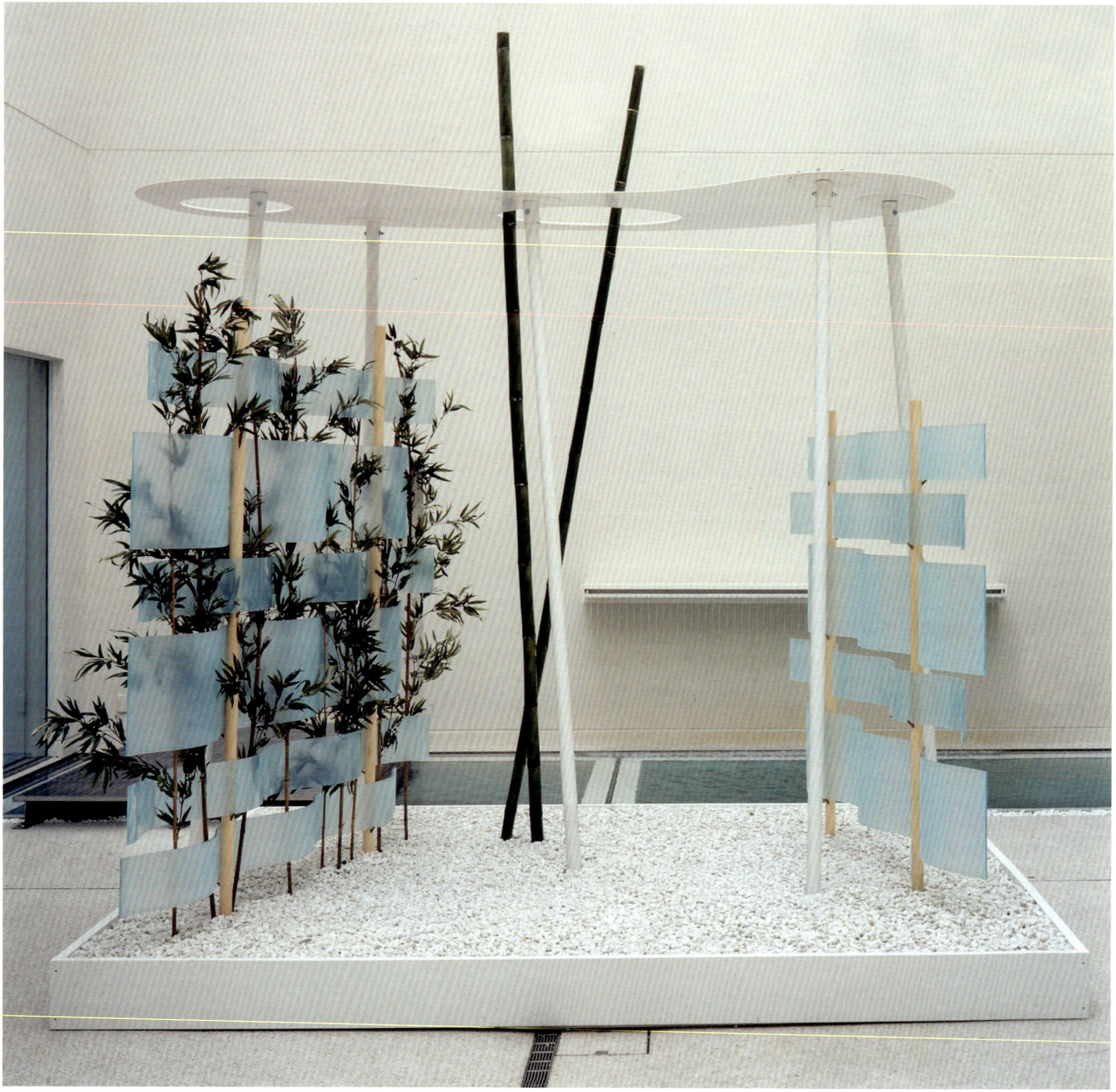

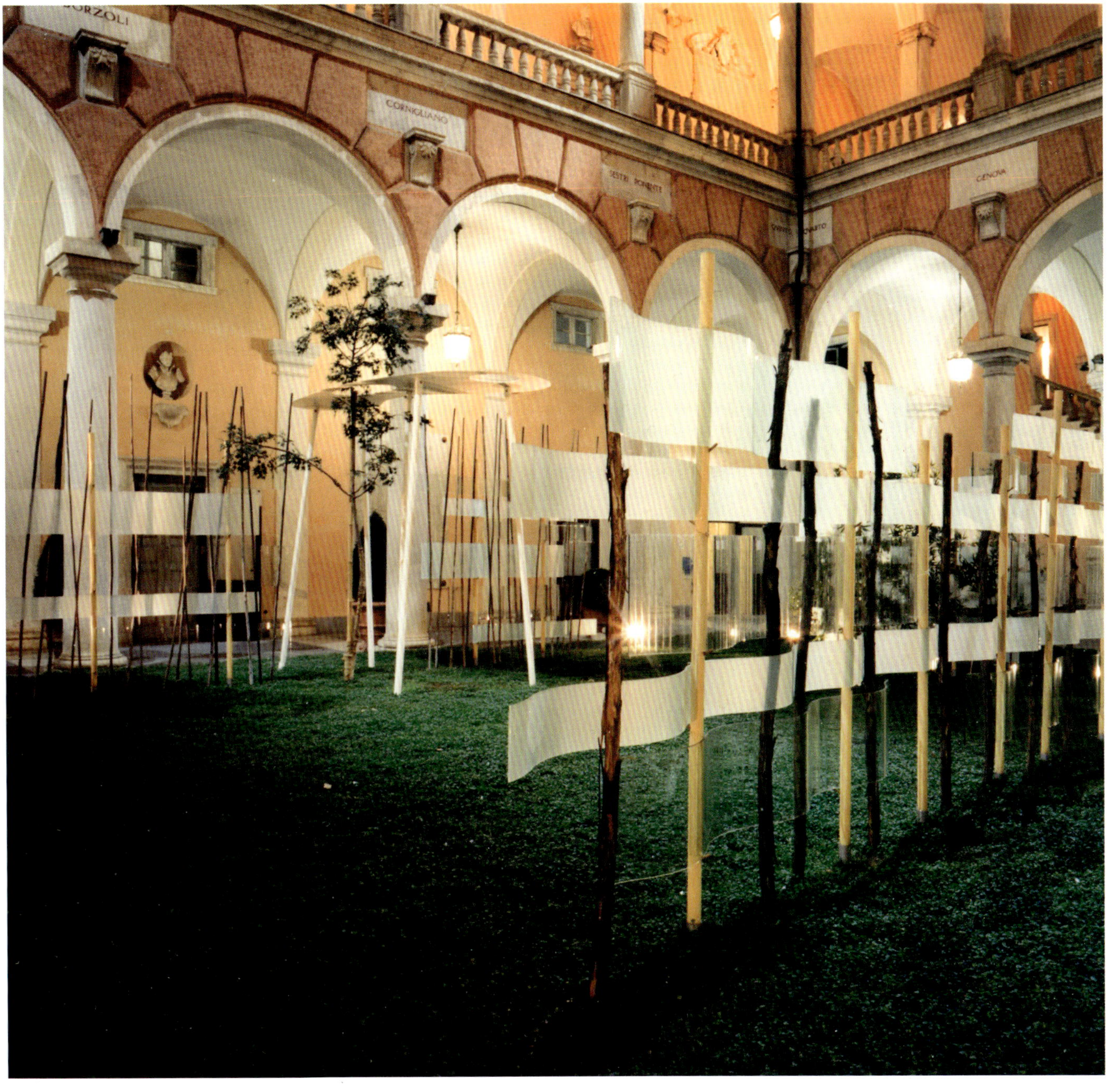
CORNIGLIANO
SESTRI PONENTE
GENOVA

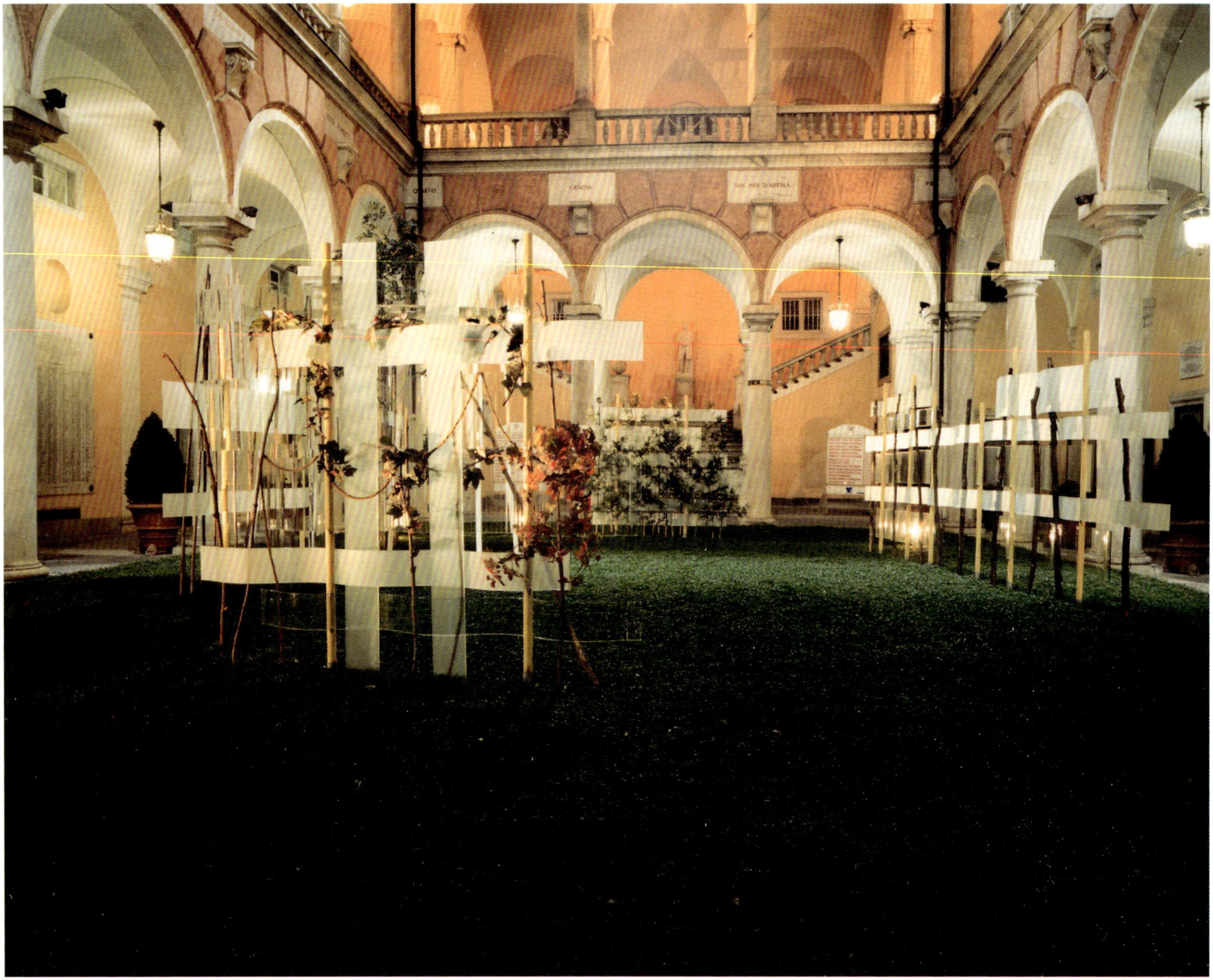

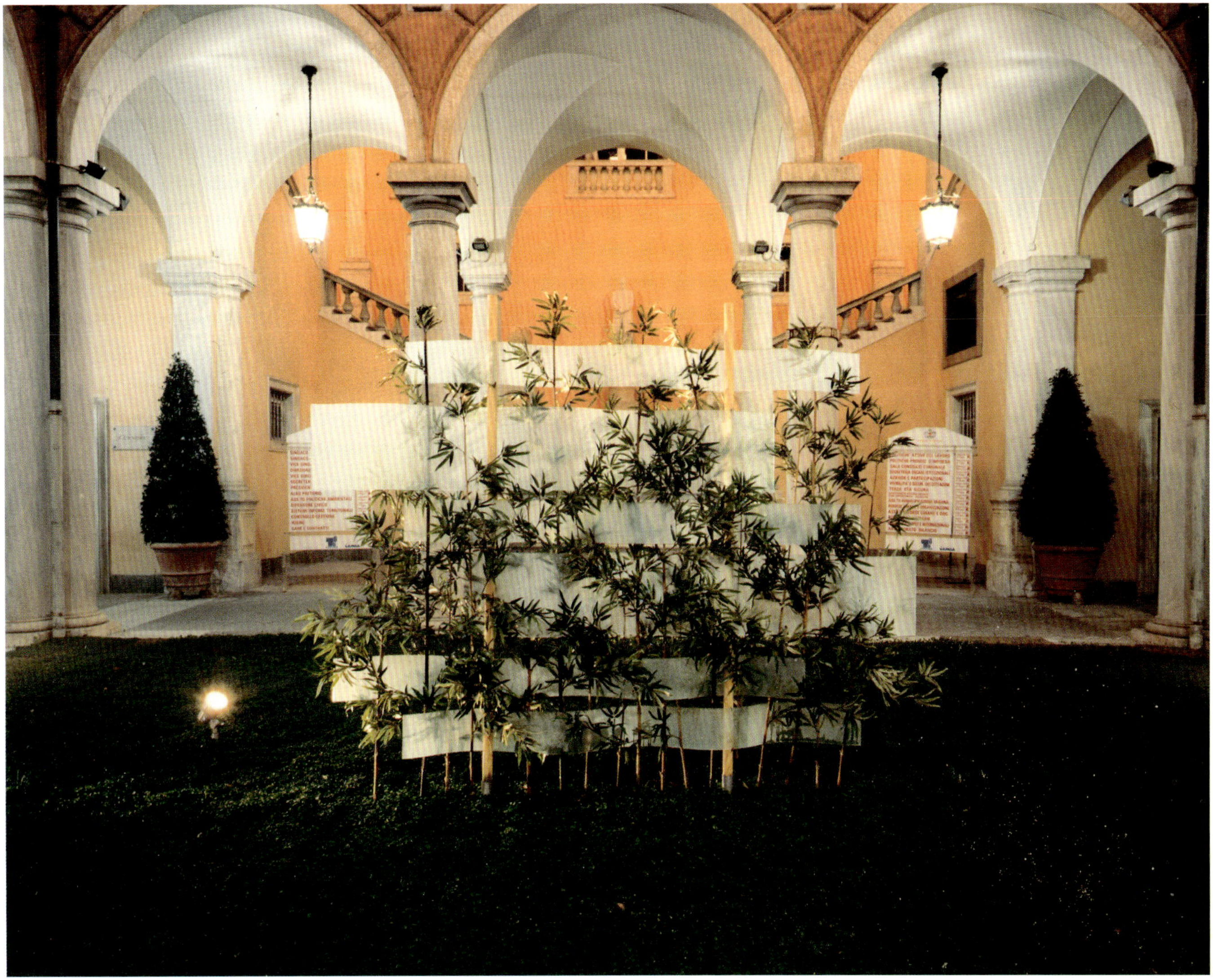

City and Music

Current interior design has before it the task of renewing some of the architectural typologies born in the twentieth century that have already quickly aged, before a transformation of the methods of use and social sensitivities: universities, hospitals, workplaces, theater spaces, and art museums are now themes that call for the beginning of a new season of experiment that will take on the charge of finding new operative devices.

This revision involves a comparison with technical and artistic cultures that have evolved and which require new functioning devices. In some way, this comparison between the new architecture and the evolving of an exterior culture needs to be established, interrupting the overly-consolidated self-referential tradition of our design culture.

The design of new concert halls does not, in fact, regard the simple evolution of a very old and noble urban typology, but rather it implies a comparison with new music, or at least with our society's new feeling of forgiveness.

The central nodes of this revolution began a half century ago with two fundamental projects, Jorn Utzon's proposal for the Sydney Opera (1955) and Hans Sharoun's design for the Berlin Philharmonie (1956).

Today, music has become a sort of sonorous semiosphere that invades our cities, creating a very extended, invasive listening network that in concert halls finds not an exclusive place of execution, but rather just a moment of high perceptive density and intense social rituality.

Within the experiential city, wholly made up of information, services, sensory knowledge, and immaterial places, the concert hall represents a genius loci of shaded borders, but high symbolic visibility.

As hip-hop thought teaches us, today music exists as an ambient reality, produced by infinite hands, innumerable synthesizers, and emitters that have the numbers of mass creativity; the new frontier exists not in creating the new, but more in knowing, championing, remounting, and using the frontier to say new things. Music (be it classical or modern) is therefore already a weak and diffuse system of social identity and the new concert halls seek to place themselves within this extended sound circuit through their own extreme visibility, creating an urban exception of an almost situationist nature that crosses over an uninterrupted flow of pre-existing musical emotions.

In other words, the urban space around concert halls is no longer empty, but already full of music.

This new historical condition should work in favor of original design intuitions because it is born of a new rapport between the auditorium and the city, and between the concert and the public that listens to it. This is a relationship of spatial continuity (music-city) on the one hand, and of strong emotional motivations on the other (music-listeners): it is a condition that calls for utterly new operative devices, with respect to the cultured music of the last century as well.

Today some of the major composers work within this type of musical buzz: Philip Glass, Brian Eno, Keith Jarrett produce horizontal music, ambient weaves that, as Pierre Boulez says, surpass the frontal mode of the concert, made up of a public and an orchestra seated one in front of the other, to create instead a fabric of theoretically unlimited sounds (therefore anti-composite) that expands through space, without a beginning and without a precise end.

This is a music that is almost similar to a new generation of air conditioning, which creates an ambient quality and belongs to the enzymatic territories of the city, where it flows continuously, like a current, a swarm, or an immaterial plankton.

But in opposition to this type of new ambient condition of music we are instead assisting in a diffuse design tendency, which on the contrary interprets concert halls as though they were an acoustic box, a device created to bring about the conditions for a scientifically perfect listening, with a closed-down perimeter from which the music must not get out, to become an aquarium separated from the world surrounding it. This tendency, going well beyond the limits of correct functionality and of the good listen, is looking for the route to a scientific refoundation of architecture, creating rigid organisms that are born of an incorrect interpretation of music, which has always developed in the wrong environments, made up of churches, courtyards, unused factories, and stadiums.

Music has always been a highly complex and imperfect phenomenon that has positively lived with the world's imperfections and background noises, creating an immaterial architecture much stronger than the material that contains it.

Even looking at the very free and varied forms of the latest designs we can surmise that in reality almost all these organisms present the nucleus of the hall, not only locked-down and rigid, but also substantially the same: fruit of the respect for the laws of acoustics, but also chained to the one international consulting institute, specialized in designing acoustically perfect halls, with an evident reduction of the internal complexity of the subject.

But the fundamental game between architecture and music is played above all in the interior spaces, which just as in the recesses of living organisms do not intervene in the external form, but produce the endocrine energies able to create the performance necessary for life and evolution.

In the place of a theater capable of filling itself like a sponge with music and from which music is dispersed throughout the environment, we often see theater designs in which music remains prisoner, segmented because it exchanged its own (cultural) role for that of perfect acoustics, a mythical (technical) role of unreachable—or, in any case, useless—perfection.

A page from Solo for Piano *of the* Concert for Piano and Orchestra *(1958) of John Cage*

Ghent – A Sonorous Sponge

Competition for the new Forum for Music, Dance, and Visual Culture, Ghent

Year
2003–2004

Design
Andrea Branzi, Toyo Ito & Associates
with
Taku Adachi, Florian Busch, Christoph Cellarius, Giuseppe Galli, Takeo Higashi, Ahihisa Hirata, Takayasu Hirayama, Daniele Macchi, Kenta Sano, Shinichi Takeuchi, Yuichi Yokokawa

Structures
Office OAK, Masato Araya, Yasushi Moribe

Acoustics
S. Motosugi, Nagata Acoustic, Tomoko Fukuchi

This design was born from a few general ideas, shared with Toyo Ito, regarding the role of interior spaces as protagonists of the contemporary city.
These are interior spaces that dynamically adapt to changes in society and culture, just as the physiological systems inside living organisms carry out functions that are invisible from the outside, but nevertheless vital and sophisticated because they produce fundamental functional and qualitative enzymes.
The figure of this design is essentially a large interior organism, contained within a sheath of transparent, indifferent glass, a sort of autonomous aquarium. This design therefore distances itself from the current tradition of concert halls wherein music is interpreted as an environmental and social separation and specialization.
Our attention focuses on a new, different conception of music, understood as an expansive and horizontal ambient quality that invades spaces and overflows the concert hall's enclosures.
It is a matter of a certain type of musical culture with which architecture must begin to compare itself—because this culture requires special systems quite different from the traditional ones, based on a rigorous separation of inside and outside, and on utterly rigid environmental limits—in order to move instead towards more fluid and open environmental situations, where music preserves its sensory and perceptive nature as part of an urban space producing experiences, acquaintances, and fewer strictly specialized places.

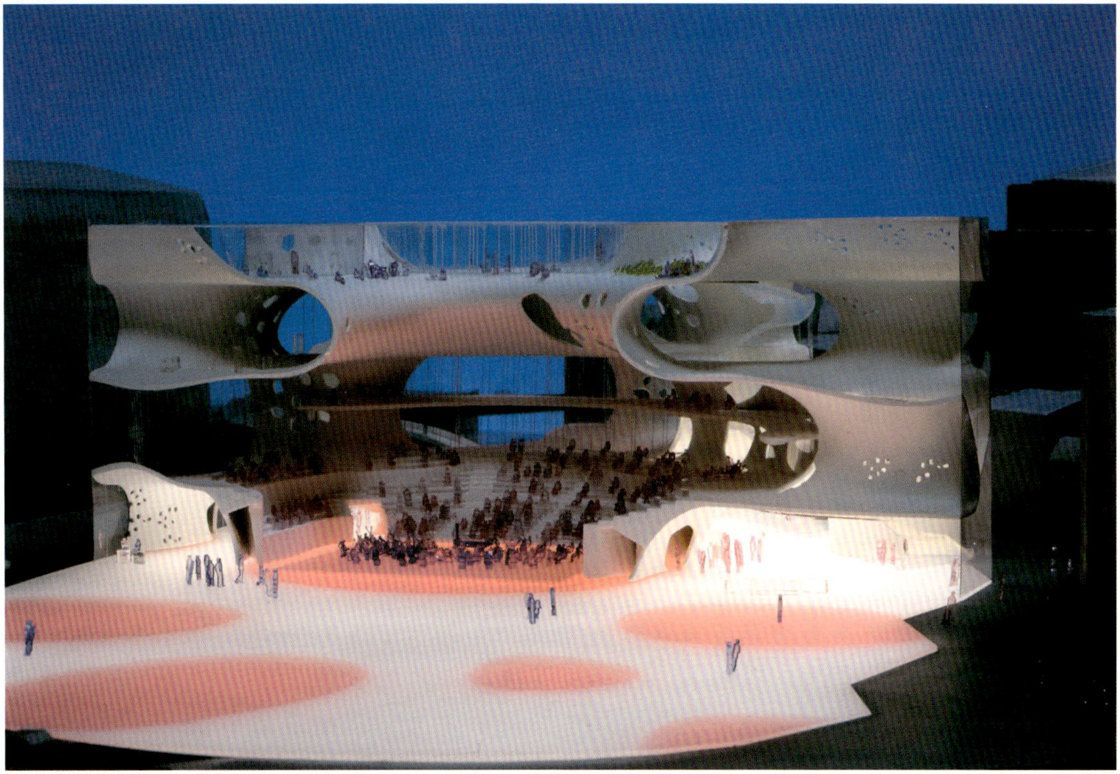

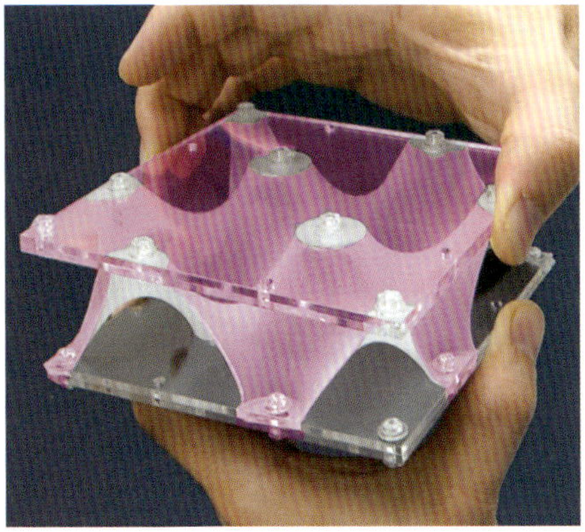

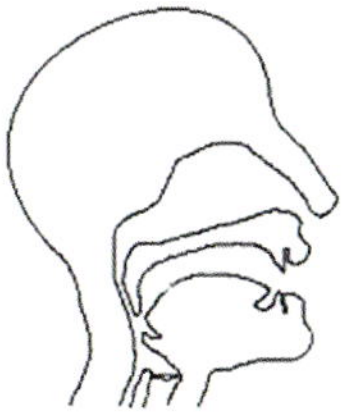

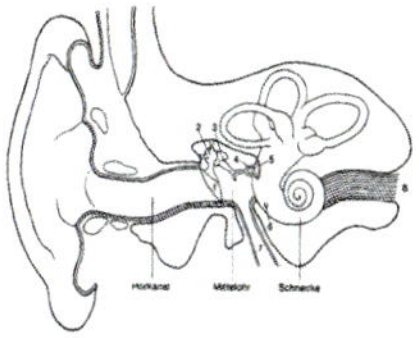
Schnecke

The interior organism is formally autonomous from the crystal sheath that houses it; its image is prevalent with respect to the building's entire form. One's gaze can cross from one part to another.

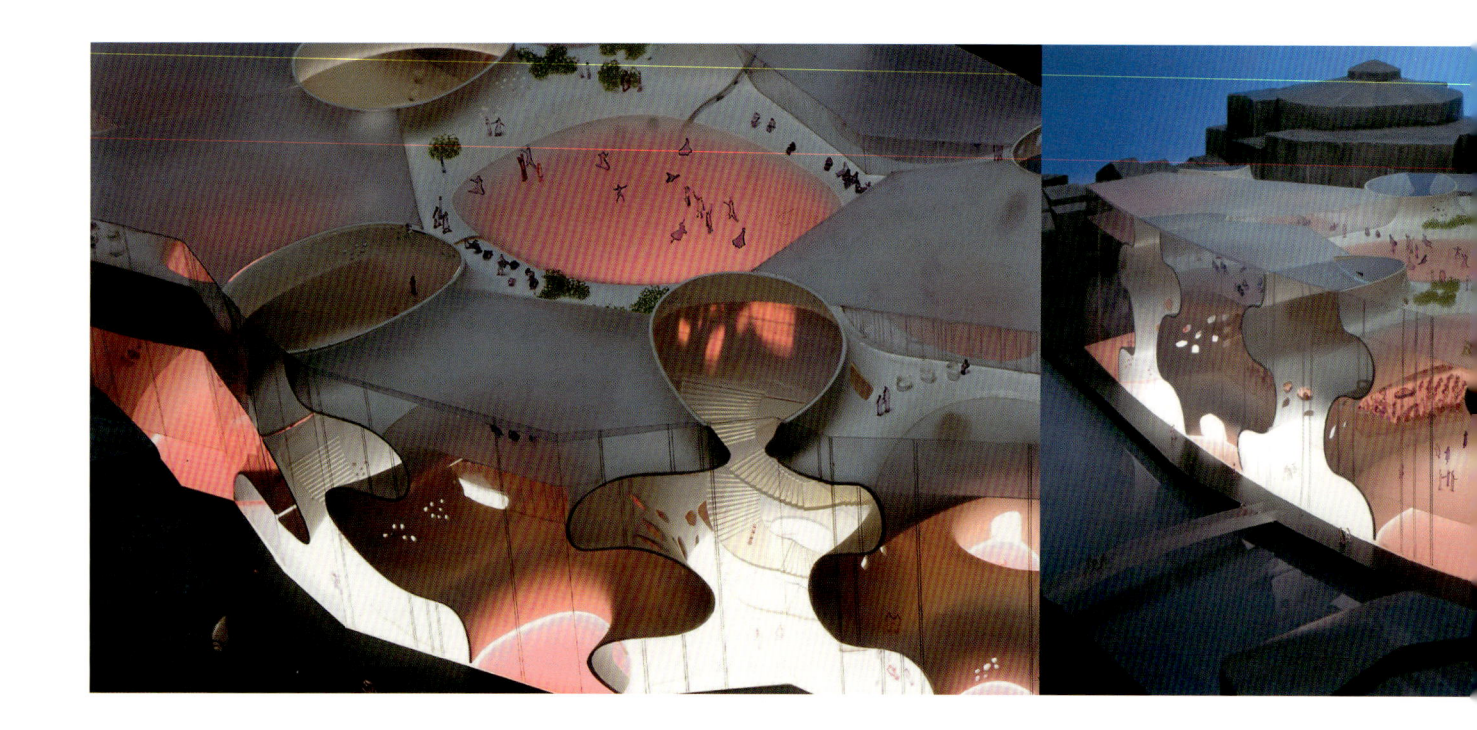

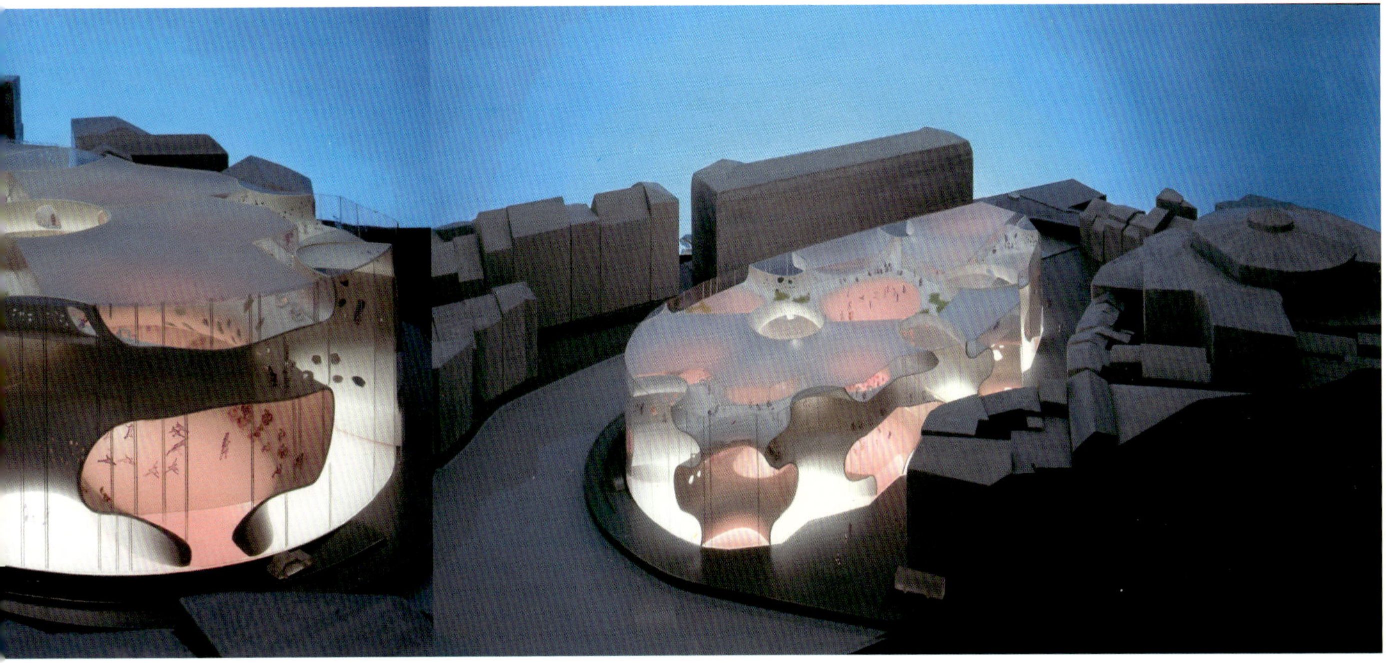

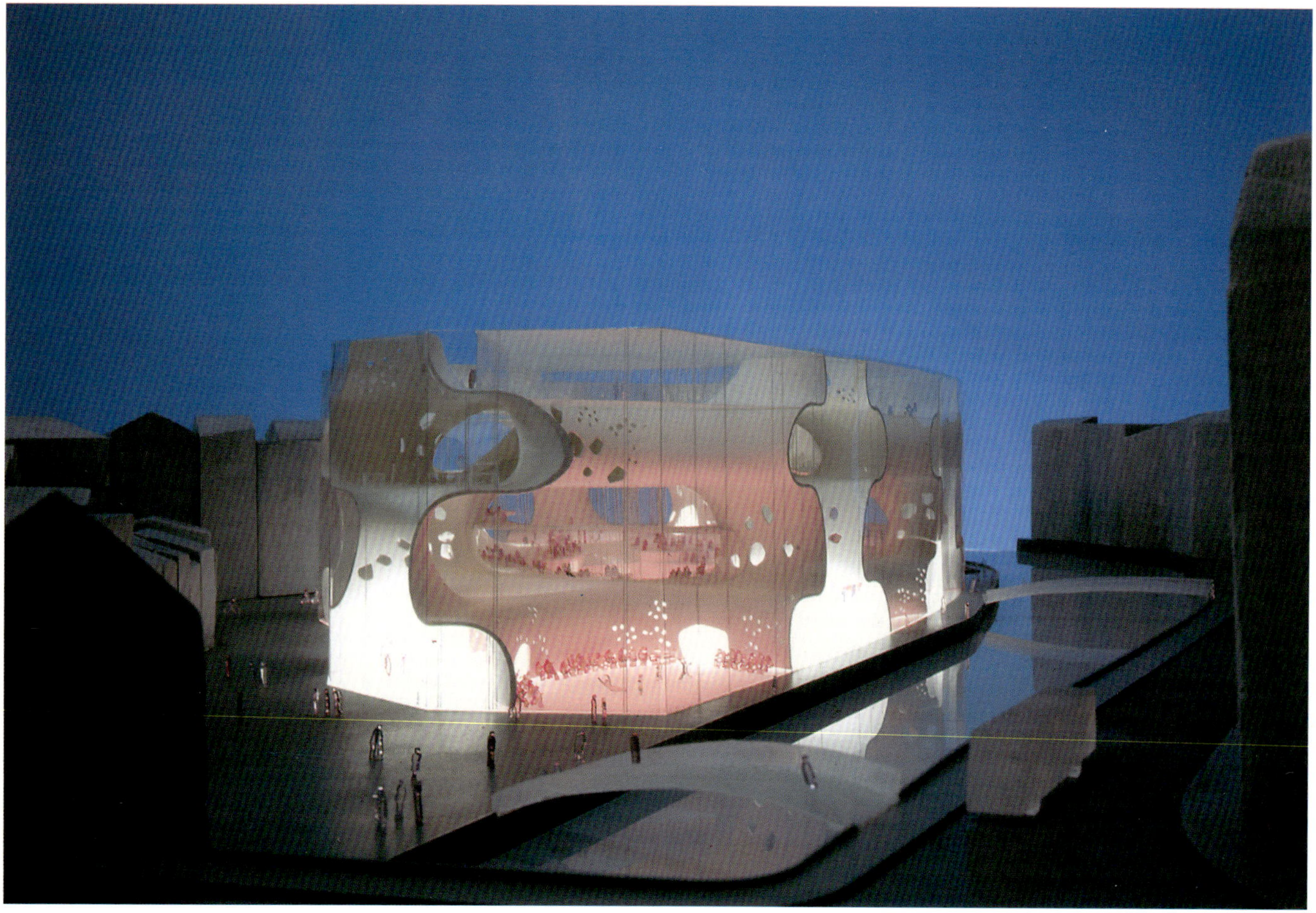

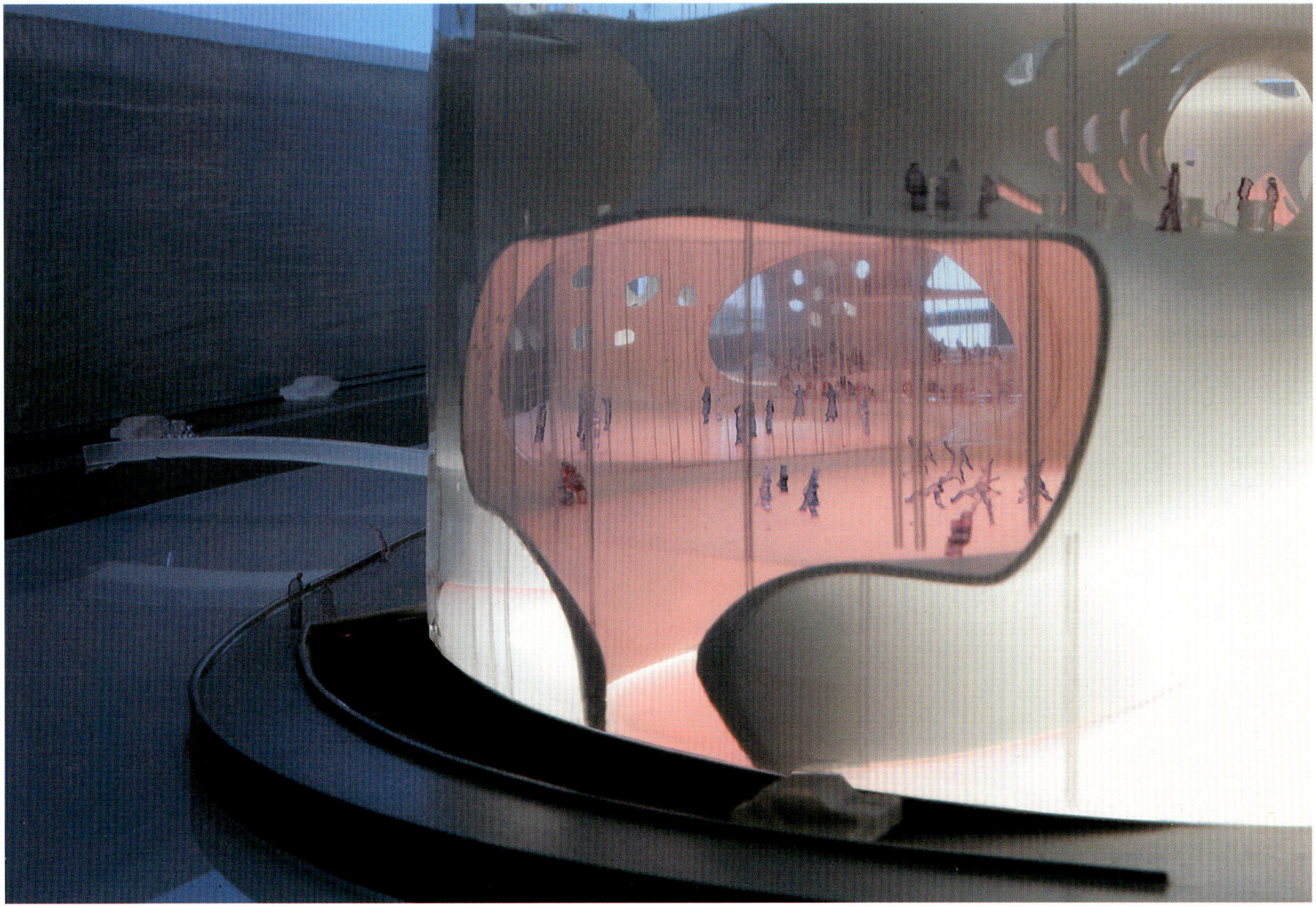

Bibliography

Essential Bibliography on the Subject
Paul K. Feyerabend, *Against Method*, NLB, London 1975.
Gianni Vattimo, *Il pensiero debole*, Feltrinelli, Milan 1983.
Rita Levi Montalcini, *Elogio dell'imperfezione*, Garzanti, Milan 1987.
David Harvey, *The Condition of Postmodernity*, Blackwell, Cambridge (Ma.) 1990.
Bart Kosko, *Fuzzy Thinking: The New Science of Fuzzy Logic*, Hyperion, New York 1993.
Various Authors, *The Solid Side*, V+K Publishing, Naarden 1995.
François Furet, Giuliano Procacci, *Controverso Novecento*, Donzelli, Milan 1995.
Jeremy Rifkin, *The End of Work*, G.P. Putman's Sons, New York 1995.
François Jullien, *Traité de l'efficacité*, Paris 1996.
Zygmunt Bauman, *La società dell'incertezza*, Il Mulino, Bologna 1999.
Zygmunt Bauman, *Liquid Modernity*, Polity, Cambridge 2000.
Richard Florida, *The Rise of the Creative Class*, Basic Books, New York 2002.
Salvatore Settis, *Futuro del classico*, Einaudi, Turin 2004.

Author's Bibliography
Andrea Branzi, *Moderno, Post-moderno, Millenario*, Studio Forma/Alchymia, Milan 1980.
Andrea Branzi, *Il Design italiano degli anni '50*, Centrokappa, Binasco 1981.
Andrea Branzi, *Merce e Metropoli - esperienze del Nuovo Design italiano*, Epos, Palermo 1983.
Andrea Branzi, *La Casa Calda - Esperienze del Nuovo Design Italiano*, Idea Books, Milan 1984 (also published by the M.I.T. Press, Cambridge (Ma.) 1984; Thames and Hudson, London 1984; L'Equerre, Paris 1985).
Andrea Branzi, *Animali Domestici*, Idea Books, Milan 1986 (also published by the M.I.T. Press, Cambridge (Ma.) 1986, Philippe Sers, 1987).
Andrea Branzi, *Learning from Milan*, M.I.T. Press, Cambridge (Ma.) 1988.
Andrea Branzi, *Pomeriggi alla media-industria - Design e Seconda Modernità*, Idea Books, Milan 1988.
Andrea Branzi, *La Quarta Metropoli*, Domus Academy, Milan 1990.
Andrea Branzi, in Various Authors, *Formes des Métropoles - Nouveaux Designs en Europe*, Centre Georges Pompidou, Paris 1991.

Andrea Branzi, in Various Authors, *Neues Europaische Design*, Ernst & Sohn, Berlin 1991.
Andrea Branzi, *Il Dolce Stil Novo (della Casa)*, Alessi, Crusinallo 1991.
Andrea Branzi, *Arezzo, verso un inurbamento maturo*, Municipality of Arezzo 1992.
Andrea Branzi, *Luoghi*, Rizzoli International, New York 1992.
Andrea Branzi, *Luoghi*, Idea Books, Milan 1992.
Andrea Branzi, *Luoghi*, Thames and Hudson, London 1992.
Andrea Branzi, *Luoghi*, Ernst & Sohn, Berlin 1992.
Andrea Branzi, *Nouvelles de la Metropole Froide*, Centre Georges Pompidou, Paris 1992.
Andrea Branzi, Nicoletta Morozzi, *La civiltà dell'ascolto - e altre note sul Giappone moderno*, Cronopio, Naples 1992.
Andrea Branzi, Francesco Guerrieri, *Villa S. Ignazio a Fiesole*, Alinea, Florence 1994.
Andrea Branzi, *Il design italiano 1964-1990*, Electa, Milan 1996.
Andrea Branzi, *I protagonisti del design italiano. Lo scenario, le storie, i prodotti, le utopie*, Dialogo Multimedia/Editoriale Domus, Rozzano 1996 (CD-ROM).
Andrea Branzi, *La crisi della qualità*, Edizioni della Battaglia, Palermo 1997.
Andrea Branzi, *Genetic Tales*, Alessi, Verbania 1998.
Andrea Branzi, *Introduzione al design italiano*, Baldini & Castoldi, Milan 1999.
Andrea Branzi, *Italia e Giappone: Design come stile di vita*, Nihon Keizai Shimbun, Tokyo 2001.
Andrea Branzi, *Oggetti e Territori*, Scharpoord Centrum, Knokke 2001 (video realized by Giuseppe Bartolini and Simonetta Fiamminghi).
Andrea Branzi, *Verso una modernità debole e diffusa*, introduction by Alberto Seassaro, Polidesign, Milan 2005.
Andrea Branzi, *No-Stop City. Archizoom Associati*, Siriaque Orléans, 2006.